Legal and Ethical Aspects of HIV-Related Research

Legal and Ethical Aspects of HIV-Related Research

Sana Loue, J.D., Ph.D.
Case Western Reserve University
Cleveland, Ohio

Plenum Press • New York and London

Library of Congress Cataloging-in-Publication Data

On file

The information contained in this text does not constitute legal advice. You are advised to seek legal counsel in the event that you have a specific situation requiring legal attention.

The hypothetical examples given in this text reflect issues that often arise in the context of HIV research. The hypothetical characters that are portrayed in such examples are just that: hypothetical. Their resemblance to any person, whether living or dead, is coincidental.

ISBN 0-306-45055-0

A Division of Plenum Publishing Corporation
233 Spring Street, New York, N. Y. 10013

10 9 8 7 6 5 4 3 2 1

Printed in the United States of America

To Robert D. Debner, Jr.

Preface

The motivation and inspiration for this book come directly from experiences with clients during the years that I practiced HIV-related law at the Legal Aid Society of San Diego, Inc. The issues discussed in this work reflect issues that arose on a recurring basis with clients participating in HIV research studies, with investigators calling for guidance on the legal implications of particular aspects of their proposed studies, and with research institutions and health care facilities struggling to make sense of legal maneuvers aimed at obtaining the records of their HIV-infected patients. It is impossible to thank each of these persons individually for their provocative questions and their insights.

The discussion of ethical and legal issues relating to the design of clinical trials reflects questions raised during discussions with Donald J. Slymen, Ph.D. Don was one of the first researchers, in my realm of experience, to pay close attention to ethical concerns, and I am greatly appreciative of his contribution to both my professional growth and the development of various scenarios discussed in this text.

The portions of this text dealing with confidentiality are the result of many hours of thoughtful discussion and analysis with Penn Lerblance, J.D., now deceased and still missed. Penn and I often participated together as presenters of in-service training programs for health professionals. Penn addressed discrimination, and I focused on confidentiality. Our long and detailed debates on legal issues yet unresolved by the courts and the legislatures helped to focus the discussion here.

Many of the examples pertaining to scientific misconduct in the context of HIV research were obtained from Peter Lurie, M.D., M.P.H. I greatly appreciate his generosity in sharing these materials with me.

I am appreciative of colleagues' comments on earlier drafts of the manuscript and of their guidance in striking a balance herein between theory and practice. Several individuals reviewed earlier drafts of the manuscript critically and provided me with extensive constructive criticism. I thank, in particular, Linda S. Lloyd, Dr.P.H., Dean Chaisson, M.D., and Lynn Sivinski, J.D., M.P.H. This book would not have been possible without the able research assistance of Jacqueline Love-Baker, J.D., and her constructive and detailed critique of earlier versions of this work.

I am also grateful to my editor at Plenum Publishing, Mariclaire Cloutier, for her support and her wonderful sense of humor throughout the writing process. Everyone should be blessed with such an editor.

Contents

Part Two Issues Arising during the Study

Introduction

As of March 31, 1993, the Centers for Disease Control and Prevention (CDC) had reported a cumulative total of 289,320 AIDS cases and 182,275 AIDS-related deaths in the United States. CDC has estimated that there are over one million HIV-infected individuals in the United States, with approximately 40,000 new infections each year (California Department of Health Services, 1993).

Figures worldwide are equally alarming. As of the end of 1991, a cumulative total of 446,636 cases of AIDS had been reported globally. The World Health Organization estimates, however, that there were 1,475,000 cumulative adult AIDS cases by the end of 1991 (Tarantola, Mann, Mantel, & Cameron, 1994). Increase in the numbers of persons infected and affected by HIV has been particularly notable in several African countries, including Zaire and Uganda, and in parts of Southeast Asia, including Thailand.

Clearly, these increasing numbers and the human and economic costs of HIV infection provide the impetus for HIV research. Currently ongoing research efforts span a large number of disciplines, encompassing both the biological and the behavioral sciences. As AIDS research efforts increase in both number and intensity, it becomes even more crucial that researchers be cognizant of the legal and ethical implications of their actions, in order to protect themselves, the research participants, and the sponsoring research institutions from harm.

This book represents an effort to advise HIV researchers and individuals interested in pursuing HIV research of the basic legal and ethical principles related to such research. The text may also be useful to attorneys, who find that they are called upon to advise researchers and research institutions of the legal implications of their actions, but who may have little or no familiarity with the scientific principles involved. The book attempts to strike a balance between theory and practice. All too often, researchers may be provided with the underlying ethical and legal concepts applicable to their situations, but with little guidance on how to actually implement those principles in a specific context.

The organization of this book follows the sequence of a study: prestudy planning, issues that may arise during the course of the study, and issues that generally arise after the conclusion of the study. The fourth portion of the text addresses roles not traditionally encompassed within the scope of scientific research, such as legislative advocacy and appearances as an expert witness. These situations may arise both during and after the course of a study.

Part One, Prestudy Planning, reviews the evolution of protections for research participants and the ethical principles governing the conduct of scientific research. Special attention is paid to the conduct of clinical trials. Part Two focuses on issues relating to confidentiality and mandatory reporting of HIV status or AIDS, potential conflicts that may arise during the course of the study, and scientific misconduct. Part Three addresses responsibilities vis-à-vis the study participants and the scientific community. Part Four provides an overview of the judicial, legislative, and administrative systems on both a federal and state level, and suggests ways in which the HIV researcher can utilize his or her expertise in these arenas. Each chapter may be read singly or in conjunction with other related sections. Cross-references to related portions are provided throughout the text.

PART ONE

Prestudy Planning

CHAPTER ONE

The Evolution of Protections for Research Participants

The need for special protections for those participating as subjects in human experimentation and research became all too obvious from events during World War II and from a series of medical research projects performed in the United States through the 1960s and 1970s. Testimony at the trials of the Nazi physicians at Nuremberg documented the use of concentration camp prisoners in experiments without their consent. Such experiments included the exposure of prisoners to cold water and low air pressure (Appelbaum, Lidz, & Meisel, 1987); the injection of dye into the eyes in an attempt to change eye color; and the inoculation of prisoners with typhus bacilli (Grodin, 1992). United States history provides accounts of the now infamous Tuskegee study, in which 251 blacks were followed prospectively in order to examine the natural course of syphilis. Penicillin became available during the course of the study, but was never offered to the participants (Thomas & Quinn, 1991; Jones, 1992).

This chapter begins with the aftermath of the Nuremberg trials, when the Nuremberg Code was developed. It examines various international documents that enunciate precepts for the conduct of human experimentation. The chapter also discusses the development of ethical review of research in the United States, including the development of institutional review boards.

1.1. BRIEF HISTORY

The Nuremberg Code evolved as a result of the discovery of uncontrolled experimentation on humans by the Nazi physicians. The Code enumerates ten basic principles which were devised to be universally applicable to human research:

1. The voluntary consent of the prospective participant is essential.
2. The experiment must be expected to produce results beneficial for society, that cannot be obtained by any other means.
3. The study should be based on the results of animal experimentation and a knowledge of the natural history of the disease in question so that the anticipated results justify conducting the experiment.
4. All unnecessary physical and mental suffering or injury should be avoided during the course of the experiment.
5. No experiment should be conducted where it is believed that death or disabling injury will occur, except where the research physicians also serve as subjects.
6. The degree of risk should not exceed the humanitarian importance of the problem to be solved.
7. The participant should be protected against death or injury through the use of adequate facilities and preparations.
8. The experiment should be conducted only by scientifically qualified persons.
9. The participant has the right to end his or her participation in the experiment if he or she has reached a point where continuation seems to be impossible.
10. The scientist in charge must be prepared to terminate the experiment if he or she has probable cause to believe that continuation would be likely to result in the injury, disability, or death of the research participant (World Medical Association, 1991b; Annas & Grodin, 1992).

The Code has been subject to a great deal of criticism, for both errors of commission and omission. It has been criticized for its failure to differentiate between therapeutic clinical research and clinical research on healthy subjects and for failing to provide a review mechanism for the researcher's actions (Perley, Fluss, Bankowski, & Simon, 1992). Ultimately, these deficiencies generated discussion and the formulation of the Declaration of Helsinki.

The Declaration of Helsinki, adopted by the World Medical Assembly in 1964, diverges from the Nuremberg Code by allowing a surrogate to consent to participate in the research, where the actual participant is legally or physically unable to provide consent. It also distinguishes between clinical research combined with professional care and nontherapeutic clinical research. The Declaration was later revised in 1975, 1983, and 1989. Later modifications included an increased emphasis on the need for the voluntary informed consent of the individual to participate in experimentation (World Medical Association, 1991a; Perley *et al.*, 1992; Christakis & Panner, 1991).

The 1982 "Proposed International Guidelines for Biomedical Research Involving Humans" developed by the World Health Organization and the Council for International Organizations of Medical Sciences have the Nuremberg Code as their foundation. Unlike the Nuremberg Code and the Helsinki Declaration, however, the Guidelines emphasize the need for ethical review of the funding proposal by both the initiating agency and the host country where the research will occur (Perley *et al.*, 1992; Christakis & Panner, 1991).

Although the U.S. government became involved in the regulation of research in the early 1960s, it was not until 1974 that it promulgated regulations for the protection of human subjects in research that was supported by what was then the Department of Health, Education, and Welfare. The refined regulations provided that no research would be funded by that agency unless the prospective grant recipient had submitted the proposal to an institutional review board (IRB) for review and approval. The IRB was to be composed of at least five persons with specifically enumerated skills. The IRB was charged with the responsibility of reviewing the proposal to ensure that the risks of the research would be outweighed by the anticipated benefit; that the rights and the welfare of the research participants would be adequately protected; and that informed consent would be obtained by adequate and appropriate means [45 Code of Federal Regulations sections 46.102(b), currently at 45 Code of Federal Regulations sections 46.107, 46.111, 1993]. The regulations further defined informed consent, which was to include an explanation of the procedures to be utilized in the study; of the risks and benefits to the research participant; of alternative procedures or treatments available if the prospective participant did not wish to participate in the study; and an advisory to the participant that he or she would be free to withdraw from the study at any time, without fear of repercussions [45 Code of Federal Regulations section 46.103(c)(6), currently at 45 Code of Federal Regulations section 46.116, 1993].

Very few states have enacted legislation governing the conduct of human research. The few that have include Virginia, New York (Glantz, 1992), and California (California Health and Safety Code sections 24170-24179.5, 1992). Other states have devised procedures for obtaining informed consent from surrogate decision-makers where a prospective research participant is unable to give consent (R. J. Levine, 1991).

1.2. THE ROLE OF INSTITUTIONAL REVIEW BOARDS

The IRB is charged with the responsibility of reviewing all proposed research to be undertaken by or at an institution to determine whether the research participants will be placed at risk. If the research involves risk, the IRB must evaluate whether the potential risks to the participant are outweighed by the potential benefit to the participant; whether the rights and the welfare of the participants will be protected adequately; and whether legally effective informed consent will be obtained in a manner that is both adequate and appropriate (45 Code of Federal Regulations section 46.111, 1993). The IRB may also require that the researcher provide additional information to the prospective research participant, including the possibility of unforeseeable risks, circumstances in which the individual's participation may be terminated without his or her consent, costs to the participant of participating in the research, and the potential impact of the participant's decision to withdraw from the research (45 Code of Federal Regulations section 46.116, 1993). The IRB may also review the procedures that have been implemented to protect participants' privacy and the confidentiality of the data.

An IRB must adopt and follow written procedures for various functions. These include (1) the initial and continuing review of the research; (2) the reporting of its findings and actions to the principal investigator and the research institution; (3) the determination of which projects require review more frequently than once a year; (4) the determination of which projects require verification from persons other than the investigators to the effect that no material changes have occurred since the last IRB review; (5) the prompt reporting of proposed changes in the research activity to the IRB; (6) the prompt reporting to the IRB and officials of the research institution of any serious or continuing noncompliance by the investigator with the requirements or determinations of the IRB; and (7) the review of research involving children (California Association of Hospitals and Health Systems, 1992).

IRBs meet at regular intervals to review proposed and ongoing research projects. Members of the IRB cannot have competing interests, so that they can perform their duties without risk of bias. Membership of the IRB must reflect a cross section of the scientific and lay communities (45 Code of Federal Regulations section 46.107, 1993).

The IRB must maintain written documentation of its activities and meetings, where applicable. This documentation should include copies of all research proposals that have been reviewed; scientific evaluations accompanying the proposals; proposed sample consent forms; investigators' progress reports; reports of injuries to research participants; copies of all correspondence between the IRB and investigators; minutes of IRB meetings, including a list of attendees and the votes on each item; a list of IRB members and their credentials; and a copy of the IRBs written procedures (California Association of Hospitals and Health Systems, 1992).

Despite the laudatory goals underlying the formulation and implementation of IRBs, IRBs have been criticized for being overly permissive in their approval of proposed research (Classen, 1986), their apparent lack of impact on the readability and understandability of informed consent forms by uneducated research participants (Hammerschmidt & Keane, 1992), and their relative inability to ensure that the researchers actually utilize only the forms and procedures that have been approved for use (Delgado & Leskovac, 1986; Adkinson, Starklauf, & Blake, 1983). The lack of standardization between IRBs (Castronovo, 1993) may create the appearance of injustice (Rosenthal & Blanck, 1993). Current procedures have also been criticized for their lack of a remedy to a researcher's violation of a protocol, apart from termination of funding by the funding source (Delgado & Leskovac, 1986).

Conversely, other critics have charged that IRBs are often overzealous in acting as gatekeepers, at the expense of scientists, who are ethically bound to do good research (Rosenthal & Rosnow, 1984). In practice, IRBs of medical schools are more likely to review the science more critically than are IRBs located in liberal arts colleges (Rosnow, Rotheram-Borus, Blanck, & Koocher, 1993).

Several writers (Reiser & Knudson, 1993) have suggested the development of a position of "research intermediary" as a possible solution to some of the IRBs systemic shortcomings. The research intermediary would assure that the research participants understand the research process by discussing the informed consent forms with the participants before and after they have signed them. The intermediary would also monitor how well the research protocol was being followed. The intermediary would be hired and trained by the IRB, and would be charged with the responsibility of reporting directly to the IRB.

IRBs are now facing particularly difficult questions. Many new therapies and clinical trials involve individuals with life-threatening diseases; HIV is but one example. The principle of fairness mandates that individuals meeting the scientific eligibility criteria for a clinical trial, for instance, be invited to participate in clinical trials without regard to ethnicity, gender, or socioeconomic status (Mitchell & Steingrub, 1988). Yet, there are numerous examples of reasonable exclusions based on these factors. For instance, researchers may want to limit their own liability by excluding from participation individuals who do not have a regular physician or medical insurance, which could be needed in the event of an adverse drug reaction. Researchers may wish to exclude individuals whose native language is not English not for scientific reasons, but because staffing becomes more difficult once you are required to provide interpretation and translation services. The question of what constitutes an incentive to participate in research, versus a coercive inducement, has also become more complex as research studies increasingly include individuals from diverse cultural backgrounds and lower socioeconomic strata. (See Section 2.3 for further discussion of payments as incentives and coercive inducement.)

1.3. ETHICAL REVIEW IN THE HOST COUNTRY

Research to be conducted in a country outside of the United States will also require ethical approval of the host country. These mechanisms vary with the country and may or may not be similar to the U.S. model. This section provides a comparison between the ethical review process in the United States and several other countries.

Australia

In Australia, ethical review committees are known as Institutional Ethics Committees (IEC). They operate under the National Health and Medical Research Council (NHMRC). The Council is charged with the responsibility of making recommendations to the government on matters relating to medical research. The Council has formulated specific guidelines for the conduct of human research, guided in part by the Helsinki Declaration. The guidelines require that research participants be adequately informed of the risks and purposes of the research, that they consent to participation in writing, and that they be informed of their right to withdraw at any time. The National Bioethics Consultative Committee is responsible for advising the government on bioethical issues (Drahos, 1989).

Like the IRBs in the United States, the Australian IECs have been criticized for their inability to sanction researchers who fail to comply with the approved protocol or the established guidelines for research. The only real sanction is a financial one, through the withdrawal of research funding (Drahos, 1989).

The Netherlands

Research Ethics Committees (RECs) began to develop in the Netherlands in the 1970s and 1980s. A 1984 Order provided for the establishment of RECs in connection with hospitals, but specifically provided that several hospitals may come under one committee for the purpose of ethical review of research. The Order also requires that hospitals guarantee that a refusal by an individual to participate in a research study will not influence his or her entitlement to optimum care.

A recent study of RECs found that most experimental research in the Netherlands is conducted in academic and general hospitals. A small proportion is carried out in specialized and psychiatric hospitals. Most institutions where the research is conducted have mechanisms for the scientific review of the proposals. Most of the research institutions (78%) carry out their own ethical review, often by an REC, but sometimes by medical staff or medical management.

Membership of an REC varies in size from 3 to 13; medical specialists are heavily represented on the REC. One study found that about half of the RECs include a member of the clergy or an ethics specialist. Lawyers are most often members of academic RECs. The RECs rarely include nonprofessional representatives of consumer groups or patients organizations (Bergkamp, 1988).

RECs have been criticized for their lack of legal authority; for the lack of clarity with respect to the scope and depth of their review; and for their inability to ensure that investigators are complying with the approved protocol (Bergkamp, 1988). One writer has suggested the formation of regional RECs to increase their ability to review proposals independently and to increase uniformity in decision making. This would concomitantly reduce the ability of investigators to "shop around" for approval from a more permissive REC (Bergkamp, 1988).

Uganda

Membership on ethical review committees in Uganda tends to include primarily medical doctors, although some committees reviewing HIV-related research proposals include behavioral scientists. The committees are both hospital- and community-based.

Mulago Hospital, one of the largest hospitals in Uganda, maintains a Hospital Ethical Committee. The Committee includes one lawyer, who is also the hospital administrator. The seven committee members all work in the hospital.

The Medical School Faculty and Postgraduate Research Committee is charged with the review of faculty and student research proposals. Membership includes both MDs and non-MDs. All members of the Committee must be members of the teaching staff.

The AIDS Research Committee is responsible on a national level for the review and approval of all HIV-related research. The Committee includes physicians, basic scientists, social scientists, experts in education, and laypersons. It is one of the few committees whose membership includes individuals from diverse institutions.

These committees have been criticized for many of the same reasons as the IRBs and other ethical review bodies described above. The review committee may not be able to function as independently as it might wish, in view of its ties to the medical school or the hospital. The review of proposals may require lengthy time periods because of the lack of a quorum at meetings. Like other ethical review bodies, the committees in Uganda have no mechanism to ensure that the investigator actually complies with the approved protocol, and they have no ability to enforce compliance. Additionally, representation on the various committees is often not reflective of the tribal diversity within Uganda.

1.4. CONCLUSION

Ethical protections for participants in biomedical research have evolved over time, often in response to egregious conduct on the part of biomedical researchers. Committees have been developed and implemented in various forms to review the design and conduct of the research, in order to assure that appropriate protections for the participants have been put into place. The role of these committees has become increasingly complex as research itself becomes increasingly complex and as ethical and legal issues become increasingly intertwined.

CHAPTER TWO

Governing Principles

The ethical conduct of HIV-related research, like all biomedical research, is grounded on the fundamental ethical principles of beneficence, respect for persons, and justice. Each is crucial to the ethical and legal conduct of the research and each is complex in its implementation.

Beneficence refers to respect for individuals' decisions and to the protection of the research participants from harm. Application of this principle requires that the researchers make efforts to secure the well-being of the research participants and further requires a favorable balance between the risks and the benefits of the proposed research. The proposed research must be intended to provide valid and generalizable knowledge (Mendelson, 1991).

Respect for persons demands that individuals be treated as autonomous agents and that individuals with diminished autonomy be afforded additional protections. The principle of respect for persons encompasses the process of informed consent (Mendelson, 1991). Informed consent is discussed in detail in Section 2.2.

The principle of justice or fairness mandates that the benefits and the burdens of the research be equitably distributed among individuals or communities and that no single group be required to bear a disproportionate share of the risk. Investigators must ensure that the rights and welfare of particularly vulnerable research participants are protected and that the consent of participants who are under another's authority is voluntary and free from duress (Mendelson, 1991).

This chapter addresses the practical application of these principles to HIV-related research, through a discussion of risk–benefit ratios, the informed consent process, and voluntariness of consent. Application of the principle of justice in the context of recruitment for HIV-related research is discussed specifically in Chapter 4. Confidentiality, which relates to the individual's right to privacy and the potential risk of its violation, is examined in detail in Chapter 5.

2.1. BALANCING THE RISKS AND BENEFITS

Assessing Risk

Researchers are required to assess the risks and benefits to prospective research participants, and to advise them of the potential discomforts, risks, and benefits. Although most researchers think in terms of physical risk only, a number of other risks, some of which are unique to HIV research, are also critical. It is important that researchers begin to think in terms of this more general notion of risk. The IRB will review a research proposal to ensure that the participants will be receiving these advisories.

Risk can take a number of forms, including inconvenience, physical risk, psychological risk, social risk, economic risk, or legal risk. Risk can be involved in the actual research process, the setting of the research, or the dissemination of the research findings. The risk can be related to a number of substantive areas, including maintenance of participant's privacy and confidentiality; maintenance of participants' well-being; invalid scientific inferences which, if applied, can lead to harm; the development and implementation of, and adherence to, appropriate informed consent procedures; the potential for deception of prospective participants; and the equitable distribution of the benefits and the burdens of the research (Sieber, 1992). Risk is very difficult to assess, sometimes because the investigators are not attuned to the economic, legal, and social context from which the participants come, and sometimes because a participant's subjective view of the research is very different from that of the researcher, who approaches it from a very rational point of view. The following examples underscore these difficulties.

Example 1: The Research Process/Economic and Social Risk

A researcher wishes to conduct an HIV vaccine trial in a developing country. HIV infection often carries with it a social stigma, which can ultimately lead to an individual's ostracism from his or her family and community and the loss of employment. The developing country has no provisions for addressing discrimination related to HIV. There is a possibility, however slight, that individuals participating in a vaccine trial who actually receive a vaccine may seroconvert on a temporary basis and become antibody positive for HIV. Although the risk of seroconversion is minimal and only temporary from the researcher's point of view, the potential social and economic consequences (risks) are devastating from the prospective participants perspective. The mere fact that an individual is participating in the trial as a volunteer, even if he or she does not seroconvert, may result in stigmatization and adverse social and economic consequences.

Example 2: The Research Process/Legal Risk and Well-Being

Individuals are being recruited in the United States for HIV vaccine trials. There is the possibility, as indicated above, that individuals who receive the vaccine may temporarily become antibody positive. A prospective research participant is interested in volunteering. However, he plans to travel to another country for a year to do research under a fellowship program. The country in question screens long-term residents for HIV infection. If his antibody test comes up positive, the host country may deny him entry, and he will be forced to find another research sponsor or to try to postpone his research until such time as he becomes antibody negative. Either scenario would require substantial modification of his plans.

Example 3: The Research Setting/Social Risk and Confidentiality

Researchers wish to assess the prevalence of HIV risk behaviors within the homeless population in a large urban area. They approach people on the street to enlist their cooperation. However, they do not make provisions to meet with individuals later in a more private setting. Individuals are reluctant to speak to the investigators because there is no real confidentiality in such a setting. An individual could be ostracized socially as the result of disclosed behaviors.

Example 4: Uses of the Research/Legal and Economic Risk and Well-Being

A researcher wishes to survey employees at different hospitals and medical clinics to ascertain levels of compliance with universal precautions for the handling of bodily fluids. The researchers intend to use the results to make recommended changes in the educational process for employees. The employees fear that the hospital administrators want access to the data to use it for disciplinary proceedings against employees who fail to follow guidelines. The employees refuse to participate in the study because of the potential legal and economic risks.

Potential solutions exist in each of these scenarios. In the cases involving the possible seroconversion of recipients receiving an HIV vaccine, these include the issuance of a study identification card or verification by letter from the research sponsor of the individuals true HIV negative status. The hospital administrators in Example 4 could issue a memorandum specifying that they will not have access to the data collected, and the researchers can maintain their data using identification numbers, rather than names. These examples do illustrate, however, the potential for differing perceptions of the risks and benefits as between the researcher and the prospective participant.

Assessing Benefits

The anticipated benefits of particular research may take several forms. The benefit may be to the participant directly, to the community, to other individuals affected by the same condition as the research participants, and to the researcher or his or her institution. Many times, the benefits of the research will not be obvious at the conclusion of an individual's participation. This is particularly true, for instance, where an HIV-infected person dies before the conclusion of the study and the study will not be completed for several more years, at which time the findings will be disseminated. It is important that participants understand that benefits to them resulting from their participation may not be visible in the short run and, in some cases, may never be realized.

Balancing the Risks and Benefits

The principle of beneficence, discussed in more detail below, requires a favorable balancing of the benefits against the risks. This requirement has been incorporated into federal regulations. It is very important, again, that in weighing the risks and the benefits, the researcher consider the balance not only from his or her perspective, but from that of the prospective participant as well. Consider the following example.

"Patient" has health insurance through his employment, but it has a very low lifetime limit. He is aware that one serious illness will result in the decimation of his health care benefits. He is very religious, and his faith requires that he be buried with all of his body parts in order to receive last rites. He is approached to enroll in a longitudinal study of HIV-infected persons with a particular opportunistic infection. From the researcher's point of view, the benefits clearly outweigh the risks. The individual will receive periodic tests, such as a neuropsychological examination, periodic serological examinations, and periodic clinical evaluations. All of this information will be provided to Patient's private physician, at no cost to Patient. The discomfort from any of the procedures, such as a blood drawing or spinal tap, will be minimal and temporary. From Patient's point of view, the risks may outweigh the benefits of having these results reported to his physician. Patient may have a fear of needles or may have heard from other patients that the pain associated with a spinal tap is far from minimal. Although the results may provide important information that can be used in the management of his clinical care, he will have to miss a significant amount of time from work in order to participate in the study. He would then stand a good chance of being fired. Without his employment, he would not have any medical coverage because he is unable to qualify for publicly funded medical insurance. If his co-workers were to discover that he were HIV positive and enrolled in an AIDS study, he would likely face social ostracism at work. Clearly, the considerations that are important to the patient are very different, and weigh very differently, than the considerations of the researcher.

The risk–benefit ratio may be a particularly difficult calculation in the case of HIV-infected children who are being considered for participation in clinical trials (clinical trials are discussed in greater detail in Chapter 3). The goal of expediting research to benefit HIV-infected children generally may be inconsistent with the needs of a particular child participant. As Ackerman (1990) explained,

> First, children recruited for phase I trials will be in the later stages of their illness, since they are usually not eligible until phase II or III drugs have proven ineffective or unacceptably toxic in their treatment. As a result, they will have incurred a substantial burden of prior suffering and may be significantly debilitated. Second, many subjects in phase I trials do not receive potentially therapeutic doses of the drugs being studied, because the increments in dosing for consecutive groups of subjects usually begin with a very conservative low dose. Third, exposure to unexpected toxicities and additional monitoring procedures may compound the suffering. . . . Further, many drugs that enter phase I testing do not yield evidence of potential efficacy. . . .

> Finally, the harm/benefit ratio of participating in a phase I trial must be compared to the alternative management strategy of using only measures that enhance the comfort of the patient.

The balancing of risks and benefits to child and adolescent participants is rendered even more difficult because children may perceive the risks and benefits quite differently than does the researcher or a parent. For example, the administration of a vaccine by injection may represent a minor discomfort to the researcher, but a child or adolescent may perceive the injection as "very painful" (Bjune & Arnesen, 1992). For additional discussion relating to children's ability to participate in a decision to enroll in research, see Section 2.3.

2.2. INFORMED CONSENT

Informed consent requires an assessment of the prospective participant's legal capacity to provide informed consent, the provision of adequate information to allow the prospective participant to decide whether or not to join the study, the individual's comprehension of the information that is provided, and a voluntary decision by the individual with respect to participation (Grodin, Kaminow, & Sassower, 1986; Mendelson, 1991).

Like review by an IRB, the informed consent procedure serves to minimize the harm resulting from the research (Capron, 1991). It cannot be emphasized enough that informed consent is a *process* that begins with the inception of the study and continues to its conclusion (United States Public Health Service, 1991). All too often, researchers have interpreted the informed consent process as consisting only of obtaining the participant's signature on an approved form, signifying the patient's understanding of, and consent to, the research to be undertaken. Far too little attention has been paid to whether the participant actually understands what has been explained, whether the participant's consent is voluntary, and whether the participant's continuing participation in the research is both informed and voluntary.

Numerous reasons exist for protecting the integrity of the informed consent procedure. First, the risks of experimentation may not be ascertainable in advance. Since the outcome is unknown, e.g., whether the new HIV vaccine will protect against infection, only the prospective participant can decide whether or not to proceed.

Second, there is no reason to defer to medical expertise in the context of biomedical research because it does not exist in experimental settings in the same sense as it does in clinical settings. The researcher intends to obtain new knowledge, rather than to apply existing knowledge for the patient's benefit. For instance, a blinded, randomized clinical trial of a new antiretroviral drug does not seek to delay the deterioration of a specific participant's immune functioning, but rather to acquire knowledge to be applied to the drug development and the benefit of patients generally. In this setting no one is better equipped to decide what to do than the individual. The patient knows better than the researcher how he or she feels each morning on awakening and how the HIV is affecting his or her ability to function normally. The patient also knows how much discomfort he or she is willing to endure to participate in the trial.

Third, participation in research does not provide a benefit certain to the participant, i.e., the vaccine may not provide protection against HIV infection.

Fourth, the researcher and the prospective participant may have conflicting interests and the participant is in the best position to protect his or her own interests. This could occur, for instance, where the researcher has a related financial interest (Finkel, 1991) or where the researcher and the participant have a conflict of values. The researcher is interested in pursuing remedies that will help other patients and add to the researchers academic standing. The potential participant, on the other hand, is concerned with the avoidance or alleviation of pain, the prolongation of life, and the diminution of bothersome symptoms. The balancing of values would lead each to assess the benefits of the research quite differently (Delgado & Leskovac, 1986).

Assessing Capacity

The determination of capacity is actually a legal determination. There are no clear standards for determining whether or not a person has capacity to give informed consent. Generally, a person will probably be deemed to have capacity if he or she is able to understand the nature of the research, the nature of his or her participation in the research, the risks and benefits potentially resulting from participation, and the alternatives to participation (High, 1992; Lo, 1990).

Clinically, a researcher can assess the prospective participant's capacity to consent to participation by conducting a short mental status test. This will provide very basic information about the individual's orientation to time and place, his or her ability for immediate recall, his or her short- and long-term memory, and the ability to perform simple calculations (Lo, 1990). Caution must be used, however, in the selection of these tests and the interpretation of the results. The apparent results may be misleading where the questions on which they were based are culture-dependent or in a language that the individual does not understand well.

Example

The mental status examination to be administered is in English and contains several questions relating to current politics, such as the names of the president and the mayor. The potential participant being screened is completely unconcerned with, and uninformed about, the political affairs of the world. She is being interviewed on a day when she is feeling particularly tired. She often finds that fatigue affects her ability to understand or respond in English, which is not her original language. She responds very poorly to many of the questions, and the interviewer concludes that she does not have capacity to understand what is being told to her and to consent. In actuality, she does have capacity, but was interviewed in an inappropriate language with culture-linked questions.

An assessment of a prospective research participant's capacity becomes particularly important with specific populations. These include HIV-infected children and individuals affected by AIDS dementia.

Participation of Children. Federal regulations governing research require that parental permission be obtained as a prerequisite to the child's participation in research. Such consent may be required even in situations where state law has recognized the capacity of the minor as a result of a particular status, such as emancipation, marriage, or pregnancy; in connection with the treatment of a sexually transmitted disease; or as a "mature minor," in connection with the evaluation of and selection from among alternative medical treatments (Brock, 1994). Some states have implemented alternative procedures to obtain consent in situations where a natural parent is unavailable or unable to consent, including a medical guardianship for the foster parent, a central review board to approve protocols and enrollment of children on a case-by-case basis, and increased assistance to the pediatric investigator (Levine, 1991a).

The requirement of parental consent rests on several premises. First, it recognizes the child's inability to decide for him- or herself to participate in the research. The underlying assumption is that the parent or parents can more capably decide the issue than can the child. Second, the requirement recognizes that the parents must bear the consequences of a decision to participate or to refrain from participating in the research and, accordingly, extends to the parents some degree of control over that decision. Third, the requirement of parental consent allows parents to resolve the issue of their child's participation in accordance with their own values, and to use the issue of participation as an opportunity to communicate those values to their child. Additionally, parental decision making may foster family intimacy and permit decision making by those individuals on whom the child would normally wish to rely (Brock, 1994).

In many situations, applicable federal regulations may require that the researcher explain the research to the child to the extent that he or she is able to understand, using language that the child can understand. Separate assent to participation in the research should be solicited from the child, in addition to obtaining parental permission, where the child is able to understand what is to be done and what the potential risks and benefits are and is able to signify assent. The requirement of obtaining a child's assent implies that the child can, at least in theory, veto the desire of the parents to have the child participate (Leikin, 1993; Melton, 1989).

In some situations, a child's age may be directly relevant to the research to be conducted. For instance, an investigator may wish to survey attitudes toward safe sex and the prevalence of risk behaviors for HIV transmission among gay adolescents. In this situation, the requirement of parental permission would most likely obviate a teenager's participation if his parents did not know that he was gay and he did not wish to have them know. The exclusion of participants in this category because of lack of parental permission could result in the loss of important information. Traditionally, parental permission would be required for participation (Holder, 1983). However, federal regulations provide for the waiver of parental permission in some circumstances, but mandate that alternative procedures be implemented to protect the interests of the minor (Nolan, 1990). Consequently, it may still be an open question as to whether an adolescent can legally or ethically consent to participate in such research without parental consent or surrogate consent, where such research entails only minimal risk of harm.

A minor can consent to participate in research without parental permission if the minor has attained the legal age that would be required for consent to treatment for that condition (Morrissey, Hofmann, & Thorpe, 1986). For instance, a minor can consent to participate in research related to the treatment of chlamydia if he or she has attained the legal age required for treatment without parental consent. It is unclear, however, whether a minor can consent to participate in research that is not directly related to treatment, as in the example involving the survey of gay HIV seropositive adolescents. A minor who has been legally emancipated, whether through court decision or the occurrence of a specific act, such as marriage, is by definition able to consent to his or her participation. (For additional discussion relating to children's ability to participate in research, see Section 2.3.)

AIDS Dementia. AIDS dementia complex occurs in 16 to 21% of HIV-infected patients who have progressed to AIDS (de Gans & Portegies, 1989; Levy & Bredesen, 1988; McArthur, 1987). The diagnosis of AIDS dementia is often one of exclusion (Portegies *et al.*, 1993). Independent factors found to be associated with the risk of AIDS dementia at the time of AIDS diagnosis include being female, being of older age, and having injected drugs (Chiesi *et al.*, 1994). The course of the dementia is progressive and may be characterized by confusion, distractibility, apathy, emotional lability, and anxiety. Patients may also experience motor coordination problems (Boccellari & Zeifert, 1994).

Several potential resolutions exist if the individual is suffering from confusion and disorientation at the time participation is being considered. If the researcher determines that the individual does not have the capacity to understand the information that is being conveyed and cannot give consent, the researcher may conclude that the individual cannot participate in the study even if he or she is otherwise eligible for enrollment based on inclusion and exclusion criteria. Federal regulations do provide for the possibility of obtaining consent to participate from an individual authorized under applicable law to make this decision where the potential research participant lacks capacity to do so (Bein, 1991). This gives the researcher initial permission to seek consent for participation from a surrogate decision maker. Whether any individual is authorized under law to give consent to another individual's participation in research may ultimately depend on governing state and federal law and regulation at the time the decision is to be made. Other considerations may impact the researcher's chosen course of action, including the time and resources that would be required to obtain this consent, the quality of the relationship between the prospective participant and the individual legally recognized to provide surrogate consent, the nature of the research to be conducted (Grodin *et al.*, 1986), and the politics of enrolling such an individual in a study.

Not uncommonly, individual's infected with HIV will execute durable powers of attorney for health care or general powers of attorney. These documents permit an individual to designate another to act as his or her decision maker in specific situations when he or she is unable to make decisions because of physical or mental incapacity. In some cases, the HIV-infected individual may have designated an individual to make determinations regarding the HIV-infected individual's participation in experimental research. In such instances, the researcher may rely on the consent of the designated surrogate if the document was executed in accordance with the applicable state law and that state law recognizes the designation of an agent for that purpose. For a more detailed discussion of durable powers of attorney for health care and the ability of the designated agent to consent for the patient or research participant, see Section 6.3 and Form 6.1.

Information

The informed consent process must provide potential participants information about the purpose of the study, the fact that it is a study and not the usual process of clinical care, the methods to be used, the potential benefits to the participant and to others that may result from the research, and the foreseeable risks or discomforts associated with participation in the research (Herxheimer, 1988; Portney & Watkins, 1993; United States Public Health Service, 1991). The participant must also be advised about any alternatives to participation that exist, the extent to which confidentiality will be maintained, and any care available to the participant if the participant were to suffer an injury as a direct result of the research. Each participant must be given a chance to ask any questions and must have those questions answered. The participant should be given the name and telephone number of a specific individual who can be contacted if questions arise in the future. Additionally, the participant must be advised whether compensation will be received for his or her participation, that his or her consent to participate is voluntary, and that he or she may cease participation at any time without loss of any benefit to which he or she would otherwise be entitled (Owens, 1987).

Questions frequently arise about the extent to which details of the study must be explained to an individual (Dal-Re, 1992; Tobias, 1988). Researchers may be concerned that full disclosure will frighten potential participants and discourage their enrollment, resulting in the prolongation of the planned recruitment period or the abandonment of the research (Lara & de la Fuente, 1990; Thong & Harth, 1991). It is important, however, that an individual be provided with sufficient information for the individual to understand how participation will impact his or her life. Such details may be related to risks and benefits specific to an individual and may impact on the individual's willingness and ability to participate in the research. (See Section 4.2 for a discussion of the researcher's failure to reveal important details of the study to participants in the Tuskegee study, conducted from 1932 to 1972, and how this withholding of information continues to impact biomedical research today.)

The voluntariness of an individual's consent to participate in a clinical trial has also been called into question where the prospective participant is not made aware of the funding mechanism for the research. Shimm and Spece (1991b) have pointed out that pharmaceutical manufacturers often contract with clinical investigators to conduct pre-market testing of new products. Shimm and Spece argue that this presents a conflict of interest because the clinician may propose participation to a patient who would be better served on an individual basis by a different treatment or no treatment. The patient, often unaware of this potential conflict, may agree to participate based on his or her faith in the clinician. They propose that informed consent forms disclose such potential conflicts and that monies earned through such a contractual arrangement be returned to the medical school, rather than the individual investigator's operating budget.

The failure to provide sufficient detail about the research prior to participation may facilitate an individual's enrollment, but may later result in the individual's withdrawal from the research study and ill feeling toward the researchers and the sponsoring institution. For instance, a longitudinal study of HIV may require that an individual visit the study site once every six months for a physical examination, blood draws, and the completion of questionnaires. Unless further detail is provided, the individual may assume that such procedures are no more detailed or lengthy than a visit to his or her primary physician, which may require at most the allocation of an hour plus transportation time. The individual may suffer unforeseen consequences, such as the loss of a day's wages for each follow-up visit were these semiannual visits to require five or six hours plus travel time. If the prospective participants knew in advance that they would miss this much time from work for each examination, they might choose not to participate in the study. A participant who experiences the latter and is then forced to choose between continued participation in the study or work-related consequences may feel that he or she was misled and may withdraw from the study. This would, of course, lead to additional costs for the researcher and the research institution.

Additional information must be provided to research participants who are to be tested for HIV during the course of the research. Individuals must be told specifically that they will be tested for HIV and that they may receive the results of the HIV test if they wish. They should be told the extent to which their HIV test results will remain confidential (World Health Organization, Global Programme on AIDS, 1993). It is generally required in the United States that research participants tested for HIV be told of their serostatus (Office for Protection from Research Risks, 1988).

In some situations it will be deemed unethical to test for HIV and not give the participant the test results. In such cases, the prospective participant must consent to be told his or her test results or else not participate. Sometimes an exception will be made when it is believed that the harm engendered by disclosure outweighs that of nondisclosure. This can occur, for instance, when a participant threatens to commit suicide if he or she learns of his or her HIV seropositivity, or when a parent threatens to withdraw a child from treatment if the physician researcher discloses to the child that the child is HIV seropositive.

The disclosure of HIV seropositivity to research participants may likewise be deemed unethical. Consider the following situation. Research is to be conducted in a developing country. The researcher wishes to determine risk factors for HIV in specific communities and use that knowledge as the basis for developing an effective intervention program. However, at the time that the serosurvey is to be conducted, there is no treatment available in that country for HIV, condoms are difficult to acquire and costly when they can be found, and persons with HIV infection are highly stigmatized and likely to lose their jobs, homes, and families if their serostatus becomes known. The government of this country believes that disclosure of an individual's test results in this context amounts to the delivery of a death sentence and will not permit research to go forward without an agreement not to disclose. In such a situation, the researcher, the funding agency, and the government must weigh the benefits of proceeding with the research under such constraints against the potential harms.

Individuals who are to receive HIV testing must be given counseling prior to administration of the HIV test. The counseling must occur in a confidential setting. Counseling should include a discussion of how HIV can be transmitted, how HIV can progress, and that the results of a blood test for HIV antibody may be positive, negative, or indeterminate. The participant should be given an explanation of what each of these results means. Additionally, the participant should be told that HIV infection is not the same as AIDS and that the HIV test cannot detect HIV infection when someone is in the window period between exposure and the development of antibody. The participant's personal risk factors for HIV should be discussed, as well as techniques to reduce or eliminate any currently existing risk factors. Arrangements should be made for the participant's return to get the test results. Pretest counseling should also include a discussion of what the participant would do were the result to be positive and likewise were the result negative (World Health Organization, Global Programme on AIDS, 1993).

Posttest counseling should occur when the individual returns to receive his or her HIV test results. Such counseling includes reporting the result of the test to the individual, explaining the meaning of the result, discussing the participant's concerns, and discussing how to avoid transmission of HIV and other sexually transmitted diseases (World Health Organization, Global Programme on AIDS, 1993). Both HIV-positive and -negative individuals should be provided with a list of resources for further information and counseling.

It is crucial that individuals to be tested for HIV be told clearly the extent to which the investigators are able to safeguard the confidentiality of the results and the potential consequences of any breach of confidentiality. For instance, disclosure of an individual's HIV seropositivity could, in some settings, result in the loss of employment or ostracism from the community. It is the investigator's responsibility to reduce the possibility of such disclosures. Various strategies can be used, including the omission of identifying information where possible, limiting access to the data (World Health Organization, Global Programme on AIDS, 1993), and including both HIV-seronegatives and -seropositives in the study so that association with the study itself is not stigmatizing.

The ethics of blinded HIV surveillance testing remains controversial. Blinded HIV surveillance testing relies on blood samples drawn for another purpose in selected settings, from which all personal identifiers have been removed (Bayer, 1993). Blinded testing has been justified on the grounds that seroprevalence data available from such studies are crucial to projections regarding the impact of HIV in particular communities (Bayer, 1993); that personal privacy is assured because there are no identifying data that can be linked to individuals; and that it is a cost-effective measure for the ascertainment of prevalence estimates. Unlinked HIV seroprevalence testing is permitted in the United States. It is supported in Canada by the Royal Society of Canada and the National Advisory Committee on AIDS; it is supported internationally by the World Health Organization (Federal Centre for AIDS Working Group on Anonymous Unlinked HIV Seroprevalence Research, 1992).

Criticisms have been leveled against blinded HIV testing in the United States for its utilization of disadvantaged populations, including drug users, runaways, the homeless, and those with other sexually transmitted diseases, without their knowledge (information) or consent, and the testing's failure to confer any benefit on the individuals tested.

These studies have been compared to the Tuskegee study of syphilis-infected blacks, who were neither told that their participation was in conjunction with research nor approached for consent to participate in research (Isaacman, 1993). Opponents of blinded testing in Great Britain have argued that such research represents poor science and mistaken public health ethics. Great Britain, like the United States, ultimately approved blinded HIV surveillance testing, but permits individuals to refuse to allow their blood to be HIV-tested. However, there is no requirement that individuals be specifically advised that their blood could be tested for HIV antibodies (Bayer, Lumey, & Wan, 1991).

State law may require additional disclosures to the research participants. For instance, California requires that research participants be given a copy of the "Experimental Subject's Bill of Rights" before the researcher can obtain consent from the individual to participate in a medical experiment (California Health and Safety Code section 24172, 1992). Consequently, state law should always be consulted prior to drafting an informed consent form.

Comprehension

All too often, researchers assume that because they understand a written consent form and accompanying information about a study, the prospective participant also understands it. Studies have shown, however, that information about research studies is often written at a level well above the participant's educational level and that written informed consent forms often require more than an eighth grade education to be understood (Hammerschmidt & Keane, 1992; Meade & Howser, 1992). Poor readability often results from the inclusion of unfamiliar words, long words, and long sentences (Rivera, Reed, & Menius, 1992). Research has also indicated that participants may not understand the information about the study as well when it is presented to them by a physician only, rather than a physician and a nurse (Lynch, 1988; Tankanow, Sweet, & Weisikoff, 1992).

Comprehension will be facilitated if the materials and the written consent form are written at an appropriate readability level. Readability is often measured using either the Fry Readability Scale or the Flesch Readability Formula (Silva & Sorrell, 1988). These scales determine the readability level by relying on computations involving the number of sentences per designated selection and the number of syllables per designated selection. Many researchers have recommended that the reading level of informed consent forms be no higher than the eighth grade. However, some funding sources now require that informed consent forms be written at a sixth grade reading level or lower. The lower the readability level is, the more likely that the prospective participant will be able to comprehend the information presented (LoVerde, Prochazka, & Byyny, 1989; Young, Hooker, & Freeberg, 1990).

Readability, however, is only one of several factors that may affect a participant's comprehension (Silva & Sorrell, 1988). Confinement to bed has been found to affect comprehension negatively (Cassileth, Zupkis, Sutton-Smith, & March, 1980). Reliance on nonmedical personnel or a third party to present and review information for informed consent has been determined to increase comprehension (Benson, Roth, Appelbaum, Lidz, & Winslade, 1988; Muss, White, Michielutte, *et al.,* 1979). Understanding may be increased if the prospective participant is given sufficient time to study the information prior to signing the informed consent document (Lavelle-Jones, Byrne, Rice, & Cuschieri, 1993; Morrow, Gootnick, & Schmale, 1978; Tankanow *et al.,* 1992). A simple, clear, and concise manner of presentation on the written consent form has been found to enhance comprehension (Epstein & Lasagna, 1969; Simel & Feussner, 1992).

Additional modifications of presentation may be necessary to facilitate comprehension, particularly where the individual has experienced loss in the ability to organize and integrate information (Peterson, Clancy, Champion, & McLarty, 1992). Organizational modifications include varying the size of the type or the spacing of information or using advance organizers (Taub, 1986), using a multicomponent program that includes both written materials and other audiovisual aids (DCCT Research Group, 1989), or the use of graphics and summary declarative statements (Peterson *et al.,* 1992). The use of a video as a way of explaining the research has been found particularly helpful with prospective participants in psychiatric research (Benson *et al.,* 1988).

It may be necessary in many situations to develop and to utilize consent forms in a language other than English, and to conduct the entire informed consent process in a language other than English. This may occur, for instance, if the researcher is conducting an assessment of HIV risk behaviors in a community in a non-English-speaking country. The conduct of research in a community in the United States that is primarily non-English speaking, such as Southeast Asian refugees to the United States, would similarly demand non-English materials even though the study is to be conducted in the United States.

It is crucial that prospective participants be able to understand the forms that have been developed for their use and that the non-English versions accurately reflect the content included in the English version. Comprehension is facilitated by the use of simple sentences, the repetition of nouns rather than pronouns, the avoidance of metaphors, the avoidance of the passive voice in the English version, and the avoidance of the subjective mood. Various translation techniques can be used to increase the accuracy of the translation, including back translation, committee review, and pretest procedures. Back translation, requiring translation from the source language to the target language by one individual and blind translation from the target language back to the source language by a second person, has been found to be particularly effective (Brislin, 1970). These various techniques can also be combined to enhance the accuracy of the translation.

There is evidence suggesting that participants in studies with informed consent processes that portray realistically the demands that will be made on the participants are more likely to adhere to the study protocol over time (DCCT Research Group, 1989). Participant adherence to the study protocol has been particularly problematic in the context of AIDS research. This may be related to individuals' desperation to access any form of potential benefit, including drugs from "guerrilla clinics," and a perception that because they have been stigmatized and excluded from mainstream society, they are not obligated to conform to the researchers protocol (Arras, 1990). The ongoing provision of accurate information to prospective and current participants in an HIV-related study may do much to engender trust between the researchers and the participants and frame the role of the study participants as "coadventurers" with input into the process of the adventure (Arras, 1990).

It is important to stress that the informed consent form is but one component of the informed consent process. It is, however, important. Despite its limitations, the form provides some protection for the participant in that it advises him or her of the nature of the research, its risks and benefits, the participant's ability to withdraw or to refuse to participate, and various other elements, previously discussed. The execution of an appropriate consent form by a competent participant indicates that the researcher and the research institution notified the participant, as required ethically and legally, of the various elements of the research. The failure to obtain appropriate consent may not only result in harm to the patient-participant, because he or she does not have sufficient information to truly comprehend the situation, but may also result in disciplinary action by the funding agency against the researcher and the research institution. In a non HIV situation, the FDA recently ordered a major research institution to cease enrollment of patients into many experimental drug studies following the death of a female trial participant who had undergone an experimental procedure. The woman had signed the wrong consent form (Dalton, 1994b).

Several sample informed consent forms follow this section. These forms attempt to communicate as much information as possible to prospective participants in a seroprevalence study of HIV. There are two separate forms for participation in one study. One form is more general in nature and discusses the objectives of the study and how it is to be conducted. The second form addresses the HIV testing specifically. Both forms are written at the sixth grade reading level as measured by the Fry Readability Scale. These forms are written in the first person so that the individual reading the form can apply the information to himself or herself more easily. A line for the signature of a witness is included on the form so that an illiterate or physically incapacitated participant's "X" on the signature line, in lieu of a signature, can be witnessed.

2.3. VOLUNTARINESS

Issues relating to the voluntariness of consent often arise in situations where the individual's consent to participate in research could potentially result from coercion or duress. The concern stems from the inherently coercive nature of certain situations. Particular concern has been voiced for individuals in vulnerable situations, such as prisoners, the terminally ill, children, those suffering from an impairment in cognitive functioning, those receiving payment as an incentive to participate, and those with no other treatment options, including participants in developing countries. Common to each of these groups is the potential for abuse by those who wield authority over them or possess a benefit of such value that its transmittal to a research participant may be coercive of his or her participation. The issue of how to assure voluntariness of consent in each of these situations has not been resolved definitively. The discussions below are designed to raise the ethical issues in each instance, and to explore mechanisms for their potential resolution.

Participation of Prisoners

Through 1989, a cumulative total of 5411 AIDS cases had been reported among inmates of federal, state, and county prison systems (Hammett & Dubler, 1990). Results of mass mandatory HIV antibody screening programs and blinded studies indicate that the HIV seroprevalence rate in many correctional populations is approximately 1% (Moini

Purpose of Study

_______________ University and _______________ Hospital are doing a study together. The study wants to know how I think they can teach people to avoid HIV infection. The study wants to know if many people have HIV.

The study will ask me questions. The researchers will test my blood for HIV.

Procedures

The researchers will ask me to answer questions about HIV (the human immunodeficiency virus). They will ask me some questions about my age and family status. This will be done privately. They will take a sample of my blood to test it for HIV. They will give me the results within two weeks of the test. They will explain the results to me. They will give me counseling. They will not tell anyone else the result.

Risks/Discomfort

Some people get sore at the place where the blood is taken. Some people get dizzy or feel faint when the blood is drawn. The researchers will give me medical care if I have a medical problem during this part. They cannot pay me if I have a problem. I might feel upset by the questions. I can skip questions. I can stop answering questions.

Joining the Study

If I decide to join the study, the researchers will give me another consent form to sign for my HIV test. If I have any questions now, I should contact
_______________. If I want to join the study, I must agree to learn my HIV result.

Benefits

I will learn my HIV test result. If I am negative, I will learn ways to stay negative. If I am HIV positive, I will learn how to keep from infecting other people. I will learn ways to stay in good health.

Alternatives

I can decide not to join the study. I can decide to leave the study at any time. If I leave, I will not lose any benefits that I would normally get.

Privacy

The researchers will do their best to keep all information about me from other people. They will not give out any information about me or my file without my consent.

Form 2.1. Informed consent.

By signing this form, I am telling you that I wish to join the study described above. If I join, the researchers will give me more information and another consent form. I can ask questions at any time.

Date: ____________________ Participant ____________________

Interviewer ____________________

Witness ____________________

Form 2.1. *Continued.*

HIV Testing

1. The HIV test will test my blood for HIV (the human immunodeficiency virus). This is the virus that can cause AIDS.
2. I should only agree to have my blood tested for HIV if I can agree freely.
3. I understand that the study will try to keep my HIV test results private from other people.

A Positive Test Result

1. A positive test result means that I can spread the HIV virus.
2. A positive test result means that I can spread the HIV virus to other people by having sex.
3. A positive test result means that I can spread the HIV virus to other people by sharing needles.
4. A positive test result does not mean that I have AIDS.
5. If my test result is positive, I may feel upset. I may feel that other people treat me badly if they learn my test result.

An Unclear Result

1. Sometimes a test result is not negative and it is not positive. I can't tell what my HIV result is.
2. This kind of result is called "indeterminate."
3. An unclear result does not mean that I have HIV.
4. An unclear result does not mean that I do not have HIV.
5. An unclear result means that I do not know if I have HIV.

A Negative Test Result

1. A negative result may mean that I do not have HIV.

Form 2.2. Informed consent and agreement to HIV testing.

2. Sometimes, a person may be infected but have a negative result. This happens because it can take 6 months or more for the test to become positive after infection.
3. Even if I have a negative test now, I can become infected by having sex unless I use condoms.
4. Even if I have a negative test now, I can become infected by sharing needles.

What Will Be Done If My Test Is Positive

1. I will be told how to stay in good health.
2. I will be told where I can go for counseling and medical care.
3. I will be told how to keep from spreading HIV infection. I can do this by avoiding sexual intercourse or by using safer sex. I can do this by not sharing needles or not using drugs. I should not donate my blood, plasma, or organs. If I am a man, I should not donate my sperm. If I am a woman, I can avoid spreading HIV by not getting pregnant.
4. No one will give my HIV test result to anyone without my consent.

What Will Be Done If My Test Result Is Unclear

1. I will be told how to stay in good health.
2. I will be told to go for testing again in 3 months. I will receive a list of places where I can go.
3. I will receive counseling.

What Will Be Done If My Test Result Is Negative

1. I will be told how to stay in good health.
2. I will be told how to keep from getting HIV infection.
3. I will be told how to keep from spreading HIV infection.

I was given a chance to ask questions about this test. My questions were answered.

I agree to have my blood drawn for the HIV antibody (or ________________) test.

Date: __________________________ Participant ______________________

Interviewer ______________________

Witness ______________________

Form 2.2. *Continued.*

& Hammett, 1990). In addition, the extent to which HIV is transmitted between prison inmates continues to be an issue of concern.

The quality of medical care available to prisoners generally, and to HIV-infected prisoners specifically, has been subject to considerable criticism. One class action lawsuit charged that New York State's medical and mental health services for incarcerated HIV-infected persons "have caused and continue to cause an accumulation of class members' deaths, an inexcusable increase in their suffering, and a loss of their very humanity" (*Inmates of New York State with HIV v. Cuomo et al.*, 1990).

Given this background, it is hardly surprising that concerns have been voiced that benefits obtained through participation in HIV-related studies to remedy systemic deprivations experienced by the participant in the prison situation are, in fact, coercive. Some writers have even suggested that an institutional review board might be able to preempt a prisoner's ability to choose whether to participate in research, based on the belief that HIV-infected prisoners cannot be educated adequately about the risks inherent in their participation and, consequently, are unable to make an informed decision like unincarcerated persons (Dubler & Sidel, 1989).

In reality, benefits such as single cells for prisoners who want them are beyond what most prison systems today can provide (Dubler & Sidel, 1989). However, health care services in the prison context may be seriously inadequate. An inmate's only hope of obtaining treatment or even diagnosis may be in the context of a research study (Dubler & Sidel, 1989; Siegal, Carlson, Falck, Reece, & Perlin, 1993). An inmate's desire for treatment may be so great that he or she is willing to risk the stigmatization that may result in the prison if his or her HIV status becomes known (Dubler & Sidel, 1989; Hammett & Dubler, 1990). On the other hand, the systematic exclusion of prisoners from HIV research because of their status as prisoners would deny them both potential medical (Hammett & Dubler, 1990; Schroeder, 1983) and nonmedical benefits, such as an enhanced self-image for doing something good (Woody, 1981), that are available to those outside of the prison context. As a result of these concerns, special protections for prisoners participating in research have been developed by regulation.

Federal regulations governing human subjects research supported by federal funds provide that prisoners may participate in research. Research is defined as "systematic investigation, including research development, testing and evaluation, designed to develop or contribute to generalizable knowledge" [45 Code of Federal Regulations section

46.102(d), 1993]. Neither HIV testing nor the collection of data that are part of routine prison entry intake or administration is considered research. When research is conducted, the institutional review board evaluating research on prisoners must ensure that the procedures to be utilized are fair to all prisoners and that the risks to the prisoners participating are commensurate with the risks that would be borne by nonprisoner research participants (45 Code of Federal Regulations sections 46.301–46.306, 1993).

The IRB reviewing research involving prisoners is subject to various mandates. First, the membership of the IRB must include at least one prisoner or a representative of prisoners' interests. A majority of the IRB members must have "no association with the prisoners involved, apart from their membership." (45 Code of Federal Regulations section 46.304, 1993). Second, the research must fall into one of the categories of research permitted by regulation. These include the following:

1. Study of the possible causes, effects, and processes of incarceration, and of criminal behavior, provided that the study presents no more than minimal risk and no more than inconvenience to the subjects.
2. Study of prisoners as institutional structures or of prisoners as incarcerated persons, provided that the study presents no more than minimal risk and no more than inconvenience to the subjects.
3. Research on conditions particularly affecting prisoners as a class (for example, vaccine trials and other research on hepatitis, which is more prevalent in prison than elsewhere, and research on social and psychological problems such as alcoholism, drug addiction, and sexual assaults), provided that the study may proceed only after the Secretary of Health and Human Services has consulted with appropriate experts, including experts in penology, medicine, and ethics, and published notice in the Federal Register of his or her intent to approve such research.
4. Research on practices, both innovative and accepted, that have the intent and reasonable probability of improving the health or well-being of the subject. In cases in which those studies require the assignment of prisoners in a manner consistent with protocols approved by the IRB to control groups which may not benefit from the research, the study may proceed only after the Secretary has consulted with appropriate experts, including experts in penology, medicine, and ethics, and

published notice in the Federal Register of his or her intent to approve such research [45 Code of Federal Regulations section 46.306(a)(2), 1993].

The IRB must also certify that the proposed research meets the following standards:

1. Any possible advantages accruing to subjects in the "limited choice environment" of the prison must not be so enticing as to impair an individual's ability to weigh and evaluate the risks and benefits of participation.
2. The risks involved in participating must be "commensurate with risks that would be accepted by nonprisoner volunteers."
3. The procedures for the selection of subjects must be fair to all of the prisoners.
4. Information provided to the prisoners about the protocol for the study and the informed consent form must be written in clear language.
5. Participation in research cannot be considered in decisions regarding parole, and prisoners must be advised that their participation cannot be considered by the parole authority in making its decision.
6. Adequate follow-up care must be provided, taking into account the varying length of the prisoners' sentences (45 Code of Federal Regulations section 46.305, 1993).

New York State HIV-seropositive inmates have been able to access experimental HIV agents through participation in Phase II and Phase III clinical trials, treatment with investigational new drugs (IND), parallel track or expanded use studies, and single use INDs. Their access to experimental agents and ability to participate in research studies has been hindered by the lack of accurate medical record information for the inmates; the lack of continuity of care; the prison health care providers' inability to maintain adequate drug dispensing records; conflicts between studies' requirements for regularly scheduled follow-up visits and correctional staff concerns relating to security; difficulty identifying an inmate's primary health care provider within the prison system; correctional facilities' failure to adhere to the study protocol's medication regimen; and the failure of the correctional institutions to notify the research physicians of the decision to parole an inmate-participant, resulting in a loss to follow-up (Potler, Sharp, & Remick, 1994).

Participation of Children

Until recently, the tendency has been to protect children from experimental therapies (Philip Pizzo, quoted in Cimons, 1990). AIDS has changed that: approximately 2% of the total number of reported AIDS cases have occurred in children under the age of 13 (Nolan, 1990).

Voluntariness of consent presents special problems with children because they lack the mental and legal capacity to consent to their own participation in research. Children themselves are more likely to understand very concrete aspects of the research, such as the ability to ask questions and the amount of time involved. They are less likely to understand abstract information relating to the research, including the fact that it is research (Susman, Dorn, & Fletcher, 1992). The voluntariness of parental consent may be questionable if the family does not have access to care for the child outside of the research setting (Nolan, 1990).

Federal regulations have been developed to protect children participating in research. The level of the child's participation in the decision-making process to enroll in a research study varies with the level of risk involved in the research. The regulations' reliance on parental consent for the child seems to rest on the traditional view of parental authority to make decisions regarding their children and on the need to protect children (Leikin, 1989). The regulations divide potential research into four different categories, based on the level of risk associated with the research and the level of the child's participation in the decision making:

1. Research involving no more than minimal risk, with the prospect of direct benefit to the child. Minimal risk involves a level of physical or psychological harm that does not exceed that level which is normally encountered in the daily life of children or in a routine medical or psychological examination of children [45 Code of Federal Regulations section 46.102(I), 1993]. Procedures involving minimal risk may include routine immunizations, developmental assessments, and collecting blood and urine specimens. Controversy exists, however, as to which procedures are properly classifiable as those "involving minimal risk" (Freedman, Fuks, & Weijer, 1993). Generally, research falling into this category requires the informed consent of at least one parent or the permission of the child's guardian, and the child's assent (45 Code of Federal Regulations sections 46.404, 46.408, 1993).
2. Research involving more than minimal risk, with the prospect of direct benefit to the child. The IRB must assess on a

case-by-case basis what constitutes more than minimal risk. These procedures might include biopsies and spinal taps. The assessment of the risk must also take into account the disease, condition, or present state of the research participants. As an example, drawing blood from a hemophiliac might be seen to present more than minimal risk. Research in this category requires the consent of at least one parent or the child's guardian, and assent of the child (45 Code of Federal Regulations sections 46.405, 46.408, 1993).

3. Studies involving more than minimal risk, with no direct benefit to the child, but with the prospect of yielding "generalizable knowledge." Such studies usually require both parents' consent and the child's consent (45 Code of Federal Regulations section 46.406, 1993).
4. Studies that would not otherwise receive approval but that could lead to the understanding, prevention, or alleviation of a serious problem affecting children's health or welfare. Studies in this category are approvable only by the Secretary of Health and Human Services, following consultation with an expert panel (45 Code of Federal Regulations section 46.407, 1993).

Regulations define "assent" as "a child's affirmative agreement to participate in research." The process of obtaining a child's assent includes providing information to the child, offering the child the opportunity to participate in the decision-making process, and respecting a child's dissent (Leiken, 1993). It may be difficult, however, to determine exactly what constitutes assent. A minor's conformity or nonconformity to authority figures may be a relevant consideration in assessing a child's assent. A child's cognitive abilities at a particular age clearly impact his or her ability to understand the information provided (Leiken, 1993). A child's cultural, ethnic, or economic background may also impact his or her willingness to voice dissent (Weithorn & Scherer, 1994).

In order for an assent to be considered valid, the assent should reflect the child's understanding of what he or she must do or what will be done to him or her as part of the research. The child must also understand the basic purpose of the research and indicate a preference to participate (Weithorn & McCabe, 1988).

Particular problems exist in the case of emancipated minors, children who are wards of the state, children whose parent or parents are unavailable or legally, mentally, or physically unable to give consent, and children who are in the care of foster parents (Grodin & Alpert, 1988;

Gray, 1989; Ackerman, 1990; C. Levine, 1991a). Some states have made alternative provisions for obtaining consent in these situations, and state law should be consulted if this issue arises in the context of a particular study. Pennsylvania, for example, requires increased efforts to communicate with an unavailable natural parent and assistance to the pediatric investigator. North Carolina, California, New Jersey, and Texas provide for case by case determinations. Maryland has instituted procedures for the appointment of a medical guardianship for foster parents. Georgia and Massachusetts have established a central review board to approve protocols and the enrollment of children on a case by case basis (C. Levine, 1991a).

Cooke (1994) has highlighted the difficulties in obtaining assent from children who are particularly vulnerable. This includes those whose parents are divorced, abusive, mentally retarded, or mentally ill; migrant or homeless children; children living in an impoverished environment; and children who are members of particular religious or ethnic groups.

Unresolved issues also exist with respect to the enrollment of an adolescent in research, without the consent of the adolescent's parent(s). Courts have recently expanded adolescents' rights in other arenas, implicitly suggesting that adolescents can make informed and voluntary decisions about matters affecting their own lives. One writer has suggested classifying research involving adolescents into four different categories based on the nature of the research involved:

1. Research in which adolescence is relevant to the condition being studied, such as abortion among adolescents. The requirement of parental consent in such a study could obviate the possibility of such a study because the adolescents may not wish to discuss their reliance on abortion with their parent(s).
2. Research in which adolescence is irrelevant to the condition being studied.
3. Studies that require participants from various age groups.
4. Research related to a condition that the adolescent participant has, but that itself is unrelated to age (Holder, 1983).

Research in any of these categories could be potentially coercive where, for instance, all members of a particular class or school were required to participate, or participation would carry points for extra credit in a class or school where many students were not doing well academically. (For additional discussion relating to the participation of children in research, see Section 2.2.)

AIDS Dementia

Questions about the voluntariness of an AIDS-demented individual's consent may arise because of the individual's emotional lability and confusion. Several alternative mechanisms for obtaining informed consent have been suggested, including decision making by a family member or by another individual chosen by the patient while still competent to make such decisions once the patient became incompetent (High, 1992; Bein, 1991). Federal regulations permit informed consent to be obtained from an "individual or judicial or other body authorized under applicable law to consent on behalf of a prospective subject" [45 Code of Federal Regulations, section 46.102(c), 1993; 21 Code of Federal Regulations section 50.3(m), 1994]. The voluntariness of this appointed person's decision regarding participation depends to a great extent on that person's independence from the researchers and the research institutions (Bein, 1991). If medical care is otherwise unavailable, or relatively unavailable, to the incompetent individual absent participation in the research, the surrogate's decision may not be voluntary in the sense that the surrogate may see no other option for obtaining care for the patient.

Several writers have noted that one solution is to prohibit research with psychiatric patients. However, such a proscription could potentially deny these individuals the right to a health benefit if the proposed research arguably represents the potential "best" of available treatments. Such a proscription would violate the basic principle of distributive justice, requiring that the risks and benefits of research be distributed equitably (Fulford & Howse, 1993).

Research in Developing Countries

Questions as to who may consent for whose participation in HIV-related research have arisen because of differences in perceptions of "personhood" between Western societies and those of other cultures. The American perspective has been summarized as follows (De Craemer, 1983):

> Taken as a whole, our conception of personhood has at least one major paradoxical attribute. Although it places a high positive value on a universalistic definition of the worth, dignity, and equality of every individual person, it tends to be culturally pluralistic, and inadvertently ethnocentric. To a significant degree, it rests on theimplicit assumption that ideas about personhood are common to many, if not most, other societies and cultures. Beyond that, it assumes that the American way of thinking about the person

> represents the way men and women of all societies and cultures should and do think about personhood when they are being supremely rational and moral.

In reality, however, decisions about participation in research may not be made at an individual level, but rather at the level of the extended family, the village, or a tribal authority (Barry & Molyneux, 1992).

Various researchers have advocated continued reliance on U.S. standards for informed consent (Miller, 1991). However, continued reliance on our concepts of voluntary consent, without any deference to the local culture, may often be perceived as "imperialistic" (Gostin, 1991; Last, 1991a; Newton, 1990). Strict adherence to a U.S. requirement for informed *written* consent may also be impractical in the context of research to be conducted in a developing country with a largely illiterate population (Brown, 1991). Several researchers have proposed informed consent procedures that represent a hybrid of these diverse views.

Christakis (1992) has developed four ethical models that address this dilemma, two of which are universalistic and two of which assume that research ethics are culturally relative. Each of the models, however, is to some extent deficient. Lurie *et al.* (1994) have advocated the continued requirement of individual consent in writing, following consultation by the prospective participant with family members, community elders, or the entire community, where mandated by local culture. The Proposed International Guidelines of the World Health Organization explicitly recognize the need to accommodate the mores of the host country:

> Where individual members of a community do not have the necessary awareness of the implications of participation in an experiment to give adequately informed consent directly to the investigators, it is desirable that the decision whether or not to participate should be elicited through the intermediary of a trusted community leader.

Unfortunately, reliance on a trusted community leader does not resolve the issue of voluntariness. It is possible, for instance, that an individual consents to participate in the research because he or she feels pressured to do so since the research is supported by the village leader, the tribal leader, or the family leader. In addition, an individual may feel that participation in research is the only way to obtain any medical care for the HIV or any of its related conditions, because the medical system in the host country is inadequate to care for all HIV-infected patients, because the prospective participant is too poor to afford otherwise available medical care, or because there is no system of care for HIV-infected patients (Palca, 1990). In any of these scenarios, the question arises as to whether the individual or community leader really has any choice about participation.

Use of Payment as an Incentive

The use of payments to encourage participation in research has been termed a "paradox" (Macklin, 1989). The anticipated benefits of research must outweigh the anticipated risks of research. Payment is considered a benefit. However, unduly large payments to encourage participation may constitute undue influence or coercion. As Macklin (1989) stated, "The higher the monetary payment, the greater is the benefit; the greater the benefit, the more acceptable is the research. However, the greater the monetary payment, the more potential subjects are unduly influenced to participate; the more coercive the recruitment, the more unacceptable is the research." The impact of financial reward on a decision to participate is not merely theoretical. In experienced, healthy research volunteers, financial reward has been found to be the primary reason for participation in the research (Bigorra & Banos, 1990).

Ackerman (1989) has proposed five guidelines for payment practices, which he premises on the perception of research participants as "ordinary workers employed on a contractual basis by the sponsor of the research":

1. The conditions under which the services are performed should not pose serious, avoidable risks to the workers' basic welfare interests.
2. Workers should receive a wage sufficient to allow them to meet their basic needs.
3. Payments should be proportional to the difficulty of the work.
4. Payments should be proportional to the social value of the work.
5. Workers should have insurance against unforeseeable injuries that occur in the course of their work and that decrease their ability to meet their essential needs.

Ackerman further proposes that the degree of additional risk to which research participants may expose themselves be strictly limited. Additionally, this proposed framework would supplement, rather than displace, reliance on unpaid volunteers for research.

Ackerman's scheme presupposes that the research participant, like an independent contractor, is free to negotiate the conditions of participation and that the bargaining power of both the prospective participant and the researcher are equal. This may be far from the case. Prospective participants in HIV research studies may have less education that the researcher. By definition, they are dealing with an illness that, at this time, is invariably fatal. They may have no access to any medical care apart from that offered through study participation. They may have minimal income as a result of the loss of their job, which itself resulted from the progression of their disease. Any payment may represent a significant amount of income. Additionally, it is rare that the research sponsor will invite the prospective participant to "name his or her price" for participating.

As an example, consider a situation in which a researcher would like to conduct a cohort study of IDUs to assess whether certain HIV prevention strategies actually result in a decrease in risky behaviors, including shared needle use and unprotected sexual intercourse. Suppose further that all of the prospective participants are living below poverty level, that they may or may not be participating in a drug treatment program, and that the community in which the study is to be conducted does not have a needle exchange program for the free exchange of used needles and syringes. The investigator is concerned that the rate at which participants will be lost to follow-up will be high, because of drug-related deaths, HIV-related deaths, and the lack of participant reliability. The researcher proposes the use of an incentive to increase participant motivation and the likelihood of maintaining the cohort over time.

In this situation, it could be argued that a payment of $100 to the participant at the commencement of the study will do little to maintain motivation if that is the only payment to be paid, and may be inherently coercive as well. A single payment does little to motivate an individual to return for follow-up visits. The money may be long gone by the date of the next visit. Further, the amount of $100 may represent a fortune to an individual living on the streets, well below poverty level. The individual may not perceive that he or she has any real choice: the $100 may well represent survival and power.

Various alternative solutions exist. A smaller amount of money could be paid out at the time of each visit. This would acknowledge the participant's contribution of time and effort at the time that it is made, and provide an incentive for the participant to return at the time of the next scheduled visit. A particularly creative solution might be to arrange with various local supermarkets and convenience stores for the issuance of food coupons. These could be given to the research participants, and redeemed at any of the participating stores at their convenience.

The Health Care Provider or Social Service Provider as Recruiter

Concern has been raised that persons recruited for HIV-related research by their health care providers or social service providers may feel less than free to refuse to participate, fearing that the quality or quantity of their care or the availability of their health care provider to them will change should they refuse (Weitz, 1987). The patient may be unable to distinguish the physician in his or her provider role from the physician in his or her role as a researcher. The patient-prospective participant may assume that the health care worker would not even raise the issue of the research if he or she did not believe that it was in the patient's best interest, because the provider has always been concerned with the patient's well-being in the past (Miller, 1991). Patients may lack the technical knowledge to even formulate appropriate questions of their providers (Woody, 1981).

The potential for such unintended pressure may be further enhanced by the fact that HIV is an invariably fatal disease at the present time and many HIV-infected patients may experience difficulty in locating a provider (Kass, Faden, Fox, & Dudley, 1992; Kelly, St. Lawrence, Smith, Hood, & Cook, 1987), despite federal and state laws prohibiting discrimination related to disability. The dilemma is further compounded where the health care provider believes that a new treatment being studied in a clinical trial is the best possible option for a particular patient, but there is always the possibility that the patient, if enrolled in the study, would be randomized to the alternative therapy, which is less than desirable in the patient's particular situation (Marquis & Stephens, 1989). There are no easy answers. Clearly, the patient should be provided with as much information as he or she needs to make a decision. It may also be advisable to have a third party explain the research protocol to the patient-prospective participant, rather than the health care worker-researcher.

2.4. CONCLUSION

The implementation of ethical principles governing biomedical research requires more than a cursory review of the principles and the drafting of forms. Rather, a careful assessment of the study design and its possible impact on the participants is essential. The biomedical researcher, particularly in the area of HIV research, must consider complex questions, including the meaning of voluntariness in the context of the proposed study population and whether "voluntariness" can really exist in that population; how much information should be given to a prospective participant and in what form to be understood; and the degree to which a participant actually understands what will be done in the context of the study and how that may impact him or her. All too often, researchers fail to address these issues in depth. Protection of the research participants requires a more complete examination of these issues in the context of a study.

CHAPTER THREE

Clinical Trials

HIV and the need to treat HIV-infected individuals have sparked vehement debates about the effectiveness and efficiency of U.S. drug testing and approval procedures, including the conduct of clinical trials. This chapter reviews current procedures for the testing of new drugs related to HIV and provisions to make new drugs available to seriously ill patients before they are approved and available for general marketing. The chapter also focuses on the ethical issues that attend clinical trials related to HIV.

3.1. BASIC PRINCIPLES OF CLINICAL TRIALS

The Design of Randomized Clinical Trials

Clinical trials of new drugs are conducted after appropriate animal tests have been conducted and after the FDA has reviewed the investigational new drug (Young, Norris, Levitt, & Nightingale, 1988; Strom, 1989). Table 3.1 and Figure 3.1 provide greater detail about the FDA review and approval processes for new drugs. Clinical trials are conducted in three phases. Phase I of a clinical trial is designed to examine the toxicity of the new drug and the route of its administration. Phase I normally involves a small number of human participants. Phase II further addresses issues of efficacy, and generally involves a slightly larger number of research participants. These two phases are often combined into one. Phase III of a clinical trial attempts to expand on the knowledge gained about the drug's efficacy and toxicity, often by

Table 3.1. The FDA Process for Approving Drugs[a]

1. The sponsor of the research submits an application to the FDA for an Investigational New Drug (IND).
2. The application must include:
   a. A description of the investigational plan
   b. A list and description of any components of any drug
   c. A statement of the methods and controls for the drug's manufacture
   d. Information about all prior investigations involving the drug, including tests on animals
   e. A list of the investigators
   f. Information about the investigators' training and experience
   g. A list of the institutions at which any part of the investigation may be conducted
   h. Copies of all labeling
   i. Copies of all forms and informational materials relating to informed consent
   j. An assurance that the investigation has been or will be approved by an IRB
3. The clinical investigation cannot begin without both IRB and FDA approval.
4. Sponsors of biomedical investigations must report to the FDA and to all investigators participating in the study any unanticipated adverse effects.
5. Sponsors must not label an investigational product in a way that implies that it is safe or effective for the use under investigation.
6. Sponsors must not unduly prolong an investigation.
7. Sponsors must promptly submit a new drug application when the results establish safety or effectiveness. They must discontinue the investigation if the data will not support FDA approval.

[a] Sources: 21 Code of Federal Regulations sections 312.1, 812.5, 812.7, 812.46, and Part 56 (1994).

measuring the investigational drug against a more standard therapy or a placebo. Phase III trials normally involve a large number of participants (Green *et al.*, 1990).

The Randomization Procedure

Randomized clinical trials are regarded as the best means of evaluating a new drug or treatment, for a number of reasons. The randomiza-

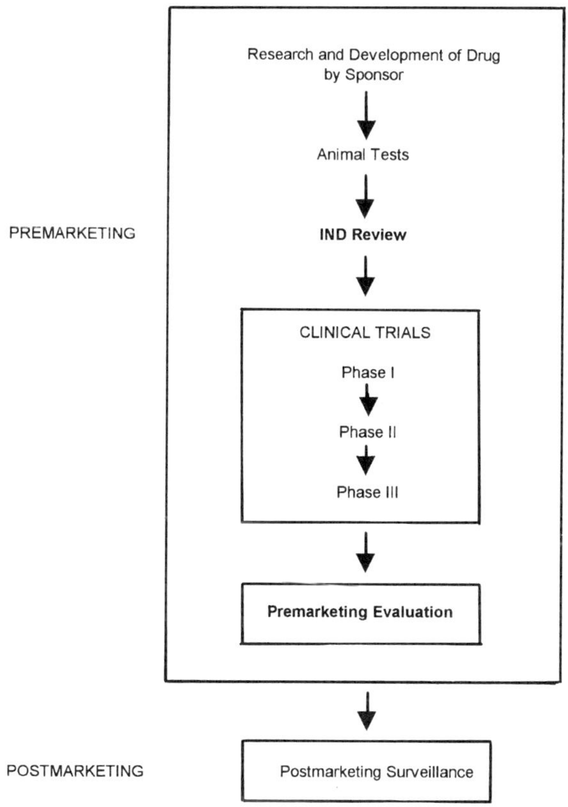

Figure 3.1. The drug development process. Bold indicates FDA function. Adapted from Young, Norris, Levitt, and Nightingale. (1988). *Journal of the American Medical Association, 260,* 2267–2270. Copyright 1988, American Medical Association.

tion of participants to different arms of the study ensures a more even distribution among study arms of potentially confounding variables that could affect the outcome of the study. Randomization also ensures a level of homogeneity among the participants so that evaluation of the results is facilitated (Sacket, 1983).

Randomized clinical trials require the use of a control group. The control group may receive a drug other than the one under evaluation, such as traditional therapy, or it may receive a placebo. The use of a placebo may be justified when the new drug under investigation is particularly toxic or when the morbidity caused by the disease for which the trial is being conducted is very low (Byar *et al.*, 1990).

The use of an alternative therapy arm, rather than a placebo arm, in HIV-related clinical trials is quite common. Randomization is justifiable only when the treatments or nontreatments of each arm are equally effective. Therefore, the assignment of ill patients to a treatment arm that is known a *priori* to yield less benefit to the patient than the treatment under investigation or a standard therapy cannot be justified. It is for this reason that control groups participating in clinical trials related to HIV treatment often receive a drug other than the one under investigation, rather than a placebo (Levine, Dubler, & Levine, 1991). Several researchers have noted that although investigators may not perceive any difference in the potential beneficial effect of the new and the standard treatment, the side effects may vary widely and these side effects, rather than the treatment, could be determinative of a patients decision regarding participation in a trial (Brahams, 1988; R. J. Levine, 1988).

Some patients may refuse to participate in a randomized clinical trial because their assignment to a particular arm of the study is outside of their control and that of the researcher or physician. Zelen (1990) has proposed utilizing a "randomized consent design" in lieu of the conventional randomized trial design to encourage more individuals to consent to participation. Using this method, the treatment is selected in advance of seeking the patient's informed consent to participate. In this scenario, the patient would agree to receive the assigned treatment if it reflects the patient's treatment preference or the patient has no treatment preference. Although this approach may facilitate recruitment for a clinical trial, the results may be difficult to interpret. Both arms of a study may appear to be equivalent in the eyes of the researcher. However, a person's own values, preferences, and characteristics may make one treatment option preferable to the other (Kodish, Lantos, & Siegler, 1990). The patient's preferences may be related to factors that could be related to the outcome measure of interest. The loss of randomization means that variables that could affect the outcome have not been randomly distributed to all arms of the study.

The design of a randomized clinical trial in a developing country may be problematic if the researchers are investigating an alternative drug to a standard therapy, and are measuring its effectiveness against a placebo rather than the standard treatment. One group of researchers has argued that the comparison of an alternative investigational drug to a placebo is not unethical when the standard drug that would be used for treatment is beyond what the host country could afford or is too cost ineffective for a society to purchase at all (Christakis, Lynn, & Castelo, 1991).

Participant Selection

Exclusion and inclusion criteria for participation in HIV-related clinical trials have been an issue of strenuous debate. Researchers may wish to exclude individuals who have had prior therapies, who are users of illicit drugs, who are taking medications for the treatment of concurrent HIV-related diseases, or who are or may become pregnant. Reliance on each of these exclusion criteria would facilitate the evaluation of the study results (Cotton *et al.*, 1993). For instance, it becomes difficult to evaluate both the effectiveness and the toxicity of a new drug under investigation if the research participant is also using other drugs that can have the same toxic or beneficial effects. Although women and men can be counseled to utilize birth control if they are to participate in studies in which the teratogenicity of a drug has not yet been determined, pregnancy and the potential effects of the drug on the fetus always remain issues even when birth control is utilized (Fletcher, 1993; Merkatz, 1993).

Outcome Measures

Study endpoints in HIV-related investigations have been the subject of continuing debate. Common endpoints include mortality, or time to development of AIDS. These particular endpoints have been criticized on a number of grounds. First, mortality is an easy standard for the researcher, but the extension of individuals' lives, only to endure an increasing amount of pain and a decreasing level of independence, may provide no benefit in the minds of the study participants and future recipients of the therapy under examination. Second, the diagnosis of "AIDS" is a definition of convenience, which encompasses infections and disorders greatly divergent in their severity and potential fatality. Third, the use of mortality as the endpoint may not be practical in the context of various studies. A clinical trial of a new drug among participants in the early stages of HIV infection would require many years of follow-up before the effect of the new treatment on mortality could be evaluated, because the participants in the early stages of HIV infection could be expected to live for many years even without a treatment. The use of a surrogate endpoint, such as the rate of decline in the participants' $CD4^+$ T cells, would permit researchers to detect the effect of the new treatment in a shorter period of time (Brookmeyer & Gail, 1994). Researchers are increasingly making use of quality of life evaluations as an endpoint in clinical trials (Gelber *et al.*, 1992).

Analysis

The analysis of the data from many clinical trials relies on "intent to treat," meaning that the data are analyzed by original treatment assignment of the study participants, rather than by treatment administered or actual time on drug. In AIDS-related trials, trial participants may not receive the drug to which they are assigned. This could happen for a number of reasons, including dose reduction as a result of adverse effects or patient modification of treatment (Ellenberg *et al.*, 1992). Some writers have argued that there is much information to be gained by taking into account the treatment that was actually administered (Efron & Feldman, 1991).

Stopping Rules

Questions also exist about the appropriateness of when to stop a clinical trial, and what criteria to use to make that decision. The researcher may have an interest in maintaining the trial over a long period of time in order to obtain more reliable conclusions based on a sufficient amount of data. However, the benefits of the investigational drug may become increasingly clear as the study progresses, so that it may become unethical to continue to randomize individuals to the placebo or alternative treatment arm. Conversely, the new treatment may actually look worse than the conventional approach. One potential solution is to formulate statistical stopping rules at the beginning of the trial, to provide clear guidance during its course. Pocock (1992) has suggested as potential criteria for the stopping of a trial the detection of a sufficiently small p value for treatment differences on a trial's primary endpoint and group sequential analyses, which permits the conduct of a limited number of preplanned interim analyses for review by a data monitoring committee.

The Mechanics of Randomized Clinical Trials

Data Monitoring Committees

Independent Data Monitoring Committees or Data Safety Monitoring Boards are often established to monitor on an interim basis an HIV clinical trial for evidence of extreme therapeutic results or excess toxicity of the investigational drug (Ellenberg, Myers, Blackwelder, & Hoth, 1993). The Committee or Board may recommend the termination of the trial, modification of the trial design, or revisions of the informed consent process based on its review of the interim results (Levine *et al.*, 1991). Fleming and DeMets (1993) have suggested that membership on such a committee:

1. Reflect participation from multiple disciplines, including medicine and biostatistics
2. Be limited to individuals without a conflict of interest
3. Be ethically and scientifically supportive of the study's objectives and design
4. Balance responsibilities to patients currently enrolled in the study, future enrollees into the study, and future patients outside of the study
5. Be knowledgeable about relevant external information
6. Be aware of data management and quality control procedures to be used in the study
7. Be the only individuals to receive interim results
8. Maintain special procedures to evaluate and act on requests from investigators or sponsors, without being unblinded
8. Make an independent recommendation as to the wisdom of continuing or stopping the trial, based on safety and efficacy results.

The members of the Committee or Board are charged with maintaining the confidentiality of their interim findings. They may not reveal trends in the data to investigators, sponsors, participants, or the general public. A breach of confidentiality could ultimately destroy the validity of the randomization or the blinding because of the public's and the participants' reactions to these emerging trends (Levine *et al.*, 1991).

Community Consultation

Community consultation in conjunction with HIV-related clinical trials has been suggested as a means of enlisting potential participants as partners in solving the problems that are raised by the research itself. Discussion may focus, for instance, on the need for randomization, the use of a placebo group versus an alternative treatment group, procedures to safeguard confidentiality, and the selection of the study participants (Valdisseri, Tama, & Ho, 1988). Through discussions with the community about these and other relevant issues, the researchers are able to communicate their respect for the potential participants as individuals

(Melton, Levine, Koocher, Rosenthal, & Thompson, 1988). The committees can also be instrumental in the development of referral networks for social services (Valdisseri *et al.*, 1988).

There has been concern raised that reliance on community consultation as a strategy may diminish individuals' ability to exercise their autonomy. If, for instance, a group is already fairly cohesive, the group may be inclined to act in a certain manner and individuals may feel particular pressure to conform. Such discussions may focus on risks to the community as a whole, resulting in individuals' confusion between potential personal risks and risks to the community (Melton *et al.*, 1988).

The distinction between "research" and "treatment" may become a point of contention and misunderstanding. Some advocates of community consultation believe that the investigators must provide clinical care to all participants in a trial. Similarly, the clinical trial itself may be perceived as "treatment" by the community members because there is no other "treatment" available (Spiers, 1991). This view is not inconsistent with public perceptions of clinical trials generally. One study found that a majority of study participants would enter a clinical trial to receive better medical care, and fully one-third of the respondents believed that participants in clinical trials receive better-quality medical care than others (Cassileth, Lusk, Miller, & Hurwitz, 1982).

Crossover Designs

Crossover designs are sometimes used, instead of randomized trials, in the evaluation of drugs for chronic diseases (Burchell, 1992). In these studies, the patient acts as his or her own control. For example, if a particular drug is under investigation, the patient would be assigned to that drug for a prespecified period of time. The conclusion of that time on drug would be followed by a "washout" period, during which time the patient's body would presumably return to baseline. At this point, the comparison drug would be administered for a predetermined period of time, in conformity with the trial protocol. A portion of the study participants would receive the treatments in an order opposite that of another portion of the participants, in order to control for period effects (Jones & Kenward, 1989).

Crossover trials present particular advantages and disadvantages. Because each research participant provides measurements on each treatment, the issue of differences between participants is minimized. The major disadvantage of crossover trials is the possibility that the effect of treatment during one period may carry over into the next (Jones & Kenward, 1989).

3.2. ETHICAL PRINCIPLES AND HIV-RELATED CLINICAL TRIALS

Beneficence

As discussed previously, the principle of beneficence requires the minimization of harm and the maximization of benefit to the research participant. However, the calculation of the risk–benefit ratio is particularly problematic in the context of an HIV-related clinical trial. A drug that is potentially powerful enough to have an effect on HIV is also likely to have an adverse effect on other cells (Macklin & Friedland, 1986). HIV-infected persons may feel that any risk is worth the potential benefit, no matter how small the chance of a benefit may be (Pogash, 1993; Boffey, 1987). As one physician stated, "The primary conflict here is between the individual who has a fatal illness and is willing to take a million-to-one or thousand-to-one shot, and larger public health considerations that require controlled studies to determine whether drugs are effective and can have a role or not" (Boffey, 1987).

Autonomy

Information

Clinical trials may last a number of years. During this period of time, other studies may provide treatment-related information that was not known at the commencement of a particular trial. This may raise issues about the need to advise trial participants of new information from sources external to the study, and the need to obtain renewed consent for participation. One writer has stated unequivocally, "[T]here is a continuing duty on the part of the patient's physician[-researcher] to . . . inform his patient about any significant new information coming out of the experiment that might bear on the patient's choice to remain in the study or to seek other types of therapy" (Fried, 1974). This ethical dilemma was exemplified during the course of one long-term clinical trial comparing early versus later zidovudine (AZT) therapy for symptomatic HIV infection. After the commencement of that trial, but prior to its conclusion, the FDA approved earlier use of zidovudine. The investigators advised the study participants of the FDA-approved revised recommendations, the findings reported by another study that supported those recommendations, and the rationale for continuing in the trial. The investigators emphasized that the continuation of blinded participation was optional and provided a revised consent form for participants' reaffirmation of participation (Simberkoff *et al.*, 1993).

The need for "continuing informed consent" could be resolved by the implementation of regular "open forums" between the investigators and the study participants. The investigators could use this opportunity to provide participants with an update on research results from other studies that may be relevant to their situations. The participants can use this time to ask general questions about the progress of the study, such as the number of people enrolled and the manner of recruiting participants. If therapies other than the one under study have been developed for the same condition, the investigator can explain what he or she knows about them at the meeting, and can request that each participant reaffirm his or her consent to continue in the study.

Voluntariness

It has been argued that the very notion of a clinical trial violates an individual's right to autonomy because the patient-participant is not equally free to choose between any therapy that might be received in the context of a randomized clinical trial and the randomization alternative, without participating in the clinical trial. For example, if an individual can only receive AZT in the context of a clinical trial, his or her ability to exercise the right of autonomy would be questionable (Kodish *et al.*, 1990). Others have framed the issue as one of voluntariness: if an individual has an invariably fatal disease and few, if any, treatment alternatives, the individual's consent to participate cannot be "voluntary" because there was no real choice (Macklin & Friedland, 1986). Others have noted that having to choose between two unpleasant alternatives is not in itself coercive (Grady, 1991).

Voluntariness may also become an issue in the context of HIV-related clinical trials as a result of an individual's deteriorating mental status, involuntary confinement, or age (Moros & Rhodes, 1991).

These issues have been discussed in Section 2.3, dealing with voluntariness specifically.

Others have raised the issue of an individual's obligation to comply with the study protocol during the course of the clinical trial. Those who view the trial as research argue that the need to give up other, potentially beneficial drugs in order to participate in the trial is one factor that the individual must weigh in making an informed decision to participate in the clinical trial. Those who perceive the clinical trial as therapy, perhaps in part because no treatment is available outside of the trial, argue that it is unreasonable to expect the participant to forgo any opportunity to utilize a potentially beneficial treatment (C. Levine, 1988).

The principle of autonomy has also formed the basis for arguments against the existence of the FDA and for the institution of unrestricted access by patients to all drugs. It has been argued that the FDA standard may measure risk differently than does the HIV-infected person; that the FDA interferes with an individual's right to contract with a physician or pharmaceutical company for specific treatment; that the FDA is paternalistic in its decision making; and that the proper role of government is to maximize, not make, choices for individuals (Shorr, 1992). However, the principle of autonomy also mandates special protections for vulnerable populations, such as the mentally ill and children. A policy of unrestricted access to all drugs by all patients would not permit this protection.

Justice and Fairness

The principle of justice demands an examination of the means by which the burdens and the benefits of the research are distributed. AIDS research in general has been criticized for its inclusion of white male homosexuals in many studies (Macklin & Friedland, 1986), and its exclusion of women, persons of color, and injecting drug users (Freedman, 1992). Often the exclusion criteria are premised on legitimate scientific concerns, such as the need for homogeneity of the study population, the risk of teratogenicity, or the inability to follow individuals who are unreliable. Vociferous criticism of conventional clinical trials has ultimately resulted in modified procedures for the release of drugs for HIV.

The AIDS Clinical Trials Group (ACTG) is one example of conventional clinical trials. The ACTG is a system of clinical trials sponsored by the National Institutes of Allergy and Infectious Diseases (NIAID). As of 1993, there were 47 separate units at 150 sites, with over 200 research protocols. The system is government-controlled and the research is conducted through established research institutions. The inclusion criteria for these studies are generally defined strictly in order to ensure homogeneity of the study participants. Consequently, individuals who are very ill or who do not fit the inclusion criteria are excluded (Levine *et al.*, 1991). There are many more individuals infected with HIV than there are such clinical trials to address potential treatments for their HIV-related illnesses. And, as one AIDS activist stated, "Few people who are sick enough to quickly reach the classical AIDS clinical trials endpoint (of new or recurring opportunistic infections or death) are well enough to abide the rigors of a clinical trial" (Eigo, 1990).

Community-based research efforts and other alternatives to randomized clinical trials grew out of the frustration and disillusionment that resulted from individuals' inability to qualify for participation in clinical trials (Clark, 1993a; Johnson, 1989) and from what has been perceived as the slow pace of research and release of new drugs (Appler, 1988). Community-based research efforts often rely on physicians in the community. The studies are generally less complicated than traditional clinical trials (Kolata, 1988a).

"Parallel track" trials of investigational drugs were developed by the National AIDS Program Office, in consultation with numerous AIDS advocacy groups, in order to expand access to these drugs to persons who were not eligible for clinical trial participation (Levine *et al.*,1991; Cimons, 1989a). Approval of the distribution of a drug under this program is based on consideration of numerous factors, including laboratory and clinical evidence of efficacy; evidence of safety; preliminary pharmacokinetic data; the nonexistence of satisfactory alternative therapies; and an assessment of the impact of the parallel track program on recruitment for conventional clinical trials for the same drug. Two drugs approved for use under this program include dideoxyinosine (ddI) and dideoxycytidine (ddC) (Levine *et al.*, 1991).

Other programs have also been developed for the distribution of drugs at a faster rate and to a broader spectrum of users than is possible through the clinical trials investigational process only. The FDA has established a procedure for the accelerated approval of investigational new drugs (IND) for treatment. This procedure permits the marketing of a new drug for the treatment of a serious or life-threatening illness if the drug is anticipated to provide meaningful therapeutic benefit to the patient over existing treatments. In order to be considered for accelerated approval, the drug must be under investigation in a controlled clinical trial or all clinical trials must have been completed. The sponsor of the drug must also demonstrate that it is actively pursuing marketing approval of the drug (Young *et al.*, 1988). The accelerated approval may be based on favorable findings with respect to endpoints other than survival or irreversible morbidity (21 Code of Federal Regulations sections 314.500–314.510, 1994). Six HIV/AIDS IND applications had been approved as of 1990 (Levine *et al.*, 1991).

One writer has criticized this scheme for expedited marketing approval, arguing that permitting the use of unproven drugs under this framework may lengthen the time it will take to find an effective drug; deny the reality of death, for no purpose; and increase the difficulty of conducting scientifically valid trials of new drugs (Annas, 1989). Others, however, have argued that this procedure strikes a needed balance between the individual's "right" to obtain experimental treatment and the states' interest in protecting terminally ill patients from untested alternative therapies (Batterman, 1990).

Individuals may also be able to access experimental drugs through the compassionate use program. The FDA maintains an informal policy permitting individual physicians to have access to experimental drugs for particular patients. This program has come to be known as "the compassionate use IND" (Johnstone, 1988). Another informal policy permits individuals with life-threatening illnesses to import for their own use prescription drugs not available in the United States (Kolata, 1989).

California has developed and implemented a system for testing drugs in the state while bypassing the FDA requirements for approval (Rivas, 1991). Although no drug can be introduced into interstate commerce without FDA approval [21 United States Code Annotated section 355(I), 1994], the state law permits the sale and testing of the drug within the state (California Health and Safety Code section 26679, 1984). Then State Attorney General Van de Kamp explained the state's approach by noting, "Thousands of dying people are forced to sneak across the Mexican border like criminals to buy experimental drugs . . . California is on the front line taking casualties, so we must be on the front ranks of research and testing" (Van de Kamp, 1987).

"Large simple trials" have been proposed as an alternative to the lengthy conventional clinical trial and as a compromise between the traditional clinical trial and the "parallel track" (Green *et al.*, 1990). Large simple trials generally include a large number of participants, use exclusionary criteria that are less restrictive than they would be in a randomized clinical trial (Kolata, 1990a), collect data on only essential variables and primary outcome measures, and use easily documentable and verifiable endpoints (Ellenberg & Foulkes, 1994; Dunbar, 1991; Kolata, 1990b). Large simple trials may alleviate problems with participant noncompliance with the research protocol because they may reduce the need for potential participants to lie about personal characteristics in an attempt to qualify for inclusion in a trial (Dunbar, 1991). The concept of large simple trials in the context of HIV research is not without support, despite the criticism of such studies for the lack of homogeneity within the study population.

3.3. THE SPECIAL CASE OF HIV VACCINE TRIALS

Since 1987, more than 1400 uninfected people have participated as volunteers in tests of HIV vaccines. These early trials were conducted to provide information about the safety of these preparations and their ability to stimulate an immune response. It is likely that it will be some time before an effective vaccine is developed (Cohen, 1994).

Various methodological issues in the design of vaccine trials have ethical implications. Researchers must compare trial participants who receive HIV vaccine to those who do not. However, behavioral interventions conducted at the same time could make it difficult to detect differences between the vaccinated and the unvaccinated groups. Some researchers feel that if a vaccine trial fails because of a strong behavioral intervention, the trial has been a success because HIV transmission has been reduced. At least one researcher, however, has argued that the behavioral intervention provided in the context of a vaccine trial should match the standard for behavioral intervention in the community in which the trial is being conducted (Cohen, 1994). This raises ethical issues, because some communities provide no counseling whatsoever. Additionally, in multicenter trials located in multiple communities, such a policy would mean that trial participants would receive different behavioral interventions depending on where they were situated. This raises not only analytical issues, but also ethical issues of disparate benefits or treatment among trial participants.

The concern has been raised that individuals receiving an HIV vaccine may become HIV seropositive as a result. Even if this seropositivity is transitory, the concern has been raised that individuals will be stigmatized and subject to discrimination in employment, insurance, and travel (Porter, Glass, & Koff, 1989). Various solutions have been proposed, including the development of an antibody test that could distinguish between vaccine-induced seroconversion and natural infection (Porter *et al.*, 1989); an identification card indicating that the individual is a participant in a vaccine trial; confidential communication at the participant's request with the agency or company, such as an insurance company, that needs verification of the individual's seronegativity; and the creation of a confidential registry of vaccine trial participants. It has been noted, however, that many of those listed on such a registry would be homosexuals or injecting drug users and may fear the consequences of stigma resulting from a breach of confidentiality (Osmond, 1992).

The process by which vaccine trial participants should be selected has raised questions relating to the distribution of both the burdens and the benefits of these trials. One researcher has suggested that if the purpose of the vaccine is to benefit those at risk of HIV infection, then persons at risk should be trial participants (Mariner, 1990). However, reliance on certain groups of persons at high risk of HIV infection may raise other ethical concerns (Arnold, 1991). For instance, prisoners may be at high risk because of the extent of sexual activity in jails and the lack of access to condoms. However, their participation may be problematic because of their confinement and the potential that their consent to participation is not truly voluntary.

Questions have been raised regarding liability for injuries resulting from, or arising out of, an HIV vaccine trial (Arnold, 1991; Newhard, 1988). A detailed discussion of theories of liability is beyond the scope of this text, and can be found elsewhere (Arnold, 1991; Peppin, 1991; McKenna, 1988; Newhard, 1988). The World Health Organization has recommended that research participants who are injured receive compensation (World Health Organization, Council for International Organizations of Medical Science, 1982). One writer has suggested that this compensation include free medical, nursing, and rehabilitative care (Mariner, 1990). Injury may extend beyond one's health, however. A vaccine trial participant might lose his or her health insurance or place of residence as a result of participating (Osmond, 1992). Christakis and Panner (1989) have suggested an industry–government collaboration in the development of an HIV vaccine and the establishment of a compensation fund for individuals injured as a result of their trial participation. The compensation fund could be similar to the HIV vaccine compensation fund model established by the state of California.

If a vaccine is developed that is, indeed, effective, questions remain regarding its distribution. It is unclear, for example, whether participants in trials will be provided vaccine if the latter is found to be effective. It has also been argued that vaccines found to be effective in the course of vaccine trials in developing countries should be provided at no or reduced cost to the populace of those countries (Lurie *et al.*, 1994).

3.4. CONCLUSION

HIV and HIV research have provoked intense debate. This debate, and the attempt to reach a balance between differing points of view, is clearly visible in the context of clinical trials. HIV researchers must balance their desire for well-controlled trials that are most easily analyzable against the concerns of HIV-infected individuals, who perceive the drug approval process as laboriously slow and inattentive to their needs, such as broader access to therapies. HIV-infected individuals have demanded a greater voice in the drug development process, and have received it, through the implementation of community consultation, parallel track trials, and access to experimental drugs through the compassionate use program. Clinical trials represents an area in which a real partnership can be forged between the researchers and the research participants, which can lay the foundation for an in-depth and ongoing examination of the legal and ethical issues involved.

CHAPTER FOUR

Recruitment

The process of recruitment for any study is intimately related to the basic principles of autonomy and justice. Individuals who are successfully recruited must know what it is that they have joined, and they must have joined voluntarily. In order for the burdens and the benefits of the research to be distributed equitably, "the selection of recipients [cannot be] based on their social worth, lifestyle, past or potential contributions to society, or value to others (such as family)" (Macklin & Friedland, 1986).

This chapter's discussion of recruitment presupposes that an appropriate informed consent procedure has been developed and is in place for the recruitment of research participants. This section addresses other aspects of recruitment to HIV-related studies, including current ethical and legal standards for recruitment; the barriers to recruitment, particularly from specific populations; participants' motivations to volunteer to be part of a research effort; and methods of recruitment.

4.1. STANDARDS FOR RECRUITMENT

Background

Women, persons of color, and injecting drug users have been underrepresented in AIDS research. There are at least four reasons for the underrepresentation of women in drug trials: (1) women may be pregnant or may become pregnant (Murphy, 1991; Halbreich & Carson, 1989); (2) women may lack access to the health care system in general and to research in particular, often because of their status as persons of color; (3) women who are drug users are perceived as "noncompliant" and therefore undesirable as research participants; and (4) many studies have focused on AIDS rather than HIV and women who were more recently infected have not yet progressed to AIDS (C. Levine, 1991b; Levine, 1990).

Women's participation in HIV research is further complicated by pharmaceutical manufacturers' fears of liability for the teratogenic effects of a drug; by communities' fears of research, particularly where there is no direct benefit to the participant; and by general lack of access to the health care system, which often acts as a funnel for persons to enroll in research studies (C. Levine, 1991b; Murphy, 1991). Fears for the health of unborn fetuses and resulting liability may often be misplaced, as these potentialities are premised on the assumption that all women who would want to participate in HIV research in general, and clinical trials in particular, are heterosexually active and fertile (Buc, 1993). These assumptions are implicit in guidelines issued by the FDA (1977):

> A woman of childbearing potential is defined as a premenopausal female capable of becoming pregnant. This includes women on oral, injectable, or mechanical contraception; women who are single; women whose husbands have been vasectomized or whose husbands have received or are utilizing mechanical contraceptives devices.

The exclusion of these groups is inconsistent with the ethical principle of justice, which seeks an equitable distribution of the burdens and the benefits of research. Communities of color have been disproportionately impacted by HIV. Between 1981 and 1984, black and Latino individuals accounted for over 40% of all reported AIDS cases, although they constitute less than 40% of the U.S. population (United States Department of Commerce, Bureau of the Census, 1993). Between 1981 and October of 1990, 14,816 cases of AIDS among women were reported to the Centers for Disease Control; this represented 10% of the adult and adolescent cases of AIDS reported during that period (Centers for Disease Control, 1990). Clearly, these communities have an interest in participating in HIV research.

A tension exists, however, between the application of the principle of justice and those of beneficence and autonomy. Beneficence speaks to a responsibility not to do harm, which includes harm to unconsenting future children. That harm may be quite difficult to measure. Others would argue that the exclusion of women of childbearing age places greater importance on the consequences to unborn, and potentially never-to-be-born, children than on women's autonomy. Still others argue that if women of childbearing age are to be excluded from participation in clinical trials, then men of reproductive potential must be similarly excluded (Moreno, 1994).

The exclusion of women, injecting drug users, and persons of color from HIV research studies is unwise in the long run. Persons from these communities who are HIV-infected will require treatment for their illnesses. Medications tested only on non-drug–using white males may not produce the desired effect in other populations (Merton, 1993; Murphy, 1993), because of differences in pharmacokinetics and pharmacodynamics (Merkatz, Temple, Subel, Feiden, & Kessler, 1993). Mirkin (1975) summarized the issue as it applies to women by stating:

> Society may choose to forbid drug evaluation in pregnant women and children. This choice would certainly reduce the risk of damaging individuals through research. However, this would maximize the possibility of random disaster from use of inadequately investigated drugs. In the final analysis it seems safe to predict that more individuals would be damaged; however, the damage would be distributed randomly rather than imposed upon preselected individuals . . . .

Ultimately, it would seem, manufacturers who fear liability face greater exposure once the drug is approved for marketing if it has not previously been tested in heterogeneous groups (Flannery & Greenberg, 1994; Merton, 1993).

Even when women are included in AIDS clinical trials, the gender–specific analyses may not reflect any concern for the potential impact of the study or the results on women's health. Faden, Kass, and McGraw (in press), in discussing a clinical trial designed to assess the effect of AZT administration during pregnancy on the rate of vertical transmission of HIV to the infant, noted that the study neither provided gynecological care to the mothers participating in the trial nor addressed the women's nonobstetrical health concerns.

Current Regulations

Current regulations permit pregnant women to participate in clinical research if the "purpose of the activity is to meet the health needs of the mother." In such instances, the degree of risk to the fetus is not considered. However, if the purpose of the research is not to meet the mother's needs, she may not participate unless the risk to the fetus is no more than minimal (Robertson, 1994). Research with the fetus is permitted if the purpose of the research is to meet the needs of the fetus and the latter is placed at risk to the "minimum extent necessary to meet such needs" [45 Code of Federal Regulations section 46.208(a), 1993]. Research that is not intended to meet the needs of the fetus may be conducted only if the risk to the fetus is minimal and the anticipated biomedical knowledge to be derived from the study cannot be obtained otherwise [45 Code of Federal Regulations section 46.209(b), 1993].

4.2. BARRIERS TO RECRUITMENT

Access to the Investigational Drug

As discussed earlier in Section 3.1, Basic Principles of Clinical Trials, the research method itself may hinder recruitment efforts. Individuals may be unwilling to leave their treatment to chance by being randomized to the research or experimental treatment or the alternative group. Others may be particularly fearful of the toxic effects of the drug under study, and are unwilling to be randomized to the investigational drug (Boffey, 1987). Such fears hampered recruitment efforts for the initial AZT studies, particularly in New York City (Kolata, 1988b).

Recruitment efforts may also be hampered by the availability of the investigational drug outside of a study. For instance, investigators experienced great difficulty in recruiting individuals for clinical trials of ddi because of the widespread availability of the drug outside of clinical trials (Cimons, 1989b).

Distrust of Public Health Authorities

Clinical studies in the past have often relied on the participation of impoverished persons of color. This sometimes occurred as a matter of convenience. For example, the researchers may have been located at teaching hospitals that served the poor (Silverman, 1989). Unfortunately, the legacy of unethically conducted research with impoverished communities and communities of color hampers efforts to reduce HIV transmission in these communities. The Tuskegee Study is a well-known example of research in the African-American community which is now considered unethical.

The Tuskegee Study was begun in 1932 in Macon County, Alabama, by the United States Public Health Service (USPHS). The study was intended to examine the natural history of untreated syphilis in 400 syphilitic black males, as compared to 200 uninfected black male controls. Penicillin became available for the treatment of syphilis in the early 1950s. The study was not stopped, however, until 1972. By that time, between 28 and 100 of the cohort had died as a result of syphilitic lesions (Brandt, 1985). During the 40-year course of the study, the USPHS offered inducements, such as burial expenses, to encourage the men to continue in the study. The USPHS actively prevented the men from obtaining proper treatment by meeting with local black physicians to ask their cooperation in not treating the men; by requesting Macon County physicians to refer these men back to the USPHS if they presented for care; and by warning the Alabama Health Department not to treat these men for their venereal disease (Brandt, 1985). The racial aspects of the study were rationalized with the observation at a USPHS meeting that the participants were "getting better medical care than they would under any other circumstances" (Brandt, 1985).

The final report of the Department of Health, Education and Welfare, issued in 1973, found that the Tuskegee Study was ethically unjustified in 1932 (Brandt, 1985). The implications of the Tuskegee Study and the HEW's findings for AIDS research and HIV prevention cannot be overstated. The conduct of the study, in the minds of many, provides clear evidence of the governments indifference to black persons. AIDS represents yet another attempt at the genocide of blacks (Cantwell, 1993; Guinan, 1993; Thomas & Quinn, 1991).

More recently, Navajo uranium miners sued the Public Health Service (PHS), charging that as participants in an epidemiological study conducted by PHS they had been inadequately informed about research findings linking lung cancer to prolonged radiation exposure. Although the court found that PHS had decided not to warn the miners of the potential hazards associated with uranium mining in order to gain the cooperation of the mine owners and retain the participants in the study, it declined to award damages, finding that PHS's decision not to warn fell within its discretionary function, thereby barring government liability (*Begay v. United States*, 1985).

Other communities have been equally distrustful of government efforts, albeit for different reasons. Injecting drug users may believe that the government continues to prohibit needle exchange programs and to underfund drug rehabilitation programs as part of an effort to eliminate injecting drug users by ensuring their deaths. Gay men have been suspicious of government efforts since the initial characterization of the disease as affecting only gays, the consequent stigmatization of gays, and the perceived unwillingness of the federal government to fund adequately research efforts and prevention programs (Cantwell, 1993).

Distrust of public health authorities has also resulted from what has been perceived as an attempt to exclude particular groups, such as women, injecting drug users, and persons of color, from participation in promising research (Levine, 1989; Steinbrook, 1989). American blacks have historically been underrepresented in clinical trials of new drugs (Svensson, 1989). Non-English speakers have often been excluded from studies because of the difficulties inherent in ensuring accurate communication. Females have been systematically excluded because of reproductive considerations (Merton, 1993). Perceptions of systemic exclusion from research participation were recently exacerbated by the appropriation of monies for a large-scale clinical trial of an HIV vaccine in military personnel and veterans, rather than "a broad-based civilian population group, extending to underrepresented minorities, injecting drug users, and others among whom the incidence of HIV infection is high" (Healy, 1993). Refer to Section 4.1 for further discussion of the reasons for the exclusion of these groups.

Stigmatization

Recruitment for HIV-related studies may be rendered even more difficult because of fears about the consequences of participating in a study. In some cultures, fatal disease is associated with witchcraft and sorcery. Individuals participating in a study may be thought to be HIV positive, even if they are not. As a result, individuals may be subject to accusations that they are guilty of witchcraft, and may be ostracized from their family or community as a result (Schoepf, 1991).

Women may be particularly vulnerable to adverse consequences. Responsibility for the disease and its transmission may be attributed to the woman, even though she contracted the infection from her male partner. Rejection by her male partner because of her infection, or even perceived infection, may carry serious emotional and economic consequences.

Economic Factors

Individuals may be unable to participate in a study because of inadequate financial support (Ballard, Nash, Raiford, & Harrell, 1993; El-Sadr & Capps, 1992). This may result directly from participation, as when individuals paid on an hourly basis must miss time at work in order to attend appointments. The financial impact may be indirect, as when the prospective participant has insufficient funds to cover transportation costs, baby-sitting costs, or the costs of meals en route to or from the study site. These factors may be a particular hindrance to the recruitment of families with children, because of the logistics of travel and multiple competing demands for parents' time (Vollmer, Hertert, & Allison, 1992), and of women, who must often assume the primary responsibility for the care of their family, regardless of their own situation (Smeltzer, 1992). These barriers may be considerably easier to overcome than those resulting from distrust of health personnel, because they can be addressed through a system of reimbursements for participation-related expenses or study-provided transportation.

Legal Difficulties

Some individuals may be hesitant to participate in HIV-related studies because of potential legal difficulties that they may face should the information divulged in the context of the study become known to others or should their participation become known to others. These concerns most often arise where the prospective participant is a member of the U.S. armed services or where the individual is not a citizen of the United States and is concerned about the potential immigration consequences.

Military Service

HIV testing of all active duty and reserve personnel on a periodic basis and of new recruits has been in place since 1985 (Department of Defense, 1985). Consequently, extensive policies and procedures have been developed to address situations in which personnel are found to be HIV-positive on testing (32 Code of Federal Regulations part 58.6, 1991; Department of Defense, 1991). An armed forces member's participation in an HIV-related study is by itself unlikely to affect his or her status.

What may be a source of concern, however, is the potential release from the study of information pertaining to the service member's sexual conduct. Many HIV-related studies collect information pertaining to individual's risk behaviors for HIV, whether the individual is seropositive or seronegative. Current policy regarding homosexuals in the military attempts to distinguish between sexual orientation and sexual conduct. Homosexual orientation is to be considered a private matter and cannot form the basis for a discharge. Homosexual conduct, however, may provide the basis for either rejection or discharge. Homosexual conduct is defined broadly to include not only verbal statements but also "language or behavior that a reasonable person would believe intends to convey the statement that a person engages in or has a propensity or intent to engage in homosexual acts" (Department of Defense, 1993). Individuals serving in the armed forces who are contemplating participation in HIV research may feel that they are between the proverbial rock and a hard place: they would like to participate and provide accurate information to the researchers, but fear the potential consequences to their careers should that information become known.

These fears are not entirely unfounded. HIV research data may be subject to involuntary release in some situations, such as when it is the subject of a court subpoena. However, various legal protections can be put in place to protect the research participants from such disclosures, such as certificates of confidentiality. For an in-depth discussion of ways to ensure confidentiality of research records, see Section 5.3.

Immigration

Current immigration law excludes from the United States aliens who are infected with HIV [8 United States Code Annotated section 1182(a)(1)(i), 1990; 56 Federal Register 25000, 1991]. In addition, certain behaviors that may increase one's risk of HIV transmission, such as drug abuse or addiction and prostitution, are themselves grounds for exclusion from the United States (8 United States Code Annotated section 1182, 1990), regardless of an individual's HIV serostatus. A waiver to override the exclusion because of HIV infection is potentially available only to an alien who intends to immigrate permanently to the United States, i.e., become a permanent resident or "green card holder," and who is the spouse or unmarried son or daughter of a U.S. citizen or lawfully admitted permanent resident, or of an alien who has been issued an immigrant visa, or an alien who has a son or daughter who is a U.S. citizen or a lawfully admitted permanent resident, or has been issued an immigrant visa [8 United States Code Annotated section 1182(g), 1990]. No waiver is available to overcome exclusion because of drug abuse or addiction. Potential exclusion can be overcome only if the alien can demonstrate that he or she has not used the substance in question for a specified number of years (United States Department of Health and Human Services, 1991).

Individuals contemplating participation in HIV research may fear that the disclosure of information relating to them could result in their detection, if they are here illegally, or could result in their deportation as a result of their past or current behaviors or their HIV seropositivity. It is important to note that these provisions can potentially affect even noncitizens who are legally in the United States; an individual need not be undocumented to have a valid basis for concern.

Various mechanisms may be available to protect the research data from involuntary disclosure, including internal mechanisms and certificates of confidentiality. These mechanisms are discussed in depth in Section 5.3.

4.3. PARTICIPANT MOTIVATIONS FOR VOLUNTEERING

One might wonder why, with so many potential barriers between a prospective participant and actual study enrollment, anyone would actually agree to volunteer for a study. Participants may often volunteer because they view a clinical trial as a means of obtaining clinical care or therapy, rather than research (Specter, 1989; C. Levine, 1988). One recent study of 43 participants in AIDS clinical trials found that 60% agreed to participate based on health reasons, while 35% said that they agreed to volunteer because participation provided them with health care. Only 29% agreed to participate for altruistic reasons (Ickovics, Ethier, Meisler, & Rodin, 1994). In another study of 43 women participating in a trial of drugs for the treatment of acute inflammation of the fallopian tube, 15 women indicated that they had consented because of the possibility of better medical care. Over one–half, however, agreed to participate because of the potential for benefiting future patients (Lynoe, Sandlund, Dahlqvist, & Jacobsson, 1991).

The misperception of a clinical trial as a means of obtaining therapy may be exacerbated when the recruiter for the study is, in essence, a "double agent," both a researcher and the patient's physician or therapist (Levine, 1992). The physician or therapist is concerned with the provision of treatments and procedures that are designed to benefit the specific patient who is seeking care. The researcher, however, is concerned with finding something that may be of no benefit to the person before him or her, but may aid other unknown persons. The ill person may be unable to differentiate between these roles. One writer has suggested resolving this potential conflict through reliance on independent clinical judgment for ascertaining the appropriateness of a patient's enrollment into a study where the potential participant's physician or therapist is also the researcher (Levine, 1992). This would provide some assurance that the prospective participant has actually understood his or her role as a research participant. Reliance on this or a similar check in the procedure could help to avoid future problems with adherence to the protocol that result from discordance between a participant's expectations and the reality of the research setting. See Section 2.3 for further discussion of social worker and health care worker recruitment of patients into research studies.

4.4. METHODS AND STRATEGIES FOR RECRUITMENT

Methods

Numerous methods exist for the recruitment of research participants. They fall into two general, broad categories: direct and indirect patient contact.

Methods of direct recruitment include the solicitation of participants through primary care or other clinics, through screening procedures, by mail or telephone calls, and by outreach through the community or other networks. Indirect patient recruitment techniques include referrals from treating physicians, retrospective record reviews, and calls for volunteers in the media.

In order to recruit effectively from a clinic, the clinic's patient-load must be sufficiently large enough to yield the sample size required for the study. Clinic recruitment at first glance seems easier than other methods. However, recruitment through a clinic or clinics can be impeded by missed appointments and a lack of staff time and expertise to recruit patients actively. It may be advantageous to designate one staff person as being responsible for all recruitment efforts, so that that person is fully informed about the study and can focus on recruitment efforts (Fowler *et al.*, 1992). This may also have the effect of reducing the inconvenience to other staff persons, which will be essential if the researcher wishes to foster the cooperation of the clinic staff (Sieber & Sorensen, 1992).

Identification and recruitment of participants via screening for a disease will be effective only when a test exists that has sufficient sensitivity and specificity to identify those with the particular disease. Ideally, that test should be relatively inexpensive and simple. Ethically, it is important that treatment for the identified condition be available either at the study facilities or via a referral once an individual is identified with the disease of interest (Roht, Selwyn, Holguin, & Christensen, 1982). As an example, a researcher might want to ascertain the prevalence of cytomegalovirus among HIV-infected patients and risk factors for the infection. This could be accomplished through a blood test. However, it is important to offer treatment or a referral to treatment to those identified with the infection.

Mailings and telephone calls are frequently used for recruitment. The initial telephone call is often structured, in order to maximize the possibility that the individual will be found eligible for the study (Shtasel *et al.*, 1991). Telephone calls and mailing are generally used in conjunction with a screening test, to verify that those who respond to the call for volunteers actually satisfy the eligibility criteria for the study. For instance, individuals recruited for HIV vaccine trials must satisfy certain medical criteria in order to be eligible, including confirmation of their HIV seronegative status (Cimons & Steinbrook, 1987).

Community networks have been used extensively to recruit for HIV-related studies. Outreach efforts through established networks of family members, friends, and neighbors have been found to be a particularly effective means of recruiting injecting drug users for participation (Finlinson, Robles, Colon, & Page, 1993). Community consultation, discussed in Section 3.1, facilitates the direct recruitment of potentially eligible individuals who may become involved in these sessions, and establishes a network in the community for the referral of others (Sieber & Sorensen, 1992).

Recruitment of study participants is often made through treating physicians. This may be an effective method if the recruiting physicians have a sufficient number of potentially eligible patients. This method of recruitment may be somewhat problematic if care is not taken to indicate to the patient that the suggestion to participate in a study is not a component of the individual's care with that physician. See Section 4.3 for further discussion. Clearly, the treatment that the person is receiving through his or her primary physician must be consistent with the study protocol.

Retrospective record reviews are particularly helpful if the researcher is looking at a condition that affects a limited number of persons, and the variables and condition under study are routinely recorded as part of the medical chart. For instance, a retrospective record review could be employed to ascertain levels of procedure utilization among AIDS patients with active *Pneumocystis carinii* pneumonia and certain clinical, demographic, and economic factors associated with utilization. Care must be taken to ensure, however, that the confidentiality of patients' is protected. If patients have not consented to the use of their records for research, and state law does not permit the release of medical records with identifying information without the patients' written informed consent, it may be necessary to have all identifying information deleted from a copy of the records prior to their transmittal to the researchers.

Appeals through mass media have often been used in the context of HIV research. Articles in the press may bring the study to the attention of the target community (Hurley & Pinder, 1992). Unfortunately, researchers cannot always control the content or tone of reporter-written pieces, and media attention has a potentially adverse, as well as beneficial, impact on recruitment efforts.

Whether prospective participants are approached through direct or indirect methods of solicitation, it is essential that recruitment efforts be sensitive to the special concerns of the community. Various strategies have been suggested to increase the effectiveness of recruitment efforts, and to increase participant adherence to the study.

Strategies

Language

The words chosen for use in the recruitment efforts may be perceived as reflecting the role that the researchers wish the participants to play and the researchers' attitudes toward the participants. The use of the term "research subjects," in lieu of "research participants" or "research partners," may evoke images of oppression or paternalism (Maddocks, 1992). Individuals may be less willing to embrace research efforts in which they will not be accorded equal standing. Communication of the research question may inadvertently reflect heterosexist bias (Herek, Kimmel, Amaro, & Melton, 1988) and alienate subgroups that could make a valuable contribution to the study. For instance, a study of adolescent risk behaviors for HIV transmission that focuses solely on behavior between heterosexuals and presupposes that adolescent same-sex attractions do not exist will alienate some potential participants in the study and will lack the scope of information that might otherwise be available.

Location

The location of the recruitment effort may also have an impact on the success of the recruitment effort. Recruitment of participants through a drug treatment clinic, for instance, may be problematic as a result of crowded conditions in the clinic (Sieber & Sorensen, 1992) and the consequent lack of privacy during the recruitment interview. Assistance with transportation may facilitate recruitment and enrollment (Stoy, 1994).

Recruiter Characteristics

Attention to recruiter characteristics may engender more sympathy for the research and increase the likelihood that individuals approached will participate in the study. For instance, recruitment of injecting drug users through former injecting drug users may be more effective because the recruiters will be more effective in locating potential participants, and because the participants may be more likely to feel that the researchers know what they are doing and that they are trustworthy (Finlinson *et al.*, 1993).

4.5. CONCLUSION

Recent efforts have expanded access to participation in HIV-related research to include greater number of women and members of communities of color. Significant barriers to recruitment still remain, including lack of access to the experimental drug, the possibility of stigmatization resulting from participation, distrust of health authorities, economic factors, and potential legal difficulties. Recruitment to participate in HIV studies can be maximized by utilizing legal mechanisms to protect the participants' confidentiality, by implementing strategies designed to make the study more "participant friendly," and by openly discussing participants' concerns and attempting to address them.

PART TWO

Issues Arising during the Study

CHAPTER FIVE

Confidentiality

Confidentiality in the context of HIV research is of primary concern. The emphasis on confidentiality stems from the basic principle of autonomy, which includes the individual's right to control personal information and to protect his or her privacy (Winston, 1991).

Concern for confidentiality is also premised on pragmatic concerns. First, individuals participating in the research are potentially vulnerable to social risks as a result of their participation (McCormick, 1990; Purtilo, Sonnabend, & Purtilo, 1983). These risks can include social isolation (McCormick, 1990), loss of employment, eviction, and discrimination in other areas of daily living (Gray & Melton, 1985). Second, the very behaviors that a research participant reports to the investigator could be grounds for the instigation of criminal charges. For instance, individuals who are injecting drug users may report the frequency of their injecting and the substances that they are using (Gray & Melton, 1985). If this information were to become known, it is not inconceivable that law enforcement officials might also learn of the activity and follow up on this information. Such consequences could deter individuals from seeking HIV testing or from participating in research studies, ultimately harming society as a whole (Gray & Melton, 1985). Individuals' fear could deter participation even under the best of circumstances.

It is important to recognize the tension between the need to protect research participants' privacy and the need for information in research. Bayer, Levine, and Murray (1984) explained this inherent tension well:

> Ethically, a balance must be struck between the principle of respect for persons (which requires that individuals should be treated as autonomous agents who have the right to control their own destinies), and the pursuit of

> the common good (which requires maximizing possible benefits and minimizing possible harms, to society as well as to individuals.) Legally—by statute, policy, and regulation—subjects, researchers, and institutions must be protected from involuntary disclosure of information. Those entrusted with confidential information must be prohibited by law from unjustifiable voluntary disclosure. As a society we must express our moral commitment to the principle that all persons are due full measure of compassion and respect.
>
> Any investigation involving a possibly communicable disease poses a tension between an individual's desire to control personal information and the desire of others to have access to that information. Although this tension is not unique to AIDS, it is particularly sharply drawn in this case because those groups that have been identified as at high risk are also highly vulnerable socially, economically, and politically.

This "tension" is not merely theoretical. The Centers for Disease Control on three separate occasions released lists of names of persons living with AIDS to local health agencies not affiliated with the federal government and without the consent of those persons. In one case, the names were released to the New York Blood Center in connection with a follow-up study of individuals who had received a hepatitis B vaccine. The second situation involved the release of names to the Los Angeles health department in connection with a "cluster study." The third release occurred when names were provided to health departments in New York, Los Angeles, and San Francisco to prevent duplicate reporting of patients (Marwick, 1983). Patient identifying information has been released to investigators in non-HIV-related studies, without patient consent, for the purpose of enrolling individuals or families into the studies (B. P. Squires, 1993; Birkett, 1993). Some researchers have argued that an exemption permitting researchers to access certain information, such as AIDS-related cause of death, should be available to researchers for specified individuals (Dannenberg, Vernick, & Kirk, 1993).

The issue of confidentiality can arise in various contexts and at various points in time during the course of developing and conducting a study. State law may appear to mandate disclosure of HIV seropositivity or an AIDS diagnosis for the purpose of disease surveillance. A court may issue a subpoena for the records relating to a particular individual. A researcher may potentially have a duty to disclose an individual's HIV status to another because of duty to warn laws. Funding agency audit procedures may impinge on the confidentiality of research participants. Management of the study data requires the design and implementation of mechanisms to protect the research data from unwanted intrusions and the research participants from the consequences of unlawful or unethical disclosure of data. Less well recognized as a possible breach of confidentiality is researcher's use of data that they may have received from federal agencies or employer groups for one purpose but which they then use for their own research (Dickens, 1991).

This chapter first addresses provisions under state and federal law that could result in the disclosure of information related to participants in HIV research. It then explores mechanisms for the protection of the data and the research participants. A timeline is provided to highlight the various strategies available to protect participants' confidentiality at various stages of the research.

5.1. STATE LIMITS ON CONFIDENTIALITY

Public Health Reporting Requirements

Table 5.1 provides a summary of state statutes relating to the confidentiality of HIV-related records. It refers to medical records and public health records. Medical records relate to the medical and personal information that is maintained by health care providers in connection with an individual's medical care. Public health records are records maintained by a health department pursuant to specific reporting requirements.

All states require that physicians report cases of AIDS to a health department; some require that cases of HIV infection be reported as part of their communicable disease reporting and control procedures. Many HIV-related research studies are conducted by nonphysicians, who are not subject to these reporting requirements. However, studies are often conducted by physician researchers. Additionally, even nonphysician researchers may be involved in studies in which participants must be tested for HIV, and some states require laboratory personnel to report cases of HIV infection. One theorist believes that requiring researchers to report research participants' HIV serostatus to a department of health is "very, very wrong" because it will diminish participants' confidence in the researchers. Another researcher believes that requiring the disclosure of individuals' HIV serostatus in conjunction with research is akin to holding them hostage: they will be denied access to particular interventions if they don't permit disclosure (Meyers, 1991). Individuals who have obtained HIV testing anonymously have reported that they would not seek out HIV testing if reporting were mandatory (Kegeles, Catania, Coates, Pollack, & Lo, 1990).

Many states permit blinded HIV testing for research purposes, where the identity of the individual tested is not linked to the HIV test

Table 5.1. Summary of State Statutes Relating to Confidentiality of HIV Information

	Protect all HIV-related medical records	Generally requires written patient authorization	Other written authorization requirements	Protects electronically stored HIV data	HIV/ AIDS reportable
Alabama		X			HIV
Alaska					none
Arizona		X	X		HIV
Arkansas					HIV
California	X	X			AIDS
Colorado	X				HIV
Connecticut					AIDS
Delaware					AIDS
District of Columbia		X			AIDS
Florida		X	X		HIV
Georgia					HIV
Hawaii		X			AIDS
Idaho					HIV
Illinois					HIV
Indiana		X			HIV
Iowa			X		HIV
Kansas					HIV
Kentucky		X			HIV
Louisiana					AIDS
Maine		X			HIV
Maryland					HIV
Massachusetts		X			none
Michigan					HIV

Minnesota				HIV
Mississippi				HIV
Missouri	X		X	HIV
Montana				HIV
Nebraska				HIV
Nevada				HIV
New Hampshire	X			HIV
New Jersey				HIV
New Mexico				none
New York	X	X		AIDS
North Carolina				HIV
North Dakota				HIV
Ohio				HIV
Oklahoma				HIV
Oregon	X	X		HIV
Pennsylvania	X			AIDS
Rhode Island				HIV
South Carolina				HIV
South Dakota				HIV
Tennessee				HIV
Texas				HIV
Utah				HIV
Vermont				AIDS
Virginia				HIV
Washington		X		HIV
West Virginia	X	X		HIV
Wisconsin	X			HIV
Wyoming				HIV

Table 5.1. *Continued.*

	HIV information obtainable by court order	Prohibits release of public health information in court	Specific protections for HIV research records	Spouse or partner notification provisions
Alabama	X	X		X
Alaska				
Arizona	X			
Arkansas				
California	X	X	X	X
Colorado				
Connecticut				
Delaware	X			
District of Columbia	X			
Florida	X			X
Georgia	X	X		X
Hawaii	X	X		
Idaho		X		X
Illinois	X			X
Indiana	X			
Iowa	X			X
Kansas	X			
Kentucky				
Louisiana				
Maine	X			
Maryland				
Massachusetts				
Michigan	X			X

Minnesota				X
Mississippi				
Missouri	X			X
Montana				
Nebraska		X		
Nevada				
New Hampshire	X			X
New Jersey				
New Mexico	X		X	
New York	X			X
North Carolina	X			X
North Dakota			X	
Ohio				
Oklahoma	X			
Oregon				X
Pennsylvania	X			X
Rhode Island				
South Carolina	X			X
South Dakota				
Tennessee	X			
Texas	X			X
Utah				
Vermont	X			
Virginia	X			
Washington	X			X
West Virginia	X			X
Wisconsin	X			X
Wyoming				

result. These data are often used to assess the seroprevalence of HIV infection in a particular geographic area or population. Anonymous unlinked HIV testing is discussed in greater detail in Section 2.2.

Abuse and Neglect Laws

All states require that specified professionals, such as physicians, nurses, social workers, and educators, report suspected child abuse or neglect. Consequently, researchers who are licensed in such occupations and are working in the field of HIV may be faced with a legal obligation to report suspected child abuse or neglect. This can create a conflict for HIV researchers, namely the obligation to maintain the research participant's confidentiality and the obligation to report the abuse or neglect. Although this situation may arise primarily in the context of pediatric HIV research, it may also arise in connection with adult HIV research. For example, a father participating in a study may bring his child to the study site because he is unable to obtain child care that day. The child is bruised and appears to be severely malnourished. The researcher must decide whether or not these circumstances indicate possible abuse. At the same time, it may be extremely difficult for the researcher to report suspected abuse because of the possibility that the study participant will feel that the researcher has betrayed his or her trust.

The definition of "abuse" may vary between states. California defines "child abuse" as a "physical injury which is inflicted by other than accidental means on a child by another person." "Child abuse" encompasses the sexual abuse of a child, willful cruelty or unjustifiable punishment of a child, unlawful corporal punishment or injury, and the neglect of a child or abuse in out-of-home care. Statute specifically excludes from the definition of child abuse confrontations between minors or injury resulting from the use of reasonable and necessary force by a peace officer in specified circumstances (California Penal Code section 11165.6, 1992 & Supp. 1994). New Jersey, however, includes in its definition of "abuse" a child engaged in employment either injurious to his or her health or dangerous to his or her morals, and the habitual use of obscene language within hearing of the child (New Jersey Statutes Annotated 9:6-1, 1993). States may define abuse to encompass not only physical abuse or neglect, but emotional abuse as well. Florida, for instance, defines abuse to include the infliction of mental injury upon a child [Florida Statutes Annotated tit. 46, section 827.04(2), 1994].

Recent efforts to expand the definition of child abuse to encompass a woman's administration of drugs during pregnancy may be particularly problematic for the HIV researcher. For instance, a female injecting drug user participating in an HIV research study may be HIV seronegative at the commencement of the study. During the study, she becomes pregnant, and continues to inject drugs and engage in high-risk sexual behaviors. If the study is being conducted in a jurisdiction that has expanded its definition of child abuse to include the administration of drugs during pregnancy to unborn children, the researcher will be faced with a possible obligation to report the participant's drug use. In some states, the definition of child abuse may be sufficiently broad to encompass the exposure of the unborn child to the risk of HIV infection (Cooper, 1994).

Partner Notification Laws

"Partner notification" refers to the notification of an HIV-infected individual's current sexual or needle sharing partner that he or she may have been exposed to HIV. It must be distinguished from contact tracing, which is a form of medical investigation that involves contacting all known sexual or needle sharing partners within a defined period of time to advise them of possible exposure to HIV, and to ascertain their possible sexual and needle sharing partners who may have been exposed (Falk, 1988).

Table 5.1 indicates which states have partner notification provisions. The provisions may take a variety of forms (Bayer & Toomey, 1992; Edgar & Sandomire, 1990). California, for instance, has a voluntary notification procedure. A physician who knows that a patient is HIV-infected may notify the person who the physician "reasonably believes" is the spouse, sexual partner, or needle sharing partner of the HIV-infected patient that he or she may have been exposed to HIV. In notifying the individual, the physician must follow procedures specified by statute. First, the physician must seek the patient's voluntary consent to notify the individual. If the patient refuses, the physician must notify the patient that he or she will notify the spouse or partner of possible exposure. In notifying the spouse or partner, the physician may not reveal the identity or identifying characteristics of the patient who may have exposed the individual to HIV. The physician must provide the notified individual with a referral for further counseling. It is important to note that the physician is under no affirmative duty to notify the partner or spouse. If the physician does notify the individual, the notification must be done with the intent to interrupt the chain of HIV transmission. Alternatively, the physician may notify the county health officer and request that the officer notify the spouse or partner of the patient (California Health and Safety Code section 199.25, 1990).

Florida's partner notification provision is also voluntary, but is quite different from that of California. In contrast to California, which permits only physicians or surgeons to notify an HIV-infected patient's spouse or partner, Florida permits "practitioners" to notify the HIV-infected individual's spouse. The practitioner must recommend that the HIV-infected patient notify his or her spouse of the positive HIV test result and that the patient refrain from engaging in sexual activities that could transmit the virus. The patient must refuse to follow these recommendations. The practitioner may then advise the spouse of the patient's HIV status and counsel the spouse about the transmission of the virus. The disclosure to the spouse must be carried out pursuant to a perceived civil duty or the ethical guidelines of the profession. The statute is silent with respect to the notification of individuals fulfilling a spousal role who are not the legally married spouse of the HIV-infected patient. A practitioner is not criminally or civilly liable for failing to disclose the patient's HIV status (Florida Statutes Annotated section 455.2416, 1991).

In sum, partner notification laws are relevant to HIV researchers if the researcher's occupation falls within the categories of persons permitted or required to notify the HIV-infected patient's partner by the governing statute. In most states, notification of the partner becomes a question of the researcher's professional judgment, because the majority of notification provisions are voluntary. In the few states that require partner notification, however, the researcher may be faced with a serious dilemma. Notification of the partner may adversely impact the research participants' confidence in the researchers and the study, and may result in less than candid responses from those individuals who do agree to participate in the study. The failure to notify a partner pursuant to the terms of the statute could potentially subject the researcher to penalties for the violation of state law. Obtaining a certificate of confidentiality from the federal government could potentially exempt the researchers from this requirement (Meyers, 1991). Certificates of confidentiality are discussed in Section 5.3.

The Duty to Warn

Apart from state statutory provisions mandating or permitting the notification of specific classes of individuals of possible exposure to HIV, a "duty to warn" may exist as the result of a line of court cases that began in 1976 with *Tarasoff v. Regents of the University of California.*

The Tarasoff family sued the University of California and a psychologist at the Berkeley campus of the university for the death of their daughter Tatiana. Tatiana had refused the advances of another graduate student at Berkeley. The latter student sought counseling from a psychologist at the school's counseling service, to whom he revealed that he intended to kill Tatiana. The psychologist and several colleagues sought the involuntary hospitalization of the student for evaluation purposes. The student was released after a brief observation period, during which it was concluded that he was rational. The student subsequently shot Tatiana.

The psychologist claimed that he could not have advised the family or Tatiana directly of the threat, because to do so would be a breach of the traditionally protected relationship between therapist and patient. The majority of the court, however, rejected this contention and held that when a patient "presents a serious danger . . . to another [person], [the therapist] incurs an obligation to use reasonable care to protect the intended victim against such danger." That obligation could be satisfied by warning the intended victim, by notifying authorities, or by taking "whatever other steps are reasonably necessary under the circumstances" (*Tarasoff v. Regents of the University of California,* 1976). The court specifically noted that the therapist–patient privilege was not absolute:

> We recognize the public interest in supporting effective treatment of mental illness and in protecting the rights of patients to privacy and the consequent public importance of safeguarding the confidential character of psychotherapeutic communication. Against this interest, however, we must weigh the public interest in safety from violent assault . . . . We conclude that the public policy favoring protection of the confidential character of patient–psychotherapist communications must yield to the extent to which disclosure is essential to avert danger to others. The protective privilege ends where the public peril begins.

Later cases have followed the *Tarasoff* court's reasoning. A New Jersey court ruled in *McIntosh v. Milano* (1979) that the doctor–patient privilege protecting confidentiality is not absolute, but is limited by the public interest or the private interest of the patient. In reaching this conclusion, the court relied on the 1953 case of *Earle v. Kuklo,* in which the court had stated that "a physician has the duty to warn third persons against possible exposure to contagious or infectious diseases." A Michigan appeals court held in *Davis v. Lhim* (1983) that a therapist has an obligation to use reasonable care whenever there was a person who was foreseeably endangered by his or her patient. The danger would be deemed to be foreseeable if the therapist knew or should have known, pursuant to his professional standard of care, of the potential harm. Courts are divided, though, on the issue of whether the patient must make threats about a specific, intended victim to trigger the duty to warn. The court in *Thompson v. County of Alameda* (1980) found no duty to warn where there was no identifiable victim. Another court, however, found that such a duty existed even absent specific threats concerning specific individuals, where the patient's previous history indicated that he would be likely to direct violence against a person (*Jablonski v. United States, 1983).*

Analogous conduct may occur in the HIV setting. A patient may discover that he or she is HIV-infected. Angry, and refusing to accept the diagnosis and recommended changes in behavior, the individual decides to continue engaging in unprotected sex with his or her current sexual partner or to continue sharing needles for injecting drugs. This type of situation is most similar to the *Tarasoff* situation: there exists a specific person who is at risk of exposure. Less clear is the situation where an individual resolves to "take as many people" with him or her by engaging in unprotected sexual relations with multiple, anonymous partners. Who, in this situation, can realistically be warned?

Legally, there is no consensus on the applicability of the *Tarasoff* doctrine to HIV-related situations. *Tarasoff* has generally been applied in situations involving violence, rather than communicable disease. HIV is less likely to be contracted through intercourse than death is likely to occur as the result of a bullet. Even if an individual is exposed to HIV, it is unclear whether an individual might be able to clear the virus from his or her system. Additionally, those with HIV infection may live for substantial periods of time, unlike individuals killed with a single shot (Traver & Cooksey, 1988).

The duty to warn may be relevant in the research setting, even absent general legal consensus as to the applicability of *Tarasoff* to HIV. Even though the situations addressed by these court cases and the HIV-related scenarios arose in the treatment setting, the research setting may involve treatment. Further, the researcher is quite often a clinician, such as a physician, nurse, social worker, or therapist.

There are many questions that remain unresolved (Knapp & Van de Creek, 1990; Appelbaum & Rosenbaum, 1989). First and foremost is the issue of whether confidentiality should ever be breached, regardless of the circumstances. Francis and Chin (1987) support the maintenance of confidentiality:

> Maintenance of confidentiality is central to and of paramount importance for the control of AIDS. Information regarding infection with a deadly virus,

> sexual activity, sexual contacts and the illegal use of IV drugs and diagnostic information regarding AIDS-related disease are sensitive issues that, if released by the patient or someone involved in health care, could adversely affect a patient's personal and professional life.

The American Medical Association takes a different view, balancing the patient's expectation of confidentiality against social concerns:

> The obligation to safeguard the patient's confidences is subject to certain exceptions which are ethically and legally justified because of overriding social considerations. Where a patient threatens to employ serious bodily harm to another person, and there is a reasonable probability that the patient may carry out the threat, the physician should take reasonable precautions for the protection of the intended victim, including notification of law enforcement authorities. [American Medical Association, 1989.

To what extent can a clinically trained researcher predict the behavior of a research participant? There are no generally accepted standards for the evaluation of dangerousness (Lamb, Clark, Drumheller, Frizzell, & Surrey, 1989; Public Health Service, 1987). To what extent should a participant's behavior provide the foundation for a breach of confidentiality? Psychotherapists have been found to differ in their assessments of the extent to which the dangerousness of an HIV-infected individual and the identifiability of a victim should mandate a breach of confidentiality (Totten, Lamb, & Reeder, 1990). Clinicians may function at various levels within a study. Are clinicians responsible only for the development of assessment instruments to be held to the same standard as the clinician-principal investigator of the study? Does the duty to warn override the protections guaranteed to the research participant by a certificate of confidentiality? What interventions would the courts deem sufficient to fulfill the duty to warn, and to whom must the warning be given? Numerous potential interventions exist, including notification of the potential victim, notification of law enforcement authorities, detention or isolation of the patient, and additional counseling of the patient (Lamb *et al.*, 1989). In resolving these issues, it is important to distinguish between those who might wish to know, and those who may have a right to know about an individual's seropositivity. It can be argued that the same duty to warn does not run to past sexual and needle sharing partners as it does to current partners, who are more clearly at risk of exposure (Fruman, 1991).

Subpoenas

A subpoena is an order from a court or administrative body to compel the appearance of a witness or the production of specified documents or records. This section is concerned with the court-ordered production of documents or records. A subpoena must be distinguished from a request to produce a document or record, which is issued by a party to litigation.

A subpoena can be issued by a court or by an administrative body with subpoena power, at either the state or the federal level. The information sought to be obtained through the subpoena may be deemed important to an investigatory proceeding, or to the conduct of a criminal or civil proceeding. The issuance of subpoenas against researchers has become increasingly common (Brennan, 1990). The following examples are illustrative.

The case of *In re Grand Jury Subpoena Dated Jan. 4, 1984* involved a waiter who was a doctoral candidate at a university. He was writing a dissertation relating to the sociology of the American restaurant. During the course of his investigation, he gathered information from a variety of sources and guaranteed confidentiality to all of them. He routinely recorded his observations and conversations in a book of field notes, which would be used to prepare his dissertation. Following a fire at the restaurant, the federal grand jury ordered the waiter to produce his notes. The waiter moved to quash (nullify) the subpoena, and claimed a scholar's privilege to maintain the confidentiality of the information. The court ruled against him, and found that the

> application of a scholar's privilege, if it exists, requires a threshold showing consisting of a detailed description of the nature and seriousness of the scholarly study in question, of the methodology employed, of the need for assurances of confidentiality to various sources to conduct the study and of the fact that the disclosure requested by the subpoena will seriously impinge on that confidentiality.

In a much later case relating to health research, rather than sociological research, a tobacco company requested the discovery, through the issuance of a subpoena, of data, tapes, questionnaires, medical records, death certificates, and other information that was part of ongoing medical research at a hospital. The tobacco company sought this material in connection with a claim that had been filed against it by the widow of an individual who had died of cancer. The 18,170 individuals who had participated in the research had requested and received assurances of confidentiality in exchange for their participation in the research. The compilation of the requested data would require an expenditure of over 1000 hours of time by the researchers. The hospital and the other parties seeking to quash the subpoena argued that forced compliance with the subpoena would also impinge on their academic freedom. The court granted the motion to quash the subpoena, after balancing the hardship of complying with the order against the need for the information, including the fact that neither the researchers nor the hospital were parties to the underlying litigation (*Application of R. J. Reynolds Tobacco Company*, 1987).

R. J. Reynolds, together with other tobacco companies, later applied for a subpoena from a federal district court in New York. Data were again sought in connection with numerous product liability lawsuits that had been filed against the tobacco companies. Again, neither the hospital nor the researchers were parties to the underlying investigations. The federal court ruled against the hospital and the researchers and ordered them to produce the information requested. The researchers and the hospital appealed to the federal circuit court, which affirmed the lower court. The companies' request was fashioned somewhat more narrowly, and sought only computer tapes and information necessary to interpret those tapes, rather than all of the raw data. However, the confidentiality of the research participants was not completely protected. The lower court order had allowed the researchers and hospital to purge the following identifying information from the data: names, street addresses, towns or villages, social security numbers, employers, and union registration numbers. However, the order would not allow the elimination of counties of residence, union local data, and dates of birth and death, although this information could be used by the tobacco companies to identify specific individuals (*Application of American Tobacco Company*, 1989; Holder, 1989).

Research records have also been subpoenaed in cases involving toxic shock syndrome (*Farnsworth v. Proctor & Gamble Company*, 1985), DES (*Deitchman v. E. R. Squibb and Sons, Inc.*, 1984; *Andrews v. Eli Lilly & Company*, 1983), and in other cases involving tobacco (Barinaga, 1992; Holder, 1993). HIV-related research records may also be subject to such orders, absent special protections. Consider, for instance, the actual (unpublished) case of an individual who suffered injuries as the result of a car accident. He was unable to obtain a satisfactory settlement with the insurance company of the driver of the other car, so he brought suit to recover for the costs of his injuries and medical treatment. The insurance company sought the production of the research record, which contained information relating not only to his HIV status, but also to the frequency of his homosexual activities, information that was completely unrelated to the issues to be litigated.

Once material is obtained via a subpoena, it is generally subject to public inspection. Research records in the above-mentioned HIV case contained not only information about an individual's HIV serostatus, but also details about the individual's sexual relations and drug usage.

Few mechanisms exist to protect HIV research data from discovery through the use of a subpoena. Several states have specific protections for HIV status and related information that is part of a research study. California provides that research records in a personally identifying form that were developed or acquired by a person in the course of conducting research or a research study relating to HIV are confidential. Those records may not be disclosed without the prior written consent of the research participant and are not subject to discovery by subpoena in most circumstances. In addition, a specific advisory must be included on transmission of the records to the party requesting them (California Health and Safety Code sections 199.30–.40, 1990). In states where such specific protections do not exist, it can be assumed that the research results remain subject to state requirements relating to public health reporting or subpoenas.

State Information Laws

Many states have laws similar to the federal Freedom of Information Act, discussed below, that allow individuals access to governmental agency records. There are many differences between the state laws, and discussion of all of them is beyond the scope of this text. A discussion of California's law is provided as an illustration.

California law declares that "access to information concerning the conduct of the people's business is a fundamental and necessary right of every person..." in the state (California Government Code section 6250, 1980). Accordingly, the law further requires that specficially enumerated government agencies establish written guidelines and procedures for access to their records. Departments under such a requirement include the Department of Motor Vehicles, the Department of Youth Authority, the State Department of Health Services, and the Secretary of State, among others [California Government Code section 6253(a), 1994]. Specific records are exempted from disclosure including, but not limited to, personnel, medical or similar files pertaining to individuals; records of intelligence information of the Attorney General; records pertaining to pending litigation to which the public agency is a party; and interagency memoranda that are not retained by the public agency in the ordinary course of business (California Government Code section 6254, 1994). These provisions attempt to strike a balance between the public's right to know and the individual's interest in safeguarding his or her privacy.

5.2. FEDERAL LIMITS ON CONFIDENTIALITY

The Freedom of Information Act

The Freedom of Information Act (FOIA) is a federal statute that provides for the public inspection and copying of specifically enumerated types of information from federal agencies. This includes the opinions of federal agencies, administrative staff manuals, and policies and interpretations that have not been published in the Federal Register. Additionally, and more importantly in the context of HIV-related research, FOIA provides for access to "records" held by a federal agency on an individual's written request. This may include federally sponsored or funded research and the corresponding data on individuals. The agency from which the records are requested may charge reasonable, standard fees for document search, or duplication, depending on the nature of the requesting entity [Freedom of Information Act, 5 United States Code Annotated section 552(a)(4), 1977 & 1993].

Statute specifies that the agency from whom the information is requested must determine within 10 days of receiving a request whether it will comply, and must advise the requester of the information of its intent to comply or to refuse to comply. An individual whose request for information is denied has the right to file an administrative appeal from that decision.

The statute provides that "[u]pon any determination by an agency to comply with a request for records, the records shall be made promptly available to such person making such request" [Freedom of Information Act, 5 United States Code Annotated section 552(a)(6)(C), 1977 & 1993]. However, Congress has not allocated sufficient resources to most agencies to allow them to do this. Consequently, an individual may have to wait a protracted amount of time to receive the response to his or her request (Sinrod, 1994). If the request for the information is denied, and the individual is again unsuccessful with his or her administrative appeal, he or she has the right to bring an action in federal court to attempt to compel disclosure of the information sought [Freedom of Information Act, 5 United States Code Annotated section 552(a)(4)(B), 1977 & 1993].

FOIA specifically protects nine classes of information from disclosure through this procedure:

1. Information that is classified or to be kept secret by Executive Order
2. Information that relates to the internal personnel rules and practices of the agency
3. Information specifically exempted by statute
4. Trade secrets or other commercial or financial information that is obtained from a person and that is privileged or confidential
5. Inter- or intraagency memoranda or letters that would not normally be available to individuals outside of a litigation context
6. Personnel and medical files, where disclosure would be "a clearly unwarranted invasion of personal privacy"
7. Specifically enumerated types of information relating to law enforcement
8. Information relating to agencies responsible for the regulation or supervision of financial institutions
9. Geological or geophysical information and data [Freedom of Information Act, 5 United States Code Annotated section 552(b), 1977 & 1993]

The term "agency record" is undefined in FOIA (Wilborn, 1990). The ambiguity is further compounded by FOIA's reference to "matters," "memorandums," and "files" (Wion, 1979). The courts have ruled that documents are not considered "agency records" based on transfer from a non-FOIA agency to an FOIA agency (*Kissinger v. Reporters Committee for Freedom of the Press*, 1980) or because their creation was financially supported by an FOIA agency (*Forsham v. Harris, 1980*). The Supreme Court has enunciated two prerequisites essential for the classification of requested materials as "agency records": the agency must either "create or obtain" a record, and the agency must be in control of the requested materials at the time that the FOIA request is made (*Department of Justice v. Tax Analysts*, 1989).

Despite this ambiguity, it is clear that some information about a specific study may be available from its very inception. The submission of a funding proposal creates an "agency record" that can be accessed through reliance on an FOIA request (*Washington Research Project v. Department of Health, Education, and Welfare,* 1974). This allows a requester to review the submission, whether or not it was ultimately funded. Raw data held by private grantees of federal funding are not, however, "agency records" for the purpose of disclosure under FOIA (*Forsham v. Harris,* 1980).

Use of FOIA to gain access to data became a focal point in "The Case of the Florida Dentist." Richard Driskill, a 31-year-old citrus worker, claimed that he contracted HIV from his dentist David Acer. CIGNA Dental Health of Florida, the dental program that provided Acer's services, and two experts hired by CIGNA, obtained data from CDC through FOIA. Using those data, they prepared their own molecular analysis and a critique of CDC's procedures, used as the basis for CDC's conclusion that Driskill may have contracted HIV while receiving dental care from Acer. The experts' receipt of the data through FOIA aroused some controversy:

> Eaton, Driskill's lawyer, complains that while it may have been legal for the researchers to use the FOIA to obtain the CDC's data, they behaved unethically. "If you take someone else's work, and you don't ask permission to use it, that's wrong." However, Barbara Mishkin, an attorney for the Washington firm of Hogan and Hartson and an expert on scientific ethics—who is not involved with this case—says that data gathered by government is fair game, "especially when it forms the basis for public policy." [Palca, 1992]

Agency Audit Requirements

The federal agency providing the funding may wish to review the records of a study for various, quite legitimate reasons. Where research is founded on the results of interviews, the agency may wish to verify that the individuals were actually interviewed. The agency, as well as the governing IRB, has an interest in the researcher's compliance with the study protocol and the protections that were devised for the research study participants. The agency may also wish to audit the study's financial records to ensure compliance with proper accounting procedures.

The ability of an agency to access identifying information about research participants may have an adverse affect on the research study. It appears that the greater the levels of protection afforded to research participants, the more likely they will be to cooperate and the more accurate the information will be (Boruch & Cecil, 1979).

5.3. MECHANISMS FOR THE PROTECTION OF CONFIDENTIALITY

The various mechanisms available for enhancing the ability to safeguard research participants from breaches of confidentiality are applicable during different phases of a study. Figure 5.1 provides a time

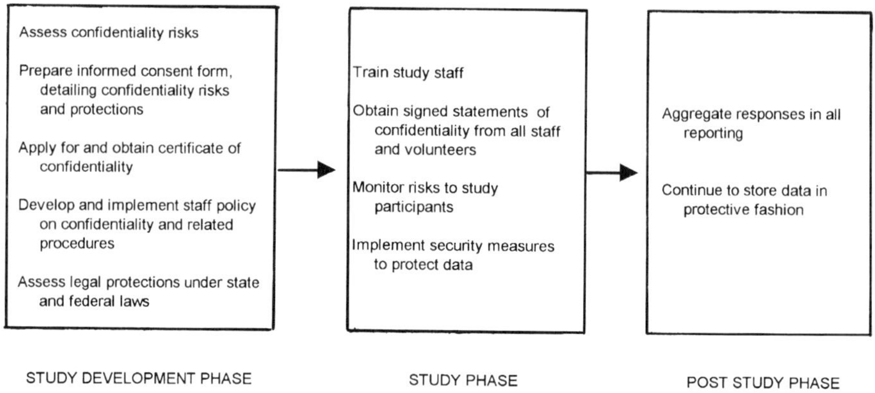

Figure 5.1. Suggested time line for the development and implementation of measures to protect confidentiality.

line for the implementation of these measures before, during, and following the conclusion of a study.

Implementing Security Measures

Unique Identifiers

Breaches of confidentiality can be minimized by assigning each research participant a unique identifier, which can consist of numbers or a combination of letters and numbers. Ideally, the identifier should be generated in such a way as to prevent its linkage with the individual's true identity. For instance, an identifier that consists of four randomly generated numbers plus the first four letters of an individual's last name will do little to protect the individual's identity. The data base should contain only the unique identifier as a means to identify the separate records. Access to the names to which the identifiers refer should be strictly limited to individuals with a need to know such information.

The Soundex code is one example of a system of unique identifiers that is being used by the states and the federal government. The Soundex code begins with a letter that is the same as the last letter in the person's name. The following four digits of the Soundex code are derived from the remaining letters in the person's name. The code has been called a "numerical alias" (Garfinkel, 1988).

Protecting Stored Data

Various practical and concrete measures can be implemented to further safeguard the data that are collected. Hard copies of data should be stored in locked cabinets, in locked offices. It is advisable to institute an alarm system so that an intrusion into data storage areas will be noticed immediately. Data stored on computer disks should be similarly stored in locked cabinets, and further protected by locked doors and an alarm system. Data stored on hard drives can be protected by locking the computer and maintaining the computer in a locked room in an area secured by an alarm or a building secured with an alarm.

Employee access to both the restricted area and the computer data and hard data should be limited. This can be accomplished by various means, including the use of a key or access card to access the area or building where the computer or data are stored, the selective distribution of keys for locked cabinets where hard copies of the data are stored or computers that house the data, and the use of passwords or codes to access the data on the computers (Torres, Turner, Harkess, & Istre, 1991).

Epidemiologists, biostatisticians, and other researchers have traditionally stored original data records for as long as possible. This facilitates reexamination of the data should additional insights arise at a later time. However, it has been recommended that the research records be destroyed once the original purposes of the study have been achieved in order to minimize the risk of inappropriate disclosure or inappropriate use of the data by nonparticipating investigators (Feinleib, 1991). It should be noted, though, that some peer-reviewed publications require authors of accepted manuscripts to maintain data for a minimum period of time following publication, should questions arise. That period may be as long as several years.

Employee Training

Employees should receive comprehensive training on the laws that govern the confidentiality of HIV-related data in their state. The training should also encompass other relevant aspects of state laws, such as protections for research records or medical records generally. The employees should be made aware of the potential consequences to research participants of an unauthorized release of information (McCarthy & Porter, 1991), and the potential civil and criminal consequences to the study staff and study institution for an unauthorized disclosure.

A procedure for the release of information should be established. All study staff and volunteers should be made aware of the procedure. Authority to release study information should be limited to specified individuals working with the study. It is advisable to have employees sign a statement of confidentiality as a condition of employment. Form 5.1 provides an example of such a form. It may also be helpful to have each employee sign for the receipt of a copy of the procedures relevant to the disclosure of information relating to study participants. Their signature should confirm that they have read and understood the policy and relevant procedures. The example of these procedures found in Form 5.2 reflects the author's experience assisting numerous nonprofit agencies and research groups with the drafting of confidentiality procedures. Form 5.3 provides an example of the release form that can be used for research participants to indicate their consent to a release of information. Form 5.4 is a checklist to be completed by an employee or volunteer as part of the disclosure procedure. This form should be completed and placed in the research participant's file, together with the original signed release form, any time that a research participant consents to the release of HIV-related information. Form 5.5, which follows the section addressing the transmission of study information, is an example of a prohibition against redisclosure to be placed on the cover sheet of all data containing participants' identity or

Employee/Volunteer Name ______________________

Employee/Volunteer Number ______________________

I understand and agree that in the performance of my duties as an employee/volunteer with ______________________, I must hold all information received through the study in confidence. In addition, I have read and reviewed a copy of the Confidentiality Policies and Procedures (attached), and agree to act in conformity with such Policy and Procedures. I understand that intentional violation of my responsibility by unauthorized disclosure of personal/confidential information may result in disciplinary action or legal action.

Date: ____________ Signature: ______________________

Form 5.1. Employee/volunteer confidentiality statement.

Policy

The research participant must consent in writing to the release of *any* information to researchers, health care providers, social service agencies, or any other person or entity outside of the research staff where the information to be provided includes either the identity or information that could be used to determine the identity of the research participant. The following procedures are to be followed with respect to any and all requests for information relating to a study participant.

Procedure

Person Responsible	*Activity/Procedure*
I. Any staff member or volunteer receiving a request for information	**1.** Forward the request to the staff person designated to handle these requests
II. Designated staff member	**1.** Evaluate the nature of the request to determine whether identifying information is required. **2.** If identity or identifying information is not required, transmit the required information. **3.** Record the nature of the data transmitted, the name and address of both the requester and the receiver of the data, the date of the request and the date of the transmittal in the Disclosure Logbook. **4.** If the requested data contains the participant's identity or identifying information, determine from the requester whether data minus the identity/identifying information would be acceptable. If it is, transmit the data following steps 1 through 3 above. If it is not, continue with step 5. **5.** If the participant's identity or identifying information must be provided, determine from the research participant whether he or she will consent to the disclosure. If the participant is willing to release the disclosure, have him or

Form 5.2. Sample confidentiality policy and procedures.

	her read, sing, and date a completed Disclosure Form (See Form 5.3.) **a.** Record the disclosure as outlined in step 3, above. **b.** Place one copy of the signed Disclosure Form in the participant's record. **c.** Place a stamp on the front cover of the information disclosed indicating that redisclosure of the information is prohibited without the express, written consent of the research participant. (See Form 5.4.) **d.** If the participant does not wish to have the information disclosed, proceed to step 6. **6.** Determine whether the requested disclosure is permitted or required under state, federal, or local law or regulation. If it is permitted, but not required , do not disclose the information. **a.** Place a record of the request and the decision not to release the information in the participant's record. **b.** Inform the requesting entity that the information requested is confidential, that the law does not require its disclosure, and that it may not be released. **7.** If the requested disclosure is potentially required by state, federal, or local law or regulation, forward the request with a memorandum detailing what has been done to date to the Principal Investigator or his or her designee.
III. Principal Investigator or Designee	**1.** Review Request for disclosure. **2.** Make a preliminary determination as to whether disclosure is required by law.

Form 5.2. *Continued.*

3. Seek advice or representation from legal counsel, if appropriate.
4. Based on assessment and legal advice, if obtained, refuse to disclose or disclose the information.
5. Document disclosure or refusal to disclose as outlined in step II-5 above.
6. Advise the research participant of the decision and outcome.

Form 5.2. *Continued.*

identifying information that is released to persons or entities outside of the study group. State and federal law should always be consulted in drafting these forms and procedures.

Protecting Transmitted Data

Researchers outside of a study may wish to have access to data, either to confirm published findings or to collaborate on particular aspects of the study. Clinicians engaged in the treatment of study participants may request information collected during a study about a specific individual to assist them in determining the proper course of care. Each of these scenarios may require a different approach to protect the participant's privacy.

Individuals participating as researchers will rarely need to know the actual identity of the study participants. The data can be transmitted to them using unique identifiers for participant records, as described above.

The release of study information pertaining to an identified individual can result in serious adverse consequences for the researcher, the participant, the study, and the study institution if not done in conformity with controlling law. A breach of confidentiality could result in serious consequences to the participant, including the loss of relationships, eviction, discrimination, loss of employment, or denial of medical care. Violation of confidentiality could reduce participants' confidence in the researchers and lead them to believe that the researcher cares only about him- or herself and not the participants. Finally, depending on the controlling law, the researcher and the research institution could be civilly or criminally liable for the breach

In all cases where information is requested with respect to a particular individual, the researcher should obtain written informed

HIV-Related Information is information that either directly or indirectly can identify you as someone who is HIV positive. Information that could do this includes the result of your HIV antibody test, your CD4 count, and whether you have had certain infections or illnesses, such as Kaposi's sarcoma, *Pneumocystis carinii* pneumonia, or oral candidiasis, among others.

Signing this form means that you are giving us your permission to give HIV-related information about you to the agency or person that is listed below. You do not have to sign the form. If you sign the form and then change your mind before the information is sent to the person or agency that is specified, we will not send the information to him or the agency. If you change your mind after you have agreed to have us send this HIV-related information, and we have already sent the information, we will not be able to interrupt the transmission of the information.

Name of person requesting information: ______________________________

Affiliation and address of person requesting information:

____

____

____

Information requested: ______________________________

____

____

Reason that information is requested: ______________________________

____

This release is valid from ______________ to ______________.

Date: ______________ Signature: ______________________________

Name (printed:) ______________________________

Address: ______________________________

____

Relationship to research participant: __________

____

Form 5.3. Sample release form.

________	Release form is completely filled out.
________	Release form is signed by the research participant or an individual who has the authority to authorize the release of information for the research participant.
________	The redisclosure warning has been affixed to the front of the information disclosed.
________	A notation has been made in the research participant's file indicating the date of the disclosure, the nature of the information disclosed, and the name of the person or agency receiving the information.
________	The original of this form has been placed in the research participant's file.

Form 5.4. Staff/volunteer checklist for disclosure of HIV-related information.

consent for the disclosure. Some states have promulgated specific provisions detailing the information that must be contained in the consent-form for the release to be considered valid. Generally, the release form should include a description of the information to be released, the name of the person to receive the requested information, the name of the person responsible for the transmission of the information, the name and signature of the participant who is consenting to the disclosure, and the date on which the participant consents. The form should also specify the duration for which the participant's consent is to be deemed valid. Many research institutions have legal departments that will draft or review such forms prior to their use, to ensure that all required information has been included. It may also be advisable, even if not required by governing state law, to stamp an advisory on a cover sheet or on each page of the transmitted information, indicating that the information is confidential and that further dissemination is subject to obtaining the written permission of the research participant. Form 5.5, modeled after California law, provides an example of a redisclosure advisory in jurisdictions where state law prohibits the release of certain information without a written release from the participant.

The transmission of records with identifying information by facsimile (fax) machine may be particularly problematic. Institutions faxing these documents are responsible for breaches in confidentiality that

This information has been disclosed to you from a confidential research record. The confidentiality of this information is protected by state law.

Any further disclosure of this information without the prior specific written consent of the research participant to whom it pertains is prohibited.

Violation of these confidentiality guarantees may subject you to civil or criminal liability.

Form 5.5. Warning against redisclosure of information/data.

occur as a result. The institution should develop and implement measures to minimize this risk. Numerous methods have been suggested, including reconfirming the fax number before transmitting the data, using cover sheets that specify that the information contained therein is confidential, and verifying that the faxed information has been received (Koska, 1992).

Certificates of Confidentiality

A "certificate of confidentiality" may be available from the federal government (Avins & Lo, 1989; Bayer *et al.*, 1984). Unfortunately, the issuance of a certificate of confidentiality is not automatic (Melton, 1988) and protects only the names of and identifying information about the research participants (Melton & Gray, 1988). What specific information may be deemed to constitute "identifying information" may be subject to debate. The governing legislation provides for the protection of the

> privacy of individuals who are the subject of [biomedical, behavioral, clinical, or other research] by withholding from all persons not connected with the conduct of such research the names or other identifying characteristics of such individuals. Persons so authorized to protect the privacy of such individuals may not be compelled in any Federal, State, or local civil, criminal, administrative, legislative, or other proceedings to identify such individuals. [42 United States Code Annotated section 241(d), 1990]

Although the certificate of confidentiality will probably safeguard study information from a subpoena, it is unclear whether it will insulate the data from states' compulsory reporting laws, such as the reporting of HIV infection or AIDS diagnoses.

Other Federal Statutory Protections

Table 5.2 outlines various federal statutory provisions that provide some protection to research participants. It is important to note that the protections afforded by these provisions may be neither automatic nor complete. Some statutes require that specific procedures be followed to apply for the protections. Some statutes may protect individuals' identity, but not identifying information.

Privacy Act

The Privacy Act protects from disclosure records maintained by federal agencies which relate to individuals, absent the individual's written consent to access. The statute permits disclosure in 11 enumerated circumstances:

1. To officers and employees of the agency maintaining the record, if they have the need for the record in the performance of their duties
2. Where disclosure is required by the Freedom of Information Act
3. For a routine use, as defined by statute
4. To the Bureau of Census for specifically enumerated purposes
5. To individuals who have confirmed in writing that they would use the information as statistical research, and identifying information is excised from the record prior to its transfer
6. To the National Archives of the United States, in various specified circumstances
7. To another agency in the United States in connection with civil or criminal law enforcement activity
8. "To a person pursuant to a showing of compelling circumstances affecting the health or safety of an individual if upon such disclosure notification is transmitted to the last known address of such individual"
9. To a congressional committee or subcommittee or either house of Congress
10. To the Comptroller General or his representatives, in the course of performing the duties of the General Accounting Office
11. Pursuant to a court order [Privacy Act, 5 United States Code, section 552a(b), 1977 & Supp. 1993].

Table 5.2. Summary of Federal Statutory Protections of Confidentiality

Statute	Scope of coverage	Automatic	Protects identity	Protects identifiable information	Administrative immunity	Judicial immunity	Legislative immunity
Privacy Act 5 U.S.C.A. sec. 552a	Personal information maintained by federal agencies as part of agency record	X	X	X			
Public Health Services Act 42 U.S.C.A. sec. 241	Mental health research		X	X	X	X	X
Drug Abuse Office and Treatment Act of 1972 42 U.S.C.A. sec. 290dd-2	Drug abuse prevention functions, including research, education, training, & treatment; applies to records only	X	X	X			
Alcohol Abuse Act 42 U.S.C.A. sec. 290dd-2	Alcohol abuse prevention functions	X	X	X			
Crime Control Act of 1973 42 U.S.C.A. sec. 3789g	Research of statistical information	X	X	X	X	X	X
Controlled Substances Act 21 U.S.C.A. sec. 872(c)	Subjects of drug abuse research		X	X	X	X	X

Criminal penalties may be imposed on any agency officer or employee who willfully discloses protected information.

Public Health Services Act

The Public Health Services Act provides that

> The Secretary [of Health and Human Services] may authorize persons engaged in biomedical, behavioral, clinical, or other research (including research on mental health, including research on the use and effect of alcohol and other psychoactive drugs) to protect the privacy of individuals who are the subject of such research by withholding from all persons not connected with the conduct of such research the names or other identifying characteristics of such individuals. Persons so authorized to protect the privacy of such individuals may not be compelled in any Federal, State, or local civil, criminal, administrative, legislative, or other proceedings to identify such individuals. [42 United States Code Annotated section 241(d), 1994]

The scope of the protection afforded is relatively broad in that it applies to both names and identifying characteristics. Additionally, the confidentiality of research participants cannot be overridden by the use of a subpoena. However, these protections are not automatic and must be requested by the researcher.

Drug Abuse Office and Treatment Act of 1972

Unlike the Public Health Services Act, the protections afforded to research participants pursuant to this legislative provision are automatic. However, the protection is limited to research involving substance abuse and does not extend to administrative or judicial proceedings. The statute provides:

> Records of the identity, diagnosis, prognosis, or treatment of any patient which are maintained in connection with the performance of any program or activity relating to substance abuse education, prevention, training, treatment, rehabilitation, or research, which is conducted, regulated, or directly or indirectly assisted by any department or agency of the United States shall . . . be confidential and be disclosed only for [specified] purposes and under [specified] circumstances. . . . [42 United States Code Annotated section 290dd-2, 1994]

Confidential information may be disclosed

> [i]f authorized by an appropriate order of a court of competent jurisdiction granted after application showing good cause therefore, including the need to avert a substantial risk of death or serious bodily harm. In assessing good cause the court shall weigh the public interest and the need for disclosure

> against the injury to the patient, to the physician–patient relationship, and to the treatment services. Upon the granting of such an order, the court, in determining the extent to which any disclosure of all or any part of any record is necessary, shall impose appropriate safeguards against unauthorized disclosure. [42 United States Code Annotated section 290dd-2(b)(2)(C), 1994]

The statute further provides that such records may be used to initiate or to substantiate criminal charges against a patient or to conduct an investigation of a patient if authorized by a court [42 United States Code Annotated section 290dd-2(c), 1994].

Crime Control Act of 1973

This Act protects research or statistical information from disclosure if it is "identifiable to any specific private person for any purpose other than the purpose for which it was obtained . . ." [42 United States Code Annotated section 3789g(a), 1994]. The information is protected from disclosure in the context of judicial, legislative, or administrative proceedings, absent the consent of the individual who originally furnished the information being sought.

Controlled Substances Act

This statute protects participants in drug abuse research from the disclosure of their "names and other identifying characteristics" in the context of federal, state, or local civil, criminal, administrative, legislative, and other proceedings. Like the Public Health Services Act, this protection is not automatic. Rather, it must be authorized by the Attorney General [21 United States Code Annotated section 872(c), 1981].

Minimizing FOIA Intrusions

The success of FOIA requests seeking access to study data can be minimized through a variety of strategies. A few of these strategies are practical measures; others are legal arguments.

Practical Measures

As indicated above, the Court in *Tax Analysts v. Department of Justice* enunciated a two-part test to determine whether records were "agency records" for FOIA purposes: whether the agency had created or obtained the records, and whether the agency had control of those records at the time that the FOIA request was made. Logically, it is less likely that data will be available pursuant to an FOIA request if either of these prongs are absent.

The federal agency cannot "obtain" the records if the latter are not provided to it. Consequently, it may be advisable for the researchers to provide the federal agency with summaries of the data, rather than the raw data itself. Additionally, the agency has not "obtained" the data if all of the latter to be examined during an agency audit are maintained at the research site so that the audit occurs on site, rather than at the agency. If the agency has neither obtained nor created the records, it cannot possibly have them under its control at the time that an FOIA request is made.

It is particularly important to remember in this context that there exists no obligation on the part of the federal agency to refuse access to information, such as by claiming one or more of the exemptions. Consequently, the less identifying information the agency has, the less likely it is that damage can be done in the event that the agency decides to disclose information pursuant to a specific request.

Legal Strategies

Unless a researcher is actually with the federal agency that receives an FOIA request, it is unlikely that the researcher will become involved directly in contesting disclosure. However, information about legal strategies may be helpful to researchers in implementing practical measures to limit intrusions.

The federal agency not wishing to disclose information will likely argue that the information requested falls under one of the exemptions enunciated by statute. In the context of HIV research, it is most likely that the exemption claimed would be one relating to personnel or medical or similar files, where the release of the information would constitute an unwarranted invasion of privacy. The burden will be on the federal agency to justify this rationale. The agency will be required to demonstrate that the requested records are properly classifiable as medical, personnel, or similar records; that the release of the information would actually result in "a clearly unwarranted invasion of personal privacy"; and that the interest in personal privacy outweighs the public's interest in the disclosure of the requested information (*Hoch v. C.I.A.*, 1984).

It is likely that even if the federal agency prevails generally, the court will find that the requested information should be released to the greatest extent possible, while still protecting individuals from the invasion of personal privacy. The statute specifically provides that "[a]ny reasonably segregable portion of a record shall be provided to any person requesting such record after deletion of the portions which are exempt . . ." [Freedom of Information Act, 5 United States Code Annotated section 552(b), 1977 & 1993]. The less identifying information the researcher has provided to the agency, the less likely it will be that something will be overlooked in the deletion of identifying information prior to furnishing the requested data to the requester.

Even absent identifying data, it may be possible for the recipient of the information to identify the individuals involved. For instance, in *Application of American Tobacco Company* (1989), the court limited the scope of the subpoena by permitting the deletion of names and some identifying information. The court did not permit, however, the deletion of other information, such as union local and county of residence, which could ultimately be used to identify individuals. A similar situation could arise in the context of an FOIA request. The release of such information could dissuade research participants from entering into or continuing to participate in the study, because their confidentiality cannot be guaranteed.

Minimizing the Impact of Audit Procedures

It may be possible to negotiate with an agency the specific parameters of an audit. The negotiated agreement should specify to what extent the auditors may have access to identifying information and whether and how reinterviews of study participants will be conducted (Boruch & Cecil, 1979). For instance, an agency that wishes to verify that interviews have actually been conducted may be willing to speak with only a subsample of the study participants, thereby limiting the number of individuals to be contacted. A review of the informed consent procedures may be satisfied by providing the agency with copies of the signed forms, after deleting the last name of the study participant from the form.

Motions to Quash Subpoenas

A motion to quash a subpoena can be used in both state and federal courts to contest a subpoena that is requesting the disclosure of research records. Because the procedures vary from state to state, this discussion will address procedures for a motion in the federal and California courts only.

Federal Court

A motion to quash a subpoena must be made promptly after the subpoena is issued. The motion must be made by the person from whom the things or records are being requested. Generally, a person who is not the person or entity from whom the records are being sought will have no right to bring a motion to quash a subpoena or a motion for a protective order (*Vogue Instrument Corporation v. Lem Instruments Corporation,* 1967). The only exception is where a person claims some right or personal privilege with respect to the documents or records that are being sought (*Norris Mfg. Company v. R. E. Darling Company,* 1961).

The court may decide to quash or modify the subpoena if it finds that it is unreasonable or oppressive [Federal Rule of Civil Procedure 45(b), 1983]. An HIV researcher could make several arguments with respect to the unreasonableness or oppressiveness of a subpoena. The disclosure of the information sought could, in the future, result in a disruption of the research and a lack of confidence in both the researchers and the study. This argument should be supported by affidavits from other researchers, physicians, or agencies who refer clients for participation in the study. If they would no longer refer clients for participation because of a breach of confidentiality, that should be stated clearly in their affidavits.

A second argument that could be made is that the search for the records requested would entail an excessive use of time and excessive dedication of resources. This could be true, for instance, where the data base for a particular study is very large and extensive resources would be required to compile the information being sought by the subpoena. This argument may not be particularly successful, because the court has the power to deny the motion to quash the subpoena conditionally on the advancement by the person or entity seeking the records of the reasonable costs of producing the documents or materials requested [Federal Rule of Civil Procedure 45(b), 1983].

A third argument that can be made is that the information being sought is not relevant to the litigation. It is difficult to make this argument successfully, because the process of discovery extends to information that is not privileged (specifically protected under certain recognized exceptions) and that is relevant to the subject matter of the pending lawsuit [Federal Rule of Civil Procedure 26(b), 1983]. As an example, consider again the case of the individual involved in an automobile accident. The insurance company wants to access his records that are part of a longitudinal study of HIV infection, claiming that these records contain medical information that is relevant to the claim for damages. The researcher can argue that the information contained in the research record is irrelevant to injuries sustained as the result of a car accident. This argument will more likely be successful where the research relates to behavioral research, which does not involve measurements related to the individual's functioning. The researcher can also argue that because he or she is not a party to the litigation, the test for relevance of the documents should not be applied as broadly as it might be if the researcher were actually a party to the lawsuit (*Collins and Aikman Corp. v. J. P. Stevens & Co.*, 1971).

Melton and Gray (1988) have argued that a common-law privilege protecting researcher–participant communications should be recognized. In order to demonstrate that such a privilege should be recognized, the communication must have taken place in the context of a confidential relationship; the maintenance of confidentiality is necessary in order to preserve that relationship satisfactorily; the relationship is important to the community; and the injury that would result from a breach in confidentiality is greater than the benefit that would be gained. The HIV researcher should be able to demonstrate that the research participants were assured of the confidentiality of the records. Other researchers or referral sources may be willing and able to provide affidavits attesting to the need for continuing confidentiality and their unwillingness to refer potential participants should a breach in confidentiality occur. The researcher can demonstrate the importance of the relationship to the community by providing data on related aspects of HIV in that community, the need to address HIV in that community, and the inability to do so if individuals are unwilling to participate in the research because of fear of unauthorized disclosures.

Form 5.6 provides an example of a motion to quash a subpoena in federal district court. An attorney should be consulted if a researcher is served with a subpoena; this form is provided for reference only. A memorandum of points and authorities, which explains the legal and factual basis for the motion to quash that is being made, is filed together with the motion.

California

The motion to quash must be supported by a memorandum of points and authorities and a supporting declaration that explains why the motion to quash the subpoena should be granted. The court may

In the United States District Court for the Southern District of California

John Plaintiff,	)	
Plaintiff	)	Civil Action No. ALJ123456
v.	)	
	)	Judge ______________
ABC Insurance Company,	)	
Defendant	)	
	)	
______________________________	)	

Motion to Quash Subpoena

Roberta Researcher moves this Court to Quash the subpoena issued against her at the request of Defendant ABC Insurance Company, a copy of which is attached. This motion is premised on the following grounds:

1. Insufficient time to respond;
2. Undue expense and burden;
3. Irrelevance of the requested materials to the litigation;
4. Availability of the records from other sources;
5. Disruption of the research that would result from a breach of confidentiality; and
6. Existence of a researcher-participant privilege.

Respectfully submitted,

____

Lenny Lawyer
Attorney for Roberta Researcher

Form 5.6. Motion to quash a subpoena (federal district court).

order that the subpoena be quashed or modified, or may direct that the researcher comply with its request. It may also order that other measures be implemented to protect the researcher from oppressive or unreasonable demands (California Code of Civil Procedure section 1987.1, 1983).

5.4. CONFIDENTIALITY PROTECTIONS OUTSIDE THE UNITED STATES

Australia

There is a general duty to maintain the confidentiality of information that was provided with the expectation of confidentiality. However, disclosures of data contained in an individual's *health record* may be ordered in the context of criminal trials or by subpoena. Australia does not have a mechanism like the certificate of confidentiality to protect the research data. An individual's health records may be accessed for research purposes without consent, despite Australia's Privacy Act, "if the research will prevent or lessen a serious and imminent threat to life or health" (Berglund, 1990). It is conceivable, for instance, that researchers will argue for the disclosure of causes of death or HIV status in order to estimate more accurately the HIV seroprevalence of a community, in order to design better prevention programs. It is unclear, though, whether such motives should override an individual's expectation of privacy and the potential for adverse consequences to the individual should the disclosure go inadvertently beyond the researchers.

Bravender-Coyle (1986) has argued that there exists a common-law duty to maintain the confidentiality of information obtained in the context of a researcher–participant relationship because it is akin to the relationship between a physician and a patient; a confidential relationship similar to that of an employer and employee; or a confidential relationship based on the duty of good faith. He further argues that the Epidemiological Studies (Confidentiality) Act imposes a statutory duty to maintain the confidentiality of data collected in the context of studies of mental, physical, or behavioral disorder that are conducted by or on behalf of the Commonwealth. What is meant by a study "on behalf of the Commonwealth" remains unclear. However, there appears to be a sufficient basis to argue that HIV research records are entitled to legal protection from discovery through legal means.

5.5. DUTY TO INFORM PARTICIPANTS

It is crucial that prospective participants in a study be informed of the measures to be taken to protect their privacy and of possible intrusions. The degree to which confidentiality can and is protected may have significant bearing on the individual's decision to participate in or to continue with a study. An HIV-infected individual, for instance, may decline to participate if he or she believes that his or her identity or sexual practices or drug-using activities may become known to individuals outside of the research staff. The American Psychological Association has enunciated this principle clearly:

> Information obtained about the research participant during the course of an investigation is confidential unless otherwise agreed in advance. When the possibility exists that others may obtain access to such information, this possibility, together with the plans for protecting confidentiality, is explained to the participant as part of the procedure for obtaining informed consent. [American Psychological Association, 1982]

5.6. CONCLUSION

A breach of confidentiality may have disastrous consequences for a participant in an HIV study, regardless of that participant's actual HIV serostatus. Breaches of confidentiality may result from action taken by members of the research team, or may be completely involuntary, as in the case of a court order to release information or agency audits. Researchers must aggressively protect the confidentiality of those participating in their studies. Various mechanisms exist, including the development and implementation of internal controls and the utilization of existing legal mechanisms. Such vigilance ultimately protects not only the research participants, but the researchers and the research institutions as well.

CHAPTER SIX

Potential Conflicts

Numerous conflicts may arise during the course of the study. For example, one or more participants may lose capacity as a result of the onset and progression of AIDS-related dementia during the course of the study. It becomes questionable whether that person can, or should, continue as a participant in the study. As a second example, new clinical trials are implemented to test the efficacy of a new drug for HIV, and participants in one clinical trial may want to participate in the new trials in order to have access to this potentially beneficial product. However, participation in both trials will make it almost impossible to evaluate the true value of either drug being tested. What is the individual's obligation as a participant of a clinical trial? This chapter examines these and other issues.

6.1. RECONCILING TREATMENT GOALS AND RESEARCH GOALS: THE NONADHERENT PARTICIPANT

This issue is most likely to arise during the course of a clinical trial. Suppose that Study A is a clinical trial that involves a comparison between two different prophylactic regimens for a particular opportunistic infection. Neither regimen is initially perceived to have an advantage over the other. The participants have been randomized to the experimental arm, which is receiving the new drug, and the comparison arm, which is receiving the standard therapy to prevent the infection. During the course of the trial, a new drug for the prevention of the same opportunistic infection is to be tested in other clinical trials. One or more research participants in Study A wish to participate in that clinical trial as well. However, participation in both trials will make it impossible to evaluate the effect of the drug being tested in Study A, because its beneficial effects, and its adverse effects, may be masked or enhanced when taken together with the new drug in Study B.

The resolution of this dilemma may depend on one's perceptions of the purpose of the trial (C. Levine, 1988). If the study participant sees the trial as an opportunity to receive the latest and the best in medical care, then it will seem unreasonable to expect that the participant forgo the opportunity to participate in Study B. If the purpose of the trial is seen as research, with possibly no benefit to the research participant but potential benefit to patients outside of the trial after its conclusion, then the requirement that participants forgo unproven remedies for the duration of the trial does not seem as harsh.

C. Levine (1988) has suggested that the enrollment of research participants as "partners with the investigators" will enhance the likelihood that the participants will follow the research protocol and forgo the use of unproven medications during the course of the trial. This issue can also be addressed in the context of the informed consent procedure. The informed consent process can include not only the form that the participant is required to read and understand prior to signing, but additional notifications that are explained both orally and in writing. The participant should be advised of the difference between the therapeutic setting and the research setting; the importance of following the research protocol, both for the health of the participant and the clarity and generalizability of the scientific findings; and the consequences to both the participant and the research as a result of failing to comply.

6.2. PARTICIPANT LOSS OF CAPACITY

Individuals recruited to participate in HIV-related studies may be competent to give consent at the time of their initial recruitment, but may lose capacity subsequent to their enrollment. This can raise both design issues and ethical issues. If the individual is no longer able to give a coherent social history, should the study rely on a surrogate as the source of that information? If the participant is no longer able to understand or remember what he or she was told at the time of his or her initial recruitment, does the original consent to participate remain valid?

Design Issues

The design issues should be addressed prior to the implementation of the study, in the context of the study protocol. Various studies have estimated that between 16 and 28% of all HIV-infected patients may develop AIDS dementia during the progression of their illness (Day *et al.*, 1992; de Gans & Portegies, 1989; Levy & Bredesen, 1988; McArthur, 1987). If the study that is to be conducted is relatively short term and involves individuals who recently seroconverted, it is unlikely that the issue will arise during the course of the study. Longer-term studies involving individuals whose illness has progressed to AIDS will be more likely to face this issue. The resolution of the design issues will depend on the nature of the study.

For instance, suppose the study was designed to assess the factors relating to the development and progression of AIDS dementia. In that case, the design of the study is not as much of an issue as are the ethical questions, because the available endpoints and measurements are consistent with the goals of the study. Suppose, however, that the study was designed to evaluate the association between the manner in which individuals contracted HIV infection (IDU versus sex partner of IDU versus homosexual) and the availability and changing nature of individuals' support network as the infection progresses. The inability of the individual to remember past or present events or to comprehend what is being asked and told to him or her will affect the quality of the information. A surrogate informant, such as a spouse or a parent, may or may not be privy to the kind of detail that is required. Reliance on surrogate informants may also introduce additional biases. For instance, the informant may want the participant to appear in the best light possible, so the informant may portray a more extensive network than actually exists, in order to emphasize the popularity and lovability of the participant. Alternatively, the informant may stress the importance of his or her role to the participant, and underreport the existence of other support available. The initial protocol should specify (1) whether to rely on the reports of surrogates, who may qualify as a surrogate informant, and the procedures to be used to ascertain and measure resulting bias, if possible, or (2) whether participants who lose capacity should be terminated from the study. In the event that the protocol provides for their termination, it is important to consider the effect of that termination on the sample size and power of the study.

Ethical Issues

Schwartz (1985), in writing about individuals suffering from Alzheimer's disease, questioned the validity of an individual's consent where that individual later becomes incompetent:

> A patient who is occasionally competent can legally give valid consent only if that consent is provided during a competent period. Whether that consent is so durable as to be valid even when the subject is no longer competent presents another, yet unresolved question.

Schwartz believed that considerations of autonomy suggest that a consent, once valid, should survive the individual's subsequent incapacity.

The writings of other ethicists underscore the complexity of this issue. Dresser and Robertson (1989) have explored the effect of an individual's incapacity subsequent to the execution of advance directives in the context of quality of life and nontreatment decisions. They have critiqued the orthodox approach of relying on a patient's prior directive or choice inferred by a surrogate's substituted judgment on several grounds. They argue first that incompetent persons are by definition incapable of making a decision. Therefore, it doesn't follow that they should be treated as if they were exercising autonomy. Second, they argue that the individual's previously expressed or inferred prior choices may not be an accurate indicator of the incompetent person's current interests. They further note that competent individuals who execute directives may be unaware that they are ultimately authorizing acts or omissions that conflict with their subsequent well-being.

The concerns of Dresser and Robertson are equally relevant in the context of HIV research. An individual may have consented to participate in research at a time when he or she could verbalize more easily and had greater mobility and energy. As the disease progresses and the individual gradually loses both mental competence and physical abilities, the effort required to continue participation in the study may be more than the individual is able to give—but the individual is unable either to assess his or her situation or to communicate it to the researcher.

Other ethical issues arise where participants begin to lose their mental capacity. Not all participants in studies have primary care physicians or regular sources of care. Some, in fact, may have no source of care. This is more likely to be true of individuals participating in social science studies than of individuals participating in clinical trials. Participants who begin to lose their mental capacity may become depressed and may often require supportive therapy (Raskin, 1988). The researchers must consider whether they have the staffing and expertise either to provide referrals to services that can be helpful or to provide the necessary supportive services themselves. Issues of confidentiality may arise where the participant becomes unable to care for him- or herself because of the extent of the mental incapacity. In such a situation, the researcher must decide whether confidentiality can ethically be breached for the protection of the participant.

6.3. ADVANCE DIRECTIVES AND THE RESEARCH STUDY

Many states permit an individual to execute an advance directive, in either the form of a living will or a durable power of attorney for health care. These documents allow a patient to specify his or her health care preferences with respect to the administration of life-sustaining treatment while he or she is still mentally and physically able to enunciate them. Many states permit the individual in the text of such a document to specify whether he or she will permit an autopsy or the donation of any part or parts of his or her body for donation or research. If the individual has not so specified his or her preferences with respect to these items, the agent appointed by the document often has the authority to make decisions with respect to these issues, consistent with the agent's understanding of the patient's preferences.

Advance directives may affect the extent of an individual's participation in an HIV study in a number of ways. For example, a study of the neuropsychological effect of HIV may contain as a part of its protocol the autopsy of participants' brains, and may seek their consent as part of the informed consent procedure to perform an autopsy and study the brain after death. However, a study participant may execute a durable power of attorney for health care following enrollment into the study, and give to his agent, in the power of attorney, the right to decide whether or not an autopsy can be performed. After the participant's death, the agent may refuse to permit the autopsy, based on his understanding of the participant's wishes as they were expressed to him subsequent to the participant's enrollment into the study. In another situation, an individual may have executed a durable power of attorney for health care and included a specific provision permitting his agent to consent to or to refuse to consent to his participation in HIV research, or to terminate his participation in the research if the agent believes that it is in the participant's best interest to do so. A researcher may then be faced with a situation where the agent of the study participant terminates the patient's participation in the research study.

The key to addressing situations that involve, or may involve, advance directives is to be proactive. For instance, the intake form for a study can ask the participant if he or she has an advance directive and, if there is one, who, if anyone, has been appointed as the participant's agent and whether the document contains any provisions relating to the individual's participation in research. If the study protocol also requires an autopsy or the examination of specific body parts after death, the intake form should request information with respect to the existence of such provisions in the directive. With the study participant's consent, the researchers can include the participant's agent in discussion about the role of the individual in the research study, the importance of that participation, and the consequences to the study and the individual if his or her participation were to cease or if the participant's involvement or commitment were to decrease. Such discussions give both the participant and his or her agent an opportunity to have their questions addressed at a time when neither of them is feeling pressured or traumatized by the participant's incapacity or impending death. Additionally, this approach may reduce the potential for discord between the research staff and the research participants and their families, friends, and agents.

Form 6.1 provides an example of a durable power of attorney for health care, valid under current California law, which includes provisions relating to both participation in research and the performance of an autopsy in conjunction with participation in a research protocol. The document gives the participant's agent express authority to consent to the performance of an autopsy as part of a study, and to authorize the patient's entry into, continuance in, or withdrawal from, a research protocol. In assessing such a document, however, it is important to keep in mind the cautionary statements of Dresser and Robertson: the individual may, by executing the document, have authorized activities that have become, at a much later date, contrary to his or her well-being. The existence of the document should not foreclose further ethical inquiry.

6.4, RESEARCHER CONFLICTS OF INTEREST

Recently drafted ethical guidelines for epidemiologists defined "conflict of interest" as occurring

> whenever a personal interest or a role obligation of an investigator conflicts with an obligation to uphold another party's interest, thereby compromising normal expectations of reasonable objectivity and impartiality in regard to the other party. Such circumstances are almost always to be scrupulously avoided in conducting epidemiologic investigations.
>
> Every epidemiologist has the potential for such a conflict. An epidemiologist on the payroll of a corporation, a university, or a government does not encounter a conflict merely by the condition of employment, but a conflict exists whenever the epidemiologist's role obligation or personal interest in accommodating the institution, in job security, or in personal goals compromises obligations to others who have a right to expect objectivity and fairness. [Beauchamp *et al.*, 1991]

STATUTORY FORM DURABLE POWER OF ATTORNEY FOR HEALTH CARE
(California Civil Code section 2500)

WARNING TO PERSON EXECUTING THIS DOCUMENT
THIS IS AN IMPORTANT LEGAL DOCUMENT WHICH IS AUTHORIZED BY THE KEENE HEALTH CARE AGENT ACT. BEFORE EXECUTING THIS DOCUMENT, YOU SHOULD KNOW THESE IMPORTANT FACTS:

THIS DOCUMENT GIVES THE PERSON YOU DESIGNATE AS YOUR AGENT (THE ATTORNEY IN FACT) THE POWER TO MAKE HEALTH CARE DECISIONS FOR YOU. YOUR AGENT MUST ACT CONSISTENTLY WITH YOUR DESIRES AS STATED IN THIS DOCUMENT OR OTHERWISE MADE KNOWN.

EXCEPT AS YOU OTHERWISE SPECIFY IN THIS DOCUMENT, THIS DOCUMENT GIVES YOUR AGENT THE POWER TO CONSENT TO YOUR DOCTOR NOT GIVING TREATMENT OR STOPPING TREATMENT NECESSARY TO KEEP YOU ALIVE.

NOT WITHSTANDING THIS DOCUMENT, YOU HAVE THE RIGHT TO MAKE MEDICAL AND OTHER HEALTH CARE DECISIONS FOR YOURSELF SO LONG AS YOU CAN GIVE INFORMED CONSENT WITH RESPECT TO THE PARTICULAR DECISION. IN ADDITION, NO TREATMENT MAY BE GIVEN TO YOU OVER YOUR OBJECTION AT THE TIME, AND HEALTH CARE NECESSARY TO KEEP YOU ALIVE MAY NOT BE STOPPED OR WITHHELD IF YOU OBJECT AT THE TIME.

THIS DOCUMENT GIVES YOUR AGENT AUTHORITY TO CONSENT, TO REFUSE TO CONSENT, OR TO WITHDRAW CONSENT TO ANY CARE, TREATMENT, SERVICE, OR PROCEDURE TO MAINTAIN, DIAGNOSE, OR TREAT A PHYSICAL OR MENTAL CONDITION. THIS POWER IS SUBJECT TO ANY STATEMENT OF YOUR DESIRES AND ANY LIMITATIONS THAT YOU INCLUDE IN THIS DOCUMENT. YOU MAY STATE IN THIS DOCUMENT ANY TYPES OF TREATMENT THAT YOU DO NOT DESIRE. IN ADDITION, A COURT CAN TAKE AWAY THE POWER OF YOUR AGENT TO MAKE HEALTH CARE DECISIONS FOR YOU IF YOUR AGENT: (1) AUTHORIZES ANYTHING THAT IS ILLEGAL, (2) ACTS CONTRARY TO YOUR KNOWN DESIRES, OR (3) WHERE YOUR DESIRES ARE NOT KNOWN, DOES ANYTHING THAT IS CLEARLY CONTRARY TO YOUR BEST INTERESTS.

THE POWERS GIVEN BY THIS DOCUMENT WILL EXIST FOR AN INDEFINITE PERIOD OF TIME UNLESS YOU LIMIT THEIR DURATION IN THIS DOCUMENT

YOU HAVE THE RIGHT TO REVOKE THE AUTHORITY OF YOUR AGENT BY NOTIFYING YOUR AGENT OR YOUR TREATING DOCTOR,

Form 6.1. Durable power of attorney for health care (California).

HOSPITAL, OR OTHER HEALTH CARE PROVIDER ORALLY OR IN WRITING OF THE REVOCATION.

YOUR AGENT HAS THE RIGHT TO EXAMINE YOUR MEDICAL RECORDS AND TO CONSENT TO THEIR DISCLOSURE UNLESS YOU LIMIT THIS RIGHT IN THIS DOCUMENT.

UNLESS YOU OTHERWISE SPECIFY IN THIS DOCUMENT, THIS DOCUMENT GIVES YOUR AGENT THE POWER AFTER YOU DIE TO: (1) AUTHORIZE AN AUTOPSY, (2) DONATE YOUR BODY OR PARTS THEREOF FOR TRANSPLANT OR THERAPEUTIC OR EDUCATIONAL OR SCIENTIFIC PURPOSES, AND (3) DIRECT THE DISPOSITION OF YOUR REMAINS.

THIS DOCUMENT REVOKES ANY PRIOR DURABLE POWER OF ATTORNEY FOR HEALTH CARE.

YOU SHOULD CAREFULLY READ AND FOLLOW THE WITNESSING PROCEDURE DESCRIBED AT THE END OF THIS FORM. THIS DOCUMENT WILL NOT BE VALID UNLESS YOU COMPLY WITH THE WITNESSING PROCEDURE.

IF THERE IS ANYTHING IN THIS DOCUMENT THAT YOU DO NOT UNDERSTAND, YOU SHOULD ASK A LAWYER TO EXPLAIN IT TO YOU.

YOUR AGENT MAY NEED THIS DOCUMENT IMMEDIATELY IN CASE OF AN EMERGENCY THAT REQUIRES A DECISION CONCERNING YOUR HEALTH CARE. EITHER KEEP THIS DOCUMENT WHERE IT IS IMMEDIATELY AVAILABLE TO YOUR AGENT AND ALTERNATE AGENTS OR GIVE EACH OF THEM AN EXECUTED COPY OF THIS DOCUMENT. YOU MAY ALSO WANT TO GIVE YOUR DOCTOR AN EXECUTED COPY OF THIS DOCUMENT.

DO NOT USE THIS FORM IF YOU ARE A CONSERVATEE UNDER THE LANTERMAN–PETRIS–SHORT ACT AND YOU WANT TO APPOINT YOUR CONSERVATOR AS YOUR AGENT. YOU CAN DO THAT ONLY IF THE APPOINTMENT DOCUMENT INCLUDES A CERTIFICATE OF YOUR ATTORNEY.

1. **DESIGNATION OF HEALTH CARE AGENT.** I, *(name and address),* do hereby designate and appoint *(name, address and telephone number of person designated as agent to make health care decisions)*, as my attorney in fact (agent) to make health care decisions for me as authorized in this document. For the purposes of this document, "health care decision" means consent, refusal of consent, or withdrawal of consent to any care, treatment, service, or proce- dure to maintain, diagnose, or treat an individual's physical or mental condition.

2. **CREATION OF DURABLE POWER OF ATTORNEY FOR HEALTH CARE.** By this document I intend to create a durable power of attorney for health care under Sections 2430 to 2443, inclusive, of the California Civil Code. This power of attorney is authorized by the Keene

Form 6.1. *Continued.*

Health Care Agent Act and shall be construed in accordance with the provisions of Sections 2500 to 2506, inclusive, of the California Civil Code. This power of attorney shall not be affected by my subsequent incapacity.

3. **GENERAL STATEMENT OF AUTHORITY GRANTED.** Subject to any limitations in this document, I hereby grant to my agent full power and authority to make health care decisions for me to the same extent that I could make such decisions for myself if I had the capacity to do so. In exercising this authority, my agent shall make health care decisions that are consistent with my desires as stated in this document or otherwise made known to my agent, including, but not limited to, my desires concerning obtaining or refusing or withdrawing life-prolonging care, treatment, services, and procedures.

4. **STATEMENT OF DESIRES, SPECIAL PROVISIONS, AND LIMITATIONS.** In exercising the authority under this durable power of attorney for health care, my agent shall act consistently with my desires as stated below and is subject to the special provisions and limitations stated below:

(a) Statement of desires concerning life-prolonging care, treatment, services, and procedures:______________________________

____

____

(b) Additional statement of desires, special provisions, and limitations: *I specifically give my agent the authority to decide whether I should participate in an HIV-related research study, or whether my participation in any research study should be temporarily or permanently terminated. I further authorize my agent to consent to my autopsy in connection with my participation in a research study relating to HIV.*

5. **INSPECTION AND DISCLOSURE OF INFORMATION RELATING TO MY PHYSICAL OR MENTAL HEALTH.** Subject to any limitations in this document, my agent has the power and authority to do all of the following:

(a) Request, review, and receive any information, verbal or written, regarding my physical or mental health, including, but not limited to, medical and hospital records.

(b) Execute on my behalf any releases or other documents that may be required in order to obtain that information.

(c) Consent to the disclosure of this information.

6. **SIGNING DOCUMENTS, WAIVERS, AND RELEASES.** Where necessary to implement the health care decisions that my agent isauthorized by this document to make, my agent has the power and authority to execute on my behalf all of the following:

(a) Documents titled or purporting to be a "Refusal to Permit Treatment" and "Leaving Hospital Against Medical Advice."

Form 6.1. *Continued.*

(b) Any necessary waiver or release from liability required by a hospital or physician.

7. **AUTOPSY, ANATOMICAL GIFTS, DISPOSITION OF REMAINS.** Subject to any limitations in this document, my agent has the power and authority to do all of the following:

(a) Authorize an autopsy under Section 7113 of the Health and Safety Code.

(b) Make a disposition of a part or parts of my body under the Uniform Anatomical Gift Act [Chapter 3.5 (commencing with Section 7150) of Part 1 of Division 7 of the Health and Safety Code].

(c) Direct the disposition of my remains under Section 7100 of the Health and Safety Code.

8. **DURATION.** This power of attorney expires on (*fill in only if you want to limit the duration of this power of attorney*).

9. **DESIGNATION OF ALTERNATE AGENTS.** If the person designated as my agent in paragraph 1 is not available or becomes ineligible to act as my agent to make a health care decision for me or loses the mental capacity to make health care decisions for me, or if I revoke that person's appointment or authority to act as my agent to make health care decisions for me, then I designate and appoint the following persons to serve in the order listed below:

(a) First Alternate Agent: (*insert name, address, and telephone number*)

(b) Second Alternate Agent: (*insert name, address, and telephone number*)

10. **NOMINATION OF CONSERVATOR OF PERSON.** If a conservator of the person is to be appointed for me, I nominate the following individual to serve as conservator of the person: (*insert name and address*)

11. **PRIOR DESIGNATIONS REVOKED.** I revoke any prior durable power of attorney for health care.

DATE AND SIGNATURE OF PRINCIPAL (YOU MUST SIGN AND DATE THIS POWER OF ATTORNEY)

I sign my name to this Statutory Form Durable Power of Attorney for Health Care on ________________ at ________ (*city, state*) ________ .

(THIS POWER OF ATTORNEY WILL NOT BE VALID UNLESS IT IS SIGNED BY TWO QUALIFIED WITNESSES WHO ARE PRESENT WHEN YOU SIGN OR ACKNOWLEDGE YOUR SIGNATURE. IF YOU HAVE ATTACHED ANY ADDITIONAL PAGES TO THIS FORM, YOU MUST DATE AND SIGN EACH OF THE ADDITIONAL PAGES AT THE SAME TIME YOU DATE AND SIGN THIS POWER OF ATTORNEY.)

STATEMENT OF WITNESSES

(This document must be witnessed by two qualified adult witnesses. None of the following may be used as a witness: (1) a person you designate as your agent or alternate agent, (2) a health care provider, (3) an employee of a health care provider, (4) the operator of a community care facility,

Form 6.1. *Continued.*

(5) an employee of an operator of a community health care facility, (6) the operator of a residential care facility for the elderly, or (7) an employee of an operator of a residential care facility for the elderly. At least one of the witnesses must make the additional declaration set out following the place where the witnesses sign.) (**READ CAREFULLY BEFORE SIGNING.** You can sign as a witness only if you personally know the principal or the identity of the principal is proved to you by convincing evidence.)

(To have convincing evidence of the identity of the principal, you must be presented with and reasonably rely on any one or more of the following:

(1) An identification card or driver's license issued by the California Department of Motor Vehicles that is current or has been issued within 5 years.

(2) A passport issued by the Department of State of the United States that is current or has been issued within five years.

(3) Any of the following documents if the document is current or has been issued within five years and contains a photograph and description of the person named on it, is signed by the person, and bears a serial or other identifying number;

- **(a)** A passport issued by a foreign government that has been stamped by the United States Immigration and Naturalization Service.
- **(b)** A driver's license issued by a state other than California or by a Canadian or Mexican public agency authorized to issue driver's licenses.
- **(c)** An identification card issued by a state other than California.
- **(d)** An identification card issued by any branch of the armed forces of the United States.

(4) If the principal is a patient in a skilled nursing facility, a witness who is a patient advocate or ombudsman may rely upon the representations of the administrator or staff of the skilled nursing facility, or of family members, as convincing evidence of the identity of the principal if the patient advocate or ombudsman believes that the representations provide a reasonable basis for determining the identity of the principal.)

(Other kinds of proof of identity are not allowed.)

I declare under penalty of perjury under the laws of California that the person who signed or acknowledged this document is personally known to me (or proved to me on the basis of convincing evidence) to be the principal, that the principal signed or acknowledged this durable power of attorney in my presence, that the principal appears to be of sound mind and under no duress, fraud, or undue influence, that I am not the person appointed as attorney in fact by this document, and that I am not a health care provider, an employee of a

Form 6.1. *Continued.*

health care provider, the operator of a community care facility, an employee of an operator of a community care facility, the operator of a residential care facility for the elderly, nor an employee of an operator of a residential care facility for the elderly.

Signature: ______________________ Residence Address ______________________

____

Print Name: ______________________ ______________________

Date: ______________________ ______________________

Signature: ______________________ Residence Address: ______________________

____

Print Name: ______________________ ______________________

Date: ______________________ ______________________

(AT LEAST ONE OF THE ABOVE WITNESSES MUST ALSO SIGN THE FOLLOWING DECLARATION.)

I further declare under penalty of perjury under the laws of California that I am not related to the principal by blood, marriage, or adoption, and to the best of my knowledge, I am not entitled to any part of the estate of the principal upon the death of the principal under a will now existing or by operation of law.

Signature:______________________

Signature:______________________

STATEMENT OF PATIENT ADVOCATE OR OMBUDSMAN

(If you are a patient in a skilled nursing facility, one of the witnesses must be a patient advocate or ombudsman. The following statement is required only if you are a patient in a skilled nursing facility—a health care facility that provides the following basic services: skilled nursing care and supportive care to patients whose primary need is for availability of skilled nursing care on an extended basis. The patient advocate or ombudsman must sign both parts of the "Statement of Witnesses" above AND must also sign the following statement.)

I further declare under penalty of perjury under the laws of California that I am a patient advocate or ombudsman as designated by the State Department of Aging and that I am serving as a witness as required by subdivision (f) of section 2432 of the Civil Code.

Signature:______________________

Form 6.1. *Continued.*

Although the guideline was written specifically for epidemiologists, the definition applies equally well to all researchers. It is important in discussing conflicts of interest to distinguish between conflicts and scientific fraud or misconduct; the two terms are not interchangeable. Scientific misconduct and fraud are examined in Chapter 7.

Researcher conflicts of interest are of concern because they may introduce bias into the research. Chalmers (1983) has defined bias as "unconscious distortion in the selection of patients, collection of data, determination of end points, and final analysis." The introduction of bias as the result of an investigator's conflict of interest can ultimately result in deficiencies in the design, data collection, analysis, or interpretation of a study. Investigator bias could potentially cause harm to the research participants and to those individuals who later rely on the research findings in making their own decisions about treatment or therapy. Even where there is no actual conflict of interest, a perceived conflict of interest may result in the erosion of trust (Beauchamp *et al.*, 1991) of the public or the participants in the research, the research institution, or the investigators. Researcher conflict of interest may stem from any of several motivating forces, including altruism, a desire for personal recognition, or the possibility of financial reward.

Altruism

Conflicts of interest in research on the part of the researcher can arise for many reasons. The researcher may see the huge toll that HIV exacts not only on those who actually suffer with the disease, but on their families, their friends, and society, as well. The researcher's desire to "do good" may overwhelm his or her desire to seek the scientific truth (Porter, 1992), and may cause the researcher to overlook important clues in the research or to refrain from delving into important subissues.

Recognition

Although not generally recognized, a researcher's desire for fame may also rise to the level of a conflict of interest (Porter, 1992). A researcher's career will be enhanced greatly if he or she can claim the discovery of the cure for HIV or for a new drug. The dispute between Robert Gallo and France's Pasteur Institute virologist Luc Montagnier over who should have received credit for discovering the AIDS virus has become infamous (Hilts, 1992). The stakes were high: grant awards, financial remuneration, and the Nobel prize.

Conflict of interest stemming for a desire for recognition maybe manifested in more subtle ways. A reviewer for a journal may recommend against the publication of a manuscript, not because the manuscript is not deserving of publication, but because the reviewer is working on similar research and wishes to receive recognition as the first researcher to address a particular issue or to note a particular finding. The *Journal of the American Medical Association* has recognized this potential danger:

> The Journal believes . . . that the term "conflict of interest" should apply not only to the possibility of financial gain for referees, but also to other, though less easily measurable, interests beyond the financial, such as the possibility of otherwise unmerited gains in priority of publication, personal recognition, career advancement, increased power, or enhanced prestige. [Southgate, 1987]

Financial Gain

Issues of financial conflict of interest have been, perhaps, the most visible form of conflict of interest in scientific research. Salahuddin, a long-time member of Gallo's laboratory at the National Cancer Institute, was under investigation for an alleged financial interest in a biotechnology company that did hundreds of thousands of dollars of business with Gallo's laboratory (Culliton, 1990). Scripps Research Institute's plans to sell its medical discoveries resulting from federally funded research efforts resulted in a proposal by the National Institutes of Health to limit financial ties between private companies and government-funded scientists (Rose, 1993). Three physicians, a venture capitalist, and a San Fernando Valley medical center have recently been sued for conspiring to use individuals in illegal human experimentation by giving them a drug that would purportedly cure HIV, without the approval of the FDA to engage in such trials, at a cost of $300 per month per patient. Two of the three physicians have lost their medical licenses in California (Pogash, 1993).

The difficulty of remaining objective while maintaining an economic interest in the outcome of one's research has been almost universally accepted. Relman (1989) noted:

> It is difficult enough for the most conscientious researchers to be totally unbiased about their own work, but when an investigator has an economic interest in the outcome of the work, objectivity is even more difficult.

The Council on Scientific Affairs and the Council on Ethical and Judicial Affairs of the American Medical Association (1990) agreed:

> For the clinical investigator who has an economic interest in the outcome of his or her research, objectivity is especially difficult. Economic incentives may introduce subtle biases into the way research is conducted, analyzed, or reported, and these biases can escape detection by even careful peer review.

Wells (1987) has stated flatly that "physicians responsible for the care of the patients or subjects in [clinical studies] should not have a significant financial interest in the company or organization."

Study Funding

Financial conflict of interest can take a number of forms. Those with a financial interest in the outcome of a particular study may be responsible for the funding of the study. This is most likely to occur in the context of clinical trials, where the clinical trial is funded by the pharmaceutical company developing and testing the new product. The opportunity for contract work for a pharmaceutical company may be beneficial to the investigator because he or she will not have to compete for funding through the peer-review process (Shimm & Spece, 1991b). The pharmaceutical company and the investigator may agree that the investigator will enter patients meeting specific entry criteria into a protocol written by the pharmaceutical company to satisfy the FDA's requirements for a Phase I or Phase II drug trial. This could occur, for instance, with the testing of a new antiretroviral therapy or a new drug for the treatment of a particular opportunistic infection. The investigator may receive a cash payment per patient enrollment, rather than a fixed amount that is unrelated to the number of patients enrolled. Investigators may also receive funding for travel to scientific meetings or consultantships (Shimm & Spece, 1991a).

Trial participants may be able to access drugs that would not otherwise be available to them. However, it is also possible that patients may be entered into a clinical trial when it is not in their best interest (Roizen, 1988), such as when an already-existing medication would be most effective for the treatment of their condition. For example, it may be more advantageous for a particular patient to begin a regimen with zidovudine than to be entered into a clinical trial to evaluate a new antiretroviral drug. This situation may be more likely to occur when the investigator is to receive a per-patient incentive and the capitation payments are small. This would require the researcher to enroll a greater number of patients to cover their fixed costs (Roizen, 1988).

Royalty Payments

A conflict may also arise in the context of royalty payments. Suppose that an investigator develops a new drug that can be used in the treatment of an opportunistic infection. The researcher then sells the product to a company in exchange for royalties. The company then asks the researcher to evaluate the product in a clinical trial. The duality of the researcher's loyalties are divided between those to the research participants and those to the company that intends to market the product. This duality of loyalty can take various forms. One study suggested that studies funded by pharmaceutical companies are more likely to favor the new therapy being tested than studies funded through other sources (Davidson, 1986).

The ownership of stock in a company may constitute a conflict of interest. Lichter (1989) has asserted that "owning stock in a company at the same time one is conducting research, the results of which can affect the stock's value, creates the potential for bias, whether intended or not. . . ." The potential for conflict of interest may not be as great where the investigator is examining a product for a very large company and the success or failure of that product is unlikely to have a large impact on the value of the company's stock. The success of even one product may determine the financial fate of a company smaller in size (Porter, 1992). In a non-HIV context, one researcher's dual role as a multimillion dollar investor in Heart Technology Inc. and as a researcher evaluating its product called "Rotablator" recently prompted review by congressional leaders concerned about conflicts of interest in research (Dalton, 1994a).

Controlling Conflict of Interest

Disclosure to Research Participants

Shimm and Spece (1991a) have argued, based on analogy to case law relating to patients and physician compensation, that research participants must be informed of all financial arrangements between the clinical researchers and manufacturers. In 1978, California enacted a statute that requires investigators to inform research participants of the source of the funding for the study (California Health and Safety Code section 24173, 1992). It does not, however, require that the investigator divulge the mechanisms for the study's funding or the amount of money that is involved. Shimm and Spece (1991b) have suggested that monies available from contracts with pharmaceutical companies for research that are in excess of the direct costs of a study be placed in an institutionwide pool. Investigators associated with the institution could compete on a local level for access to this pooled funding for their research.

Peer Review

Peer review has been suggested as a "key form of control" (Shipp, 1992). Peer review is helpful as a means of control because the investigator's work will be reviewed by others with similar skills and expertise. Other scientists will have a greater understanding of the fact that scientists make honest mistakes and that research findings may be subject to various interpretations.

It has been recognized, however, that peer review cannot be the sole source of control. A conflict of interest may not be visible to those reviewing the work (Shipp, 1992; Council on Scientific Affairs and Council on Ethical and Judicial Affairs, 1990). Peer review is most likely to occur after the work has been done and the results disseminated. In such situations, the discovery of the conflict and the public dissemination of its occurrence will undermine the credibility of the researcher involved and of scientists generally (Shipp, 1992).

Institutional Review

Various models have been developed for the identification and review of conflicts of interest. Institutions may prohibit specific activities, classify activities by level of scrutiny and control, or review activities on an individual basis to determine whether a conflict exists (Shipp, 1992). Various models also exist for the disclosure of possible conflicts of interest, including annual submissions of disclosures or ad hoc submissions. A committee may be in place to review the disclosures and the potential for conflict of interest.

Institutions differ in both the prescribed manner of disclosure and what must be disclosed. The requirement of disclosure may be institution-initiated or investigator-initiated. The institution may require that any, or all, of the following be disclosed: outside professional positions, equity holdings, outside professional income, gifts, honoraria, or loans (Shipp, 1992).

Activities may be found to be unacceptable and therefore prohibited. Some activities may be permissible, but may be problematic. The resolution of such situations could include the public disclosure of relevant information; the reformulation of the research; closer monitoring of the research; divestiture by the investigator of his or her personal interests; a cessation of the investigator's participation with the research project, or the reduction of his or her involvement; the termination of inappropriate student involvement in the project; or the termination of outside relationships that introduce the conflict (Association of American Medical Colleges, 1990).

Federal Requirements

The Public Health Service, which funds a great deal of biomedical research, requires that grantees maintain conflict of interest policies. The 1990 PHS Grants Policy Statement requires that recipient organizations

> establish safeguards to prevent employees, consultants, or members of governing bodies from using their positions for purposes that are, or give the appearance of being, motivated by a desire for private financial gain for themselves or others such as those with whom they have family, business, or other ties. Therefore, each institution receiving financial support must have written policy guidelines on conflict of interest and the avoidance thereof. These guidelines should reflect State and local laws and must cover financial interest, gifts, gratuities and favors, nepotism, and other areas such as political participation and bribery. [Public Health Service, United States Department of Health and Human Services, 1990].

The 1993 NIH Reauthorization Act created the Commission of Research Integrity, which is now examining the role of the federal government in the regulation and enforcement of scientific integrity. The role of the federal government is discussed more fully in the context of scientific fraud and misconduct, in Chapter 7.

6.5. CONCLUSION

It would be difficult to conceive of a study in which a potential conflict of interest could not arise. This is particularly true in the context of HIV research, because of the many different interests involved and the need to find an acceptable balance of those interests. Many actual conflicts can be avoided if the researcher is aware at the outset of their potential occurrence and is proactive in addressing these situations. Often, frank discussions with the participant or other designated persons may alleviate a potential conflict. Strict adherence to institutional guidelines and federal regulations may reduce the possibility of investigator conflict of interest.

CHAPTER SEVEN

Scientific Misconduct

7.1. DEFINING SCIENTIFIC MISCONDUCT

Federal regulations define "scientific misconduct" as "fabrication, falsification, plagiarism or other practices that seriously deviate from those that are commonly accepted within the scientific community for proposing, conducting, or reporting research" (42 Code of Federal Regulations section 50.101, 1993). Scientific misconduct does not refer to "honest error or honest differences in interpretations or judgments of data."

One commentator (Benson, 1991a) has noted the difficulty of categorizing behaviors as "misconduct" when they fall outside of fabrication, falsification, and plagiarism. Benson, citing Binder (1989), suggested the arrangement of scientific "sins" into a "concentric circle of unacceptable practices." The most unambiguous cases of fraud include plagiarism, falsification, and fabrication, constituting the ninth through the seventh concentric rings. Those who fail to credit others for their work by omitting citation fall into the sixth circle. The fifth through the first circles encompass, respectively, scientists who selectively report data, who use inappropriate statistics, who trim data to massage the results, who use historical controls instead of actual controls for an experiment, and who divide a scientific project into the least divisible unit to produce a multitude of scientific papers. Onek (1994) has questioned the propriety of equating scientific misconduct and "other serious deviations from accepted research practices," which may be detrimental to the research process, but which do not constitute scientific misconduct.

There have been several instances of alleged scientific misconduct in the context of HIV research. In 1986, Daniel Zagury injected himself and 18 seronegative offspring of HIV-infected mothers in Zaire with vaccinia recombinant expressing gp160. Ten of the children were 2 to 9 years of age; eight were between the ages of 10 and 18. Although Zagury was severely criticized by the NIH, he was exonerated by French authorities (Lurie, 1995).

A second instance involved Dr. Robert Redfield, of the United States Army. Dr. Redfield presented results at at least one professional conference indicating that the use of gp160 therapeutic vaccine resulted in a decreased viral load among its recipients. However, he later admitted that he had not included all of the research participants in the analyses and that he had used an inappropriate control group (Hendrix & Boswell, 1992). Despite these errors, the published results have never been retracted (Lurie, 1995; Hendrix & Boswell, 1992). An Air Force subcommittee reviewing Dr. Redfield's conduct found that

> the information presented by Dr. Redfield threatens his credibility as a researcher and has the potential to negatively impact AIDS research funding for military institutions as a whole. His allegedly unethical behavior creates false hope and could result in premature deployment of the vaccine. [Public Citizens Health Research Group, 1994]

A third instance of alleged misconduct involved the Immune Response Corporation. The Food and Drug Administration concluded, based on the results of an inspection conducted as part of its Bioresearch Monitoring Program, that the Immune Response Corporation had committed several "violations of regulations that govern the use of investigational drugs." These violations consisted of (1) the inclusion of research participants in the clinical trial who did not meet the entry criteria; (2) the modification of adverse experience information with no documentation of the reasons for such changes; (3) retrospective post-unblinding changes in categories and changes based on a review of a subset of data; and (4) the exclusion of two subjects from analysis although the journal article in which the results were published claimed that the analysis included all treated subjects. The FDA specifically found that "[a]s a result of these deviations from protocol, a significant result was published in the article." The FDA further found violations in the informed consent procedures in that (1) the consent forms contained statements that appeared to make claims for the effectiveness of the study drug and discount the effectiveness of the established drug, zidovudine, and (2) research participants were promised receipt of the test drug after completion of the study, although the protocol provided for only three injections (Simmons, 1995).

The Role of Investigator Intent

It is generally accepted that a researcher must have intended to make a false statement for scientific misconduct to have occurred. The

Guidelines for the Conduct of Research at NIH defines scientific misconduct as "fabrication, falsification, plagiarism, or other practices motivated by intent to deceive" (Onek, 1994). Plagiarism has been termed "the most blatant form of misappropriation of credit" (Committee on the Conduct of Science, National Academy of Sciences, 1989). Plagiarism ranges from paraphrasing materials without giving proper credit to the original author, to quoting directly without indicating either that the excerpt is a quote or the source of the excerpt, to stealing research proposals (Kuzma, 1992). Shapiro and Charrow (1985) defined fraud as involving "deliberate misrepresentation of the data, in the form of either 'fudging' (altering the results) or 'dry labbing' (generating data without performing the study)."

7.2. SCIENTIFIC MISCONDUCT INVESTIGATIONS

Procedures

Publications

In general, disciplinary procedures are not in place to address issues of plagiarism or multiple publication of the same material. Nigg and Radulescu (1994) demand that scientific misconduct be met with "strong action by the employer and by journal editors." They have advocated that scientific journals develop written policies regarding scientific misconduct and that they respond to allegations of misconduct.

Institutional/Funding Source Procedures

The Office of Research Integrity (ORI) is an independent office in the Department of Health and Human Services (42 United States Code Annotated section 289b, 1994). This office is responsible for establishing procedures to respond to reports from research institutions filing reports of investigations, conducting investigations, monitoring institutional compliance, and protecting whistleblowers.

Federal regulations require that "[i]nstitutions . . . foster a research environment that discourages misconduct in all research and that deals forthrightly with possible misconduct associated with research for which [Public Health Service] funds have been provided or requested" (42 Code of Federal Regulations section 50.105, 1993). An institution's failure to do so could result in a loss of funding or an investigation of the institution by the ORI.

If there are allegations of misconduct and the allegations involve federally funded research, the institution that received the federal money must follow procedures mandated by federal regulation. These include the following:

1. Establish uniform policies and procedures to investigate and report potential misconduct (42 Code of Federal Regulations section 50.101, 1993)
2. Inform its scientific and administrative staffs of the policies and procedures and the importance of compliance
3. Take immediate and appropriate action as soon as misconduct is suspected or alleged
4. Inform the ORI of all investigations (42 Code of Federal Regulations section 50.103, 1993)

The federal regulations also provide for the protection of those who reported the misconduct and the privacy of those under investigation (42 Code of Federal Regulations section 50.103, 1993).

Pascal (1994) has outlined the steps to be taken by the institution when a charge of misconduct arises:

1. Assess the allegations to determine whether they are frivolous and whether the situation falls within the scope of the PHS regulations
2. Protect the data and other research documents during the investigation
3. Conduct a full investigation if warranted by the results from the preliminary inquiry
4. Obtain adequate scientific expertise to assist in the investigation
5. Protect the procedural rights of both the researcher under investigation and the individual(s) who initiated the complaint
6. Report the investigation and its findings to the ORI
7. Advise individuals involved of the potential criminal consequences for any false written or oral statements made to the ORI or any other component of Health and Human Services (HHS) as part of an investigation

A researcher has the right to request a full and complete new hearing before the HHS Departmental Appeals Board (DAB) if he or she disagrees with the findings of the ORI. The ORI has the burden of proving its case (Onek, 1994).

Sanctions

There exist a range of sanctions for scientific misconduct, which include attempts to recover the federal funds from the grant recipient;

debarment from the receipt of federal grant or contract monies for a specified period of time; termination or withholding of ongoing PHS grant support; acceptance of a voluntary agreement not to apply for federal research funding for a specified period of time; requiring the investigators to certify the integrity of their future proposals; requiring that reviewers of future proposals be informed of the misconduct; and prohibiting the scientist from participating on PHS committees (Settle, 1994; Dresser, 1993). Settlements may provide that the institution amend procedures for addressing scientific misconduct (FDC Reports, 1994).

7.3. REDUCING THE POTENTIAL FOR SCIENTIFIC MISCONDUCT

Several studies have found that serious problems with research often decline in response to the initiation of an ongoing audit program. A study by Shapiro and Charrow (1989) found that the initiation of an FDA audit program reduced serious problems. Weiss *et al.* (1993) found that scientific improprieties decreased following the initiation of on-site peer review of investigator performance in the Cancer and Leukemia Group B cooperative group. Improvements included a decrease in consent form deficiences; increased compliance with federal regulations for oversight by an institutional review board; and a reduction in major protocol deviations in drug dosing.

7.4. CONCLUSION

Reasonable minds may differ on what conduct actually constitutes scientific misconduct. There is general agreement, however, that certain offenses constitute misconduct, including plagiarism and the falsification of data. Investigator intent is crucial to a determination that misconduct has occurred. This permits a distinction between those situations in which an investigator has deliberately engaged in misconduct, and those in which the investigator was acting in good faith, but in error. Procedures are now in place to investigate allegation of researcher misconduct, which attempt to protect the privacy of both the researchers and the research participants. These procedures will undoubtedly evolve over time as additional legal and ethical issues are raised.

PART THREE

Following the Study

CHAPTER EIGHT

Participants and Records

Numerous legal or ethical questions can arise toward the end of a study. A study participant may sue for harm, claiming that he or she suffered injury as a result of the protocol, and that the consent given was not informed because crucial information was withheld. Colleagues not connected with a study may request that the raw data be transmitted to them in order to conduct additional analyses. This chapter addresses researcher obligations with respect to participants and other researchers. It focuses on the potential for legal liability to research participants for injury during the course of the study.

8.1. LEGAL LIABILITY FOR INJURY TO RESEARCH PARTICIPANTS

The recent Quebec case of *Weiss v. Solomon* (1989) is one of the few reported instances of a research participant claiming that he suffered injuries arising out of participation in a clinical trial. Weiss's surgeon recruited him in 1981, at the age of 62, to participate in a nontherapeutic trial designed to assess the ability of indomethacin drops to reduce retinal edema subsequent to cataract surgery. Following the administration of the indomethacin drops, a series of three fluorescein angiograms were to be administered in order to assess the drug's effect. Weiss experienced an extreme drop in blood pressure and pulse immediately following the first injection of fluorescein. He could not be revived.

Following Weiss's death, his wife and children brought an action against the principal investigator, the recruiting physician, and the hospital in which Weiss had been a patient and the research had been conducted. The claim alleged that Weiss had had a long history of hypertrophic cardiomyopathy and should have been excluded from the study because of an increased risk of cardiac arrest. The plaintiffs further claimed that Weiss should have been informed of the increased risk of this procedure and that the hospital's resuscitation efforts were unsuccessful because the hospital failed to have the proper resuscitation equipment available. The Quebec Superior Court found both the hospital and the principal investigator liable. The recruiting physician was not found liable because of his limited participation in the conduct of the research.

The judge found that Weiss should have been screened for hypertrophic cardiomyopathy, without stating how Weiss should have been screened. The judge also reasoned that all of the known risks had not been divulged to Weiss prior to obtaining his consent to participate, implying that consent was not truly informed. The judge referred not only to Canadian law, but also to the Declaration of Helsinki, as a basis for his decision.

The judge's opinion left unanswered the scope of knowledge required of a research ethics committee reviewing a proposal that is before it. The judge faulted the committee for failing to require revisions in the protocol that would have excluded individuals with cardiomyopathy from the trial or that would have required the availability of resuscitation equipment in the event of a cardiac arrest. The judge further found that the consent form had minimized the risk of fluorescein angiograms, when the risks should have been explained in detail.

Clearly, Canadian law is not binding in U.S. courts. However, the Weiss court's reliance on the Helsinki Declaration as a basis for its decision, rather than on Canadian law alone, makes it more likely that a U.S. court would look to the Weiss case in evaluating the adequacy of disclosure and informed consent in the nontherapeutic research setting. This has implications, particularly in the context of HIV vaccine trials. First, the HIV vaccine trial participants will not derive any therapeutic benefit as a result of their participation. The failure to provide sufficient information as part of the consent procedure could potentially constitute nondisclosure and obviate the validity of the consent obtained.

Issues remain, as well, with respect to liability for unforeseen injuries suffered by research participants during the course of the research. Such injuries may occur in the absence of investigator fault. The United States currently has no compensation system for individuals injured in this context. The failure to establish such a system could ultimately impact on the willingness of individuals to volunteer for research and increase the difficulty of recruitment (Zak, 1991).

8.2. SHARING DATA

Data sharing has received considerable support (Hogue, 1991). Sieber (1988) has identified nine situations in which the sharing of data may be requested:

1. Research contract requiring delivery of the data to the funding source following completion of the contract
2. A research grant requiring storage of the data and its sharing with any other researcher on request
3. A journal requirement that raw data be made available to reviewers of an article and to readers following publication
4. A collaborative relationship with a colleague
5. A request from a colleague to borrow data as a sample for training students
6. A decision to archive data to allow access to future borrowers
7. Government funding for the collection of data, which may then be used by another government organization that may use the data for policy-making
8. A court subpoena compelling disclosure of the data
9. A request from a competitor for the raw data from confidential research conducted without funding

Several of the situations relate to the voluntary sharing of data. Hedrick (1988) has advanced ten reasons to encourage voluntary sharing:

1. To reinforce open scientific inquiry;
2. To verify, refine, or refute the original results
3. To replicate research findings with multiple data sets
4. To explore new questions
5. To create new data sets by linking data files
6. To encourage multiple perspectives
7. To reduce the incidence of inaccurate or fabricated results
8. To develop knowledge relating to analytic techniques
9. To provide resources for training
10. To reduce unnecessary duplication of collecting data and its resulting burden on the research participants

Involuntary data sharing, as exemplified by Sieber's last three situations, can result in potentially negative effects. These include additional time constraints and financial burden on the original primary investigator, the lack of reward for sharing the data, the loss of control over the use of the data, and a possible slowing of scientific progress (Stanley & Stanley, 1988).

Both voluntary and involuntary data sharing become particularly problematic in the context of HIV research. Data sharing cannot violate either guarantees of confidentiality provided to the participants or state laws relating to the release of such data. (See Chapter 5 for a detailed discussion of confidentiality.) Sharing information with government agencies may be particularly problematic. The Centers for Disease Control, for instance, is charged with the responsibility both to conduct research and to prevent disease. That prevention function potentially includes the use of quarantine as a means of protecting a community, making the supply to CDC of data with identifiers somewhat problematic (Boruch, 1984).

8.3. CONCLUSION

Injury to study participants may occur, even in the absence of fault. It is important to identify areas of potential problems as early as possible, so that precautions can be taken to avoid them to the extent possible. Measures to reduce or eliminate the potential of injury include, but are not limited to, the imposition of exclusionary criteria, the drafting of complete and accurate informed consent forms and the implementation of an effective informed consent procedure, and careful follow-up of the research participants.

The sharing of research data is not unrelated to the issue of potential injury to the research participants. The involuntary sharing of data, such as that required by court order or agency audit, may compromise the confidentiality that was promised to the participants, resulting in injury. Even the voluntary sharing of data, which is to be encouraged for multiple reasons, must be done carefully to avoid harm to the research participants.

CHAPTER NINE

Publication and Dissemination of Research Results

9.1. AUTHORSHIP AND PROFESSIONAL PUBLICATION

Researchers in general are accustomed to seeing multiple authors credited with the conduct of research. At times, authorship of collaborative publications may be in the double digits. Four explanations have been advanced as the basis for this proliferation of authorship: the development of social structures supportive of collaborative research; the interdisciplinary nature of scientific research; the development of larger teams to address complex scientific problems; and the growing role of the federal government in funding research (Benson, 1991b).

Problems inherent in multiple authorship are easily identified. Coauthors may have no direct knowledge of the accuracy of the underlying data. Scientists relying on periodicals to share information and to establish reputations may be misled.

Various measures have been developed in an attempt to address these problems, including journal requirements that authors sign statements of responsibility, numerical rankings of authors according to their level of contribution, multiple categories of authors, and the alphabetizing of all authors. Benson (1991b) has asserted that such measures are inadequate and that "the cure is to return to the traditional definition of author: only persons who conduct and write the research should be allowed to be listed as the author." A return to such a policy would eliminate the use of authorship as a political favor and would provide greater assurance that those credited with the research have actual knowledge of the data and the accuracy of their interpretation.

The issue of authorship may arise frequently in the conduct of HIV research. Research may involve the collection of data in multiple countries or at multiple sites. Individuals who have participated in the collection of the data, such as interviewers and phlebotomists, may feel that the study could not have occurred without their assistance and may demand inclusion as authors. Researchers responsible for the clinical care of patient participants or recruitment may also demand authorship, despite their unfamiliarity with research principles and their inability to contribute to the compilation of a paper.

Stanley and Stanley (1988) have encouraged the use of written agreements in the context of data sharing. That recommendation is equally valid in the context of authorship. A written agreement between proposed authors, even in the form of a mutual letter, would set forth the commitments to be fulfilled by each author. Failure to fulfill the commitment would justify the elimination of the individual's name from the list of authors. This approach may be particularly helpful in situations where authors are geographically distant and active participation in the writing process must be facilitated.

Most manuscripts will be submitted for review and publication to peer-reviewed journals. The peer review process has often been criticized for bias toward the inclusion of studies evidencing positive results, nonblinded review (Laband & Piette, 1994), and the inability to detect fraudulent results (Whitely, Rennie, & Hafner, 1994). Increasing evidence of editorial misconduct has given rise to recommendations for the establishment of an International Medical Scientific Press Council, responsible for addressing grievances and imposing sanctions (Altman, Chalmers, & Herxheimer, 1994). The possibility of such problems arising in the context of HIV research may be particularly acute considering the desperation resulting from mounting numbers of individuals infected with HIV and institutional pressures on researchers to produce and publish significant findings. (See Chapter 6 for a discussion of conflict of interest.)

Research has suggested that blinding results in more unbiased reviews and that nonblinded reviewers may be affected by various types of bias (Fisher, Friedman, & Strauss, 1994). Professional rivalries can easily and even unintentionally influence a critique of research and the willingness to see a competitor be the first to publicize important results. This has been particularly evident in the context of HIV research (Shilts, 1987). Blinded review of research should be utilized whenever possible to reduce the possibility that such consideration enter into the evaluation of the work.

9.2. COMMUNICATING RESULTS TO THE PUBLIC AND TO PARTICIPANTS

Acknowledging Uncertainty

Medical and health researchers have been criticized for arrogance in their communication with the public (Sandman, 1991). This has been particularly evident in the well-publicized battle between Robert Gallo and French researchers for the ultimate credit for the isolation of HIV. Sandman (1991) has stressed the need to acknowledge uncertainty when uncertainty exists, in lieu of adopting arrogance as a professionally defensive tactic. Although he limited his comments to epidemiologists, they are equally applicable to HIV researchers from other disciplines.

Sandman enumerated four factors underlying the need to acknowledge uncertainty. First, findings may be far from conclusive. When this is the case, principles of ethics demand that the lack of conclusiveness be acknowledged (Schulte, 1991). Second, the scientific process is tentative. Third, a researcher invites attack by claiming more confidence than can be justified. Fourth, the study results cannot be applied appropriately without an understanding of how certain or uncertain they are (Sandman, 1991).

Dynamics specific to HIV research further mandate acknowledgment of uncertainty. The number of individuals infected with HIV continues to grow. Existing treatments have limited benefit and are not universally available (Altman, 1993). A failure to acknowledge the uncertainty of study results relevant to drug development, for instance, and to verify the results obtained, can falsely raise the hopes of those infected with and affected by HIV, and slow scientific research on other potentially beneficial treatments.

Communicating Results and Errors

Even the accurate communication of study results to the public may entail difficulties. The identification of a "high-risk group," for instance, may provoke fear in individuals so labeled and may result in social stigmatization of individuals. AIDS, for instance, has been called the "Gay Plague" (Seligmann, Gosnell, Copola, & Hager, 1983). Researchers' initial emphasis on high-risk groups, rather than high-risk behaviors, may have resulted in the unintentional stigmatization of the groups identified and the maintenance of high-risk behaviors for HIV transmission among individuals not classifiable as a "high-risk" group member.

Schulte (1991) has noted that the identification of a high-risk group, particularly in the absence of a clear definition of risk, may provoke anxiety in members of that group. The clear delineation of known factors contributing to an increased risk will permit individuals to more adequately evaluate their own risk. The mere fact of someone's homosexuality, for instance, does not increase the risk of HIV infection, absent behaviors facilitating such transmission.

Mistakes in research and the publication of research results later found to be fraudulent can be as distressing to the public as to the scientific community. In 1993, for instance, Chow and his colleagues announced the discovery of the "Achilles' heel" of HIV, and the potential benefits of a triple-drug combination to halt replication of the virus. Shortly thereafter, however, the researchers acknowledged an error in their interpretation of laboratory data and their failure to detect a mutation in the virus used in the experiment. AIDS activists charged that the researchers deliberately manipulated the system to increase the size of the trial. Volunteers in the trial became confused (Altman, 1993). Ultimately, the publication of erroneous results may have reduced public confidence in the scientific process and the integrity of researchers.

Admirably, Chow and his Harvard colleagues acted quickly to publicize corrections. Other scientists, working in less visible areas of research, may have been less quick to do so (Altman, 1993).

Participants as a Special Class

Participants in research may be owed a more extensive obligation. Although general news articles have been shown to be effective in purging fraudulent results from the scientific literature (Whitely *et al.*, 1994), this approach may be inadequate as a means of notifying study participants of errors. The question has been raised regarding the extent to which a university or other entity must use its own resources to find, notify, and assist individuals who participated in the research. The argument has been made that the imposition of such a requirement would serve as a disincentive to the initiation of new research. Schulte (1991) ultimately concluded that the research institution may be responsible for the notification of study participants.

9.3. CONCLUSION

Authorship carries with it many responsibilities, including the accurate reporting of findings to professional colleagues and the public, and the retraction of inaccurate statements. It is important that authors communicate uncertainty to their colleagues and to the public, if uncertainty exists, when they are communicating their interpretations of their findings. Further, the communication of study results must be done in a socially responsible manner, to avoid as much as possible the stigmatization of groups or media misinterpretation of findings. Investigators and the research institution may have special duties to research participants to inform them of errors in their findings or their interpretations.

PART FOUR

New Roles for the HIV Researcher

CHAPTER TEN

An Overview of the Legal System

The HIV researcher is challenged by the possibility of new roles outside of the strictly scientific or social science arena. For instance, a researcher may be called in as an expert witness in a court proceeding where the plaintiff is suing the defendant for damages in a personal injury lawsuit, alleging that the defendant knowingly infected her with HIV. In a second scenario, the researcher may wish to support or protest legislation that has been introduced at the state level. Alternatively, the researcher may wish to see legislation on a particular point introduced, and is willing to draft the legislation for presentation by a state representative.

This chapter outlines the basic workings of the legal system: the judiciary, the legislature, and the regulatory agencies. Additional detail is provided in subsequent chapters in the context of actual situations involving an HIV researcher.

10.1. THE CONSTITUTION

The Constitution has been called the "supreme law of the land." All statutes and all regulations, whether at the local, state, or federal levels, must be consistent with the principles enunciated in the Constitution.

The Constitution is divided into two parts, the main portion and 26 amendments. The main portion of the document establishes the three branches of the government and defines the responsibilities of each. The legislative branch is charged with the promulgation of statutory laws. The executive branch is charged with the enforcement of the laws. The judicial branch is charged with the responsibility of interpreting the laws.

The first ten amendments following the main portion of the Constitution are known as the Bill of Rights. These include the freedom of speech, the free exercise of religion, the right to a trial by jury, and the right against self-incrimination, among others.

The Constitution grants specific powers to the federal government. Under the Ninth Amendment, powers not granted to the federal government are reserved to the states. Federal powers include the levying of taxes, the ability to declare war, and the power to regulate interstate commerce.

Each state also has a constitution. A state's constitution may provide the citizens of the state with more rights than the federal, but cannot provide fewer rights than are guaranteed by the federal constitution. For instance, a state constitution may provide greater privacy rights to its citizens than does the federal constitution.

10.2. STATUTES

Statutes are laws that are enacted by legislative bodies. At the federal level, the legislative body consists of the House of Representatives and the Senate. At the state level, statutes are enacted by the state legislature. At the local level, ordinances may be promulgated by a city council or county board of supervisors.

The courts are charged with the responsibility of interpreting the statutes and their applicability to cases before the courts. This may be particularly difficult where statutory provisions are in conflict or where the wording of a statute is vague or ambiguous. Cases may also be brought to the courts in which a party is alleging that a particular statute that has been implemented is unconstitutional, that it is inconsistent with one or more provisions of the federal or state constitution.

10.3. RULES AND REGULATIONS

Regulations and rules are promulgated by agencies at all levels of government. The regulations and rules must be consistent with the statutes that have authorized their promulgation and with the federal constitution. Rules and regulations promulgated by a state agency must also be consistent with the constitution of the state in which the agency sits. Examples of agencies with authority to promulgate rules and regulations include the Interstate Commerce Commission, the Internal Revenue Service, and the Food and Drug Administration. At the state level, examples include workers' compensation boards, medical licensing boards, and environmental agencies.

10.4. THE JUDICIARY

Judicial decisions must be consistent with the constitution. They must also be consistent with the statutes, as long as the statutes are consistent with the constitution. The judiciary is charged with the responsibility of reviewing the constitutionality of statutes and regulations that are challenged in the courts as unconstitutional.

The courts will often decide cases in reliance on the doctrine of *stare decisis.* This means that courts will try to resolve cases before it on the basis of earlier cases involving the same issue, or precedents. This doctrine is applied vertically, in that equal or lower courts in the same system will be bound by prior decisions. For instance, a Superior Court in California will be bound by a decision of the California Supreme Court where that decision involved similar facts and legal issues. However, a Florida court would not be bound by the California Supreme Court decision. A federal district court would be bound by the decisions of the Court of Appeals for the circuit in which it sits, but would not be bound by the decisions of a Court of Appeals for another circuit. For example, the United States District Court for the Southern District of California would be bound by the decisions of the Ninth Circuit Court of Appeals, because it sits in the Ninth Circuit, but it would not be bound by the decisions of the United States Court of Appeals for the Fifth Circuit. In reality, however, one circuit court may take note of another circuit court's decision on the same issue, although it will not be bound by it.

10.5. CONCLUSION

The legal system is an intricate system of checks and balances, between the judicial, legislative, and administrative branches of government. Even within each branch, numerous checks and balances have been implemented, many of which will be discussed in subsequent sections in the context of HIV-related issues.

CHAPTER ELEVEN

The HIV Researcher as an Expert Witness

A basic understanding of both the court system and procedures used in litigation is crucial to the researcher who assumes the role of an expert witness. An expert witness can be called in at various points during the course of litigation, including depositions or the trial itself.

11.1. THE COURT SYSTEM

The Federal Court System

The basic federal court system can be thought of as a three-tiered pyramid. At the bottom tier are the federal district courts. These courts hear criminal cases involving federal misdemeanors and felonies; civil rights cases arising under federal statutes or the U.S. Constitution; and a diversity of citizenship cases, where the party suing is from a different state than the party being sued and the dollar amount in controversy exceeds a threshold amount. Figure 11.1 illustrates the basic structure of the federal court system.

In some situations, the federal district court is the only venue in which a claim can be heard. For instance, a lawsuit brought under a federal civil rights statute must be heard in federal court; a state court does not have the authority to hear the case. In other situations, a lawsuit may be brought in either federal or state court.

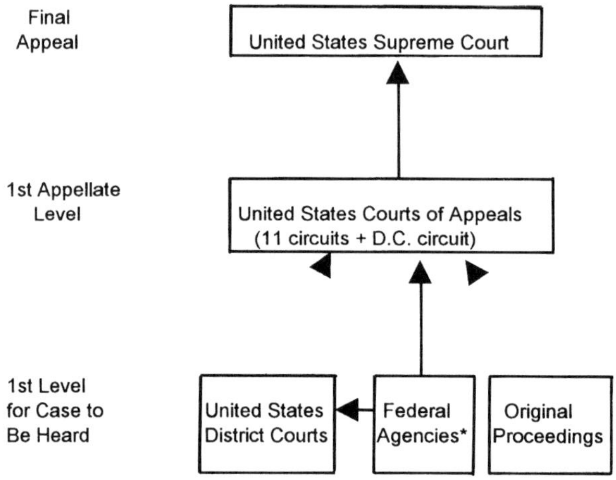

Figure 11.1. Schematic representation of the federal court system. (*Some types of cases may be adjudicated administratively by a federal agency. A party might ask for review in federal district court. The decision of the federal district court might then be appealed to a Court of Appeals.)

Decisions can be appealed from the federal district court to the Court of Appeals for the Circuit in which the federal district court sits. There are 11 federal circuits, plus the circuit for the District of Columbia. A 13th Court of Appeals for the Federal Circuit hears appeals arising under certain federal laws, such as patents, trademarks, and appeals from the U.S. Court of Claims.

An appeal from a decision of a Court of Appeals to the U.S. Supreme Court is not automatic. The Supreme Court hears appeals from state supreme courts and from federal courts of appeals in cases involving federal statutes, treaties, or the U.S. Constitution. The Supreme Court can limit the number of cases it hears through the process known as the writ of certiorari. This is a petition to the Supreme Court to file an appeal. Writs are not granted very often. When they are granted, it is often because the issues presented reflect a conflict between various circuit courts of appeals.

The State Court System

The court system of each state is different, and the details of the 50 state court systems cannot be presented here. However, the following description of California's court system is instructive.

Figure 11.2 depicts the basic court system. The court system can be thought of as a multitiered pyramid. At the bottom of the pyramid are the municipal courts and justice courts. There are 88 Municipal Courts in California, with a total of 566 judges, and 76 Justice Courts in the state, with a total of 76 judges. These courts have jurisdiction to hear cases involving amounts in controversy of $25,000 or less and certain offenses, such as traffic violations. Appeals from these courts are taken to the Appellate Department of the appropriate Superior Court.

Superior Courts have jurisdiction to hear cases involving more than $25,000 in controversy and criminal cases involving misdemeanors and felonies. There are a total of 58 Superior Courts in California, one for each county. There are a total of 725 Superior Court judges. Appeals from decisions of the Superior Courts are taken to the Courts of Appeal.

Finally, the California Supreme Court hears appeals from the Courts of Appeal. Examples of cases that the Supreme Court might hear include a claim that a person's right of privacy under the California State Constitution was violated by agents of the state, or an appeal from a trial for a felony in which capital punishment was imposed.

11.2. THE PROCESS OF CIVIL LITIGATION

Civil litigation, in which one party sues another, is premised on numerous objectives, including discovery of the truth and an attempt to

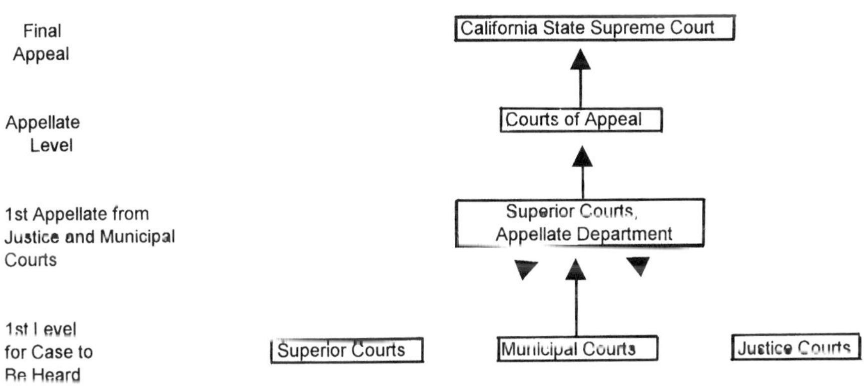

Figure 11.2. Schematic representation of the California court system.

make whole the party who was injured. In a civil case relating to HIV, a person might be suing for monetary damages to "make them whole" or for the payment of medical expenses. A case goes through many stages prior to actually being heard in the courtroom.

Complaint and Answer

A lawsuit is normally commenced with the filing of a complaint in the court of appropriate jurisdiction. Prior to the filing of the complaint, the attorney for the plaintiff may have tried to reach a settlement with the defendant for the recovery of the damages that are alleged to have occurred. This may have been in the form of a demand letter, requesting payment of a certain sum of money prior to a specific date. For instance, suppose that Patty Plaintiff recently discovered that she was HIV positive. She claims to have had protected sex with every individual with whom she has had sexual relations in the last five years. She asserts that she goes regularly (every six months) for HIV testing, and only recently seroconverted. She just learned that her most recent and long-term sex partner, David Defendant, has been HIV seropositive for several years, but did not inform her of this prior to having sexual relations with her. She is seeking a sum of money from David Defendant sufficient to cover her lifetime costs of medical care, plus attorney's fees and court costs, plus damages for pain and suffering. Abel Attorney has sent a demand letter to David, which he initially ignored and then passed on to his attorney, Linda Lawyer. David represented to his attorney that he did not know that he was HIV seropositive at the time when he had relations with Patty. Because the parties cannot agree to liability or damages, Abel Attorney files a complaint on behalf of his client, Patty Plaintiff.

The format for a complaint may differ between jurisdictions. Generally, a complaint must state facts sufficient to support a claim, and must state the legal basis of the claim. In the case involving Patty Plaintiff and David Defendant, the complaint must state the facts that would support a claim that HIV could have been transmitted, such as the parties involved, the dates of the occurrences, and other relevant data. The complaint must usually state the legal theory on which the complaint is being premised. In this case, it might be that David owed Patty a certain duty and that duty was breached, giving rise to personal injury. Alternatively, it might be that Patty consented to the sexual relations based on David's representations to her that he was HIV seronegative; that she would not have consented if he had disclosed his HIV seropositivity; that David's touching of her was consequently nonconsensual;

and that she is seeking monetary damages as a result. Many jurisdictions may also require that the plaintiff verify the complaint, indicating under penalty of perjury that he or she has read the complaint and that the contents of the complaint are true to the best of her knowledge.

Following the filing of the complaint, and within a prescribed time line, the defendant has the right to file an answer to the complaint. The answer may admit or deny the allegations of the complaints or a portion of the allegations. Sometimes, the defendant will enter a "special appearance" to contest the court's jurisdiction. Sometimes the answer will also contain counterclaims, which are claims being made by the defendant against the person who filed the original complaint.

Discovery

An expert witness may be called on to testify during the discovery process, before a case ever reaches trial. Discovery refers to established processes to obtain information relevant to the case prior to the actual trial. Although discovery can take several forms, those most relevant to the researcher include depositions and the issuance of a subpoena by a court to produce records. Because subpoenas have already been discussed at great length in Section 5.1, this section will focus exclusively on procedures related to depositions.

Lawyers generally take depositions for one of two reasons: to obtain evidence or to record the testimony for use at trial when the attorney suspects that the individual testifying may not be available at the time of trial. For instance, an extremely busy HIV researcher with several grants in various parts of the world may not be able to commit to appearing at a trial on a particular day. However, his or her testimony will be available if it was previously recorded as part of a deposition.

Very often, it will be the attorney for the party for whom the expert is not testifying who will want to take the expert's deposition. In the case of Patty Plaintiff, for instance, suppose Rene Researcher is testifying for Patty on the issue of the transmissibility of HIV through sexual relations and HIV as the causative agent of AIDS. It is more likely that David Defendant's attorney will arrange to depose Rene Researcher, because the information that he obtains through the deposition will allow him to appraise more accurately the strength of David's case in relation to the strength of Patty's case. He will also have a more accurate idea of the points that Rene Researcher will make that will have to be refuted at trial if David is to prevail in the lawsuit. Abel Attorney, who represents Patty

Plaintiff, would most likely not want to depose Rene Researcher unless she will be traveling or will be otherwise unavailable during the anticipated dates of the trial. In that case, he might depose Rene Researcher in the form of a video, which could be preserved for trial. Usually, his deposition of his own witness would be of more benefit strategically to David Defendant than it would be to Patty Plaintiff.

Lawyers often disagree on how soon during the course of a lawsuit a deposition should be taken. Some lawyers might prefer to wait until close to trial to take Rene Researcher's deposition, because they would have had more time to conduct an investigation of all of the underlying facts and may be better prepared themselves for the deposition.

Lawyers also have very different techniques for the preparation of their witnesses prior to a deposition. Keeton (1973) has recommended that attorneys prepare the witness for a deposition as fully as would be done for the trial itself. The preparation of Rene Researcher for her deposition might include a practice session with Abel Attorney, in which he asks her questions that David's attorney, Linda Lawyer, might ask herself. It is likely that Abel Attorney will also stress the need for Rene Researcher to think about each question before she answers; to feel free to say that she does not understand a question if she does not understand; and to consult with Abel Attorney during the course of the deposition, if necessary. Abel Attorney will inform Rene Researcher that any inconsistencies between her deposition testimony and her later testimony at trial may be harmful to Patty Plaintiff's case because the jury may make inferences about her credibility based on these changes. It is for this reason that Rene Researcher's responses to questions asked must be concise and specific to the question that is actually asked.

It would not be unusual if David Defendant's attorney, Linda Lawyer, were friendlier and more gracious to Rene Researcher during the course of the deposition than during the course of the trial. This technique is often used as a way of appealing to a witness's more human side, the theory being that the witness will then be more open and forthcoming with information. A change in Linda Lawyer's demeanor from the time of the deposition to the time of the trial might also affect Rene Researcher by putting her off balance.

The deposition itself may last a very short time, or may be quite protracted and last several days. The length of the deposition is often determined by the complexity of the particular subject and the questions themselves, and the lawyers' abilities to understand both the issues and the responses that the witness provides. For instance, Rene Researcher's deposition is likely to require at least several hours if Linda Lawyer's questions include queries about the nature of the human immunodeficiency virus itself and the basis for Rene Researcher's conclusions about the transmissibility of HIV through sexual intercourse.

Sometimes the lawyer for whom the witness is testifying will want to ask questions of his or her own witness. This is most frequently done when the lawyer feels that a particular point made in response to a question needs further clarification, particularly to avoid the appearance of inconsistency at a later date. This process can also lengthen the amount of time required for the deposition.

Sometimes the two lawyers at a deposition will disagree about whether a particular question can be asked at the deposition. If the disagreement is about a question that is perceived as very important, they may actually stop the deposition. In other cases, the attorneys will decide to proceed with the rest of the deposition but to submit their dispute on a particular question to a court to decide whether or not it can be asked. These types of discussion can be very confusing to an expert witness, who does not know whether or not to answer a question that was posed. In this situation, the expert witness should follow the instructions of the attorney for whom the witness will be testifying at trial.

11.3. THE PROCESS OF CRIMINAL LITIGATION

It is not likely that an HIV researcher would be called on very often to testify in the context of a criminal trial. However, several situations may arise in which either the prosecutor or the defense attorney would want a researcher's testimony at the time of trial. This would be most likely to occur in cases arising under state, rather than federal, criminal law. For instance, an HIV-seropositive defendant may have been charged with attempted murder after having unprotected sexual intercourse with an individual who not only did not know that the defendant was positive but, to the contrary, had been told specifically by the defendant that he was negative. The prosecutor may want the researcher to testify about the probability of HIV transmission associated with an individual act of unprotected intercourse. Conversely, the defendant's attorney may also wish to have testimony on the same point. He or she may believe that, although the defendant may have wished to alarm the person with whom he had intercourse, the low risk of transmission associated with one act of intercourse negates the possibility that the defendant possessed the requisite intent to kill at the time that he committed the act. A basic understanding of procedure in criminal cases will help the researcher to understand the role that he or she is playing in the overall process.

The procedures governing the processing of a criminal case vary from state to state. This discussion will provide a general review of existing procedures in California.

The crime for which an individual is to be charged is classified as a misdemeanor or a felony. Some crimes may be placed in either category, depending on the surrounding circumstances. Misdemeanor cases are often heard in municipal court. A complaint for a misdemeanor serves as the warrant to arrest the accused individual and the legal pleading that formally accuses the individual of the crime. Felonies are heard in superior court. In felony cases, the complaint serves as the basis for the issuance of a warrant of arrest by the judge. Later, a pleading will be filed which formally accuses the individual of the crime. This legal pleading is known as the information.

After an individual is arrested, he or she will be "booked", fingerprinted, and photographed. Depending on the circumstances of the arrest and the crime charged, the individual may be subject to involuntary testing for intoxication or for HIV infection. The individual may also be tested for drug addiction, but only with his or her written consent.

Arrestees can be held for only a specified period of time before bringing them before a judge. The judge will determine whether there is "probable cause"--sufficient legal and factual basis to hold the defendant to answer. This part of the proceeding is known as the peliminary examination. It gives the defendant some idea of the prosecution's case, permits the testimony of witnesses who may be unavailable at the time of the actual trial, and affords the defendant an opportunity to raise various issues. The right to a preliminary examination can be waived by the defendant by pleading guilty before the judge at the time that the complaint is read to him or to her.

At the time of the preliminary examination, the judge can decide whether or not to reduce a felony charge to a misdemeanor. If the judge finds that there exists sufficient cause to believe that the named defendant committed the crime charged, the judge may issue an order that the defendant answer or a commitment, directing that the defendant be taken into custody. The judge may decide whether the defendant may be released, either on bail or on his or her own recognizance.

At the arraignment, the accused will be called into court and given an opportunity to hear the charges and to plead to them. Entering the plea is not part of the arraignment, but is considered a separate act. The defendant may enter into a plea bargain. If the defendant pleads not guilty, the case will be set for jury selection and trial.

11.4. CONSIDERATIONS IN SERVING AS AN EXPERT WITNESS

The Ethics of Participating as an Expert Witness

The issue of whether a scientist or researcher should appear as an expert witness has been a matter of controversy for some time. The question has been raised, for instance, as to whether the researcher is willing to foster misimpressions by his or her testimony because of the fee that he or she receives in exchange for the testimony (Cole, 1991). Individuals viewing the legal system from the outside would correctly see that both the plaintiff and the defendant offer testimony from expert witnesses who disagree with each other. Cole (1991) has explained that this is not the case of "sell-out by witnesses," but rather of "selections by attorneys" of experts. As Cole aptly explains, "it is the fact that a scientist holds to a position, and can articulate that position authoritatively, clearly and convincingly that causes him to be sought after as an expert witness and to be well paid."

The attorney for one party may try to disqualify the credibility of the expert witnesses for the other party through cross-examination, notwithstanding the experts' stature in their fields or their command of their disciplines. This is part of the adversarial process. It can be analogized in some ways to the competitive grant review process, whereby grant proposals are reviewed and scored by researcher's peers. Those proposals that can withstand minute scrutiny are most likely to be funded. Those parties in litigation whose arguments and facts "hang together" and can withstand cross-examination are most likely to be successful.

There are some aspects of testifying that should be given extensive thought prior to agreeing to testify. If the researcher is relying in whole or in part on his or her research findings as the basis of an opinion, the research data on which the researcher is relying will most likely be deemed relevant. This means that the opposing party may, in some instances, be granted the right to examine portions of the data relevant to the researcher's opinion (Federal Rules of Evidence 401, 705, 1992). For instance, if the researcher is testifying that, based on his or her research, there exists a certain probability of HIV transmission associated with a single act of vaginal intercourse, the researcher may be called on to produce the data that support that conclusion. This brings into issue whether the data collection and maintenance procedures have been structured in such a way to protect the privacy of the research participants. (See Section 5.3 for a detailed discussion of protection of data.)

Motivations for Participating as an Expert Witness

Cole (1991) has identified several motivating factors that could persuade a researcher to participate as an expert witness: advocacy of the truth; professional satisfaction; fear of illness; fear of death; desire for financial retribution; social, political, or economic advocacy; prestige; power; or remuneration. Each of these will be examined in turn.

According to Cole, participation as an expert witness allows a researcher to advocate the truth, rather than to pursue it. As a result, he asserts, the researcher can feel some professional satisfaction at having played this role. In the case of Patty Plaintiff, for instance, the defendant's expert witness may be able to ascertain from Patty's medical history that there were other risk factors for HIV transmission which she and her attorney may have minimized or overlooked. The HIV researcher may feel professional satisfaction in providing additional insight into the situation, which may ultimately assist the jury in reaching a decision regarding liability and damages.

The researcher may find that the opportunity to advocate for the truth may arise at different times during the litigation process. Prior to commencing litigation, a plaintiff's attorney may consult with the researcher to assist in determining whether the plaintiff actually has a good factual claim. The defendant's attorney may consult with a researcher to determine whether there is a solid factual basis to the plaintiff's claims and, using that assessment, may decide whether or not it is advisable to settle a claim without proceeding to litigation. A researcher may also be called on to testify in the context of a trial.

Cole asserts that the motives of fear of illness, fear of death, and the desire for retribution are rarely the motivations of the expert witness, but are often motives of the plaintiff in a personal injury action. In the HIV context, however, these emotions may play a part in the decision of a researcher to participate as an expert witness. Suppose, for instance, that the agent appointed pursuant to a durable power of attorney for health care has requested the cessation of life-sustaining treatment that is being administered to a patient. It may be appropriate to call on a clinician-researcher to testify on any of several points, depending on the specific details of the situation. These may include the research patient's capacity at different points in time, the progression of the individual's illness, and whether the patient is suffering from a "terminal condition." The researcher may not have been the participant's physician, but, in many instances, may be called on to testify based on his or her review of the patient's medical records and the expert's knowledge of current and recommended procedures for the treatment of specific conditions. The researcher's own views of lengthy and incapacitating illness and of death may play a role in his or her decision to testify. The researcher's views of the relationship between patients and systems may play a similar role in the decision to testify. A researcher who views the medical care system as nonresponsive to the needs of terminally ill patients may see the opportunity to testify as a way of seeking reform.

It is difficult to quantify power and prestige that result from serving as an expert witness. It can be assumed that a researcher who performs honestly and ethically as an expert witness will have additional opportunities in the future to serve again as a witness, presumably increasing his or her power or prestige. Although expert witnesses are often charged with "selling out" because they have received a fee for their services, Cole (1991) notes that it is more appropriately a question of "doing one's job and being paid for it."

11.5. STANDARDS FOR THE EXPERT WITNESS

The Admissibility of Evidence

The standards for qualification as an expert witness and for the admission of testimony as that of an expert vary between jurisdictions. This section will focus on the standards in federal courts, which have been adopted by many of the states.

Federal Rule of Evidence 402 permits all "relevant" evidence to be admitted, unless otherwise prohibited by the Constitution, other rules of evidence, or the Supreme Court. "Relevant" evidence is evidence that has "any tendency to make the existence of any fact that is of consequence to the determination of the action more probable or less probable than it would be without the evidence" (Federal Rule of Evidence 401, 1992). Federal Rule of Evidence 702 provides:

> If scientific, technical, or other specialized knowledge will assist the trier of fact to understand the evidence or to determine a fact in issue, a witness qualified as an expert by knowledge, skill, experience, training, or education, may testify thereto in the form of an opinion or otherwise.

The supreme Court in *Daubert v. Merrill Dow Pharmaceuticals, Inc.* (1993) analyzed the meaning and applicability of this Rule. The Court stated that the term *scientific* "implies a grounding in the methods and procedures of science." The Court further stated that for an assertion or inference to qualify as *scientific knowledge,* it "must be derived by the scientific method."

The Court enunciated four criteria that can be used in determining whether the subject of the expert's testimony qualifies as scientific knowledge and whether that knowledge will help the trier of fact to determine or to understand an issue. First, in order to qualify as scientific knowledge, the theory or technique may have been tested or may be amenable to testing. Second, the court may consider whether the theory or technique has been subjected to peer review. Third, the court may consider the known or potential rate of error associated with a particular method or technique. Fourth, the court may assess whether the method or technique is generally accepted within the relevant scientific community.

There has been a great deal of controversy about the potential impact of the *Daubert* decision on the conduct of litigation (Annas, 1994; Simon, 1993; Hutchinson, 1993). It is unclear, without actual cases as a guide, how the *Daubert* decision will impact the role of expert witnesses in cases involving HIV-related issues. However, the following scenario may well be possible.

Assume that the case of Patty Plaintiff versus David Defendant is going to trial. Patty is claiming that the sexual touching was nonconsensual because she would not have consented if David had disclosed the facts to her and that David Defendant calls as one of his expert witnesses a scientist who claims that HIV is not the causative agent of AIDS and that HIV is not transmitted via sexual intercourse or contact with other bodily fluids. Several threshold issues confront the court before David's witness will be allowed to testify.

First, the court must determine whether or not the proffered witness is actually an expert, based on education, knowledge, skill, or experience. The court must then determine whether the testimony to be offered is "scientific" and whether the admission of that testimony will assist the trier of fact to understand or determine an issue. It is impossible to predict how the court would ultimately resolve the issue. However, we can attempt a resolution by applying the principles enunciated in *Daubert*. First, the theory that HIV is not the causative agent of AIDS has not been tested, but it can be tested using the scientific method. At the present time, the majority of the scientific community believes that HIV is the causative agent of AIDS and that HIV is transmissible via blood and other bodily fluids. Consequently, the testing of this theory in humans is not possible ethically, because it would mean injecting the virus into susceptible individuals and tracking the development of the disease. There remains the issue of whether an experiment using an animal model is sufficient to answer the question of transmission in humans, particularly in view of the difficulties finding a suitable animal model for HIV research. Second, research substantiating the theory that HIV is not transmissible by blood or sexual intercourse has not been subjected to peer review. Additionally, this theory is not generally accepted within the scientific community. Under such an analysis, it is not at all certain that the expert would be allowed to testify to this theory of transmission or causation.

Reconciling Legal Causation and Scientific Causation

It is important that researchers testifying in court keep in mind the differing goals and processes of law and science. Litigation is designed as an adversarial process to resolve disputes between private parties and to compensate injured parties. Litigation also serves as a deterrent of future harm by holding the party at fault accountable for his or her actions. The judge or jury must decide the issues presented based on the facts and knowledge that are available at the time that the case is heard, even if those facts are incomplete. The decision is binding on the private litigants, except to the extent that it is modified or vacated on appeal to a higher court. Conversely, science permits continual revision of theories; the scientific method focuses on disproving accepted precepts as a means of gaining additional knowledge (Popper, 1965).

The differences in the goals of the legal and scientific processes are reflected in the operationalization of causation by each discipline. In a civil lawsuit for negligent harm, the plaintiff must establish four elements: (1) that the defendant owed the plaintiff a duty to act in a particular manner, with a degree of care; (2) that the defendant failed to act in the requisite manner; (3) that the plaintiff suffered harm; and (4) the harm suffered by the plaintiff was the result of the defendant's breach of duty, i.e., the defendant's conduct was the cause of the harm to the plaintiff. The plaintiff must prove his or her case "by a preponderance of the evidence", i.e. it must be more likely than not, or a 50.1% probability. Liability is assigned based on the determination that the plaintiff has or has not met this burden, even if there exists plausible alternative explanations for the injury claimed by plaintiff. In effect, the judge or jury is being asked to make a three-pronged determination: first, whether the defendant was negligent; second, whether that negligence caused the injury to the plaintiff; and third, whether the defendant should be held legally responsible for the harm suffered by the plaintiff (Keeton, Dobbs, Keeton, & Owen, 1984).

Epidemiology, for instance, defines causation quite differently. An exposure will be deemed a cause if it "initiates or permits, alone or in conjunction with other causes, a sequence of events, resulting in an effect" (Rothman, 1976). Some causes are sufficient, in that they will inevitably produce a specific effect. Other causes are necessary causes, in that the disease will not occur in their absence. Necessary causes, however, are not always sufficient causes (Rothman, 1986). As an example, many patients with HIV may develop tuberculosis, which results from *M. tuberculosis.* However, *M. tuberculosis* is not a sufficient cause of tuberculosis. If it were sufficient, then other factors would have no relevance to the development of tuberculosis. Such other factors might include the degree of an individual's immunosuppression, diet, and access to preventive therapy.

Susser (1991) has enumerated various factors to be considered in determining the existence of a causal association between an exposure and an effect. These include the size of the estimated risk, considering probability levels and confidence intervals; whether a given effect has a unique cause and whether a given cause has a unique effect; the persistence of an association on repeated testing; the extent to which the hypothesized causal association is consistent with preexisting knowledge and theory; and whether the causal hypothesis can predict an unknown fact that is consequent on the initial association. Hill enumerated nine factors that could be used to distinguish causal associations from noncausal associations: (1) strength; (2) consistency; (3) specificity, in that the cause under investigation leads to a single effect; (4) temporality, meaning that the supposed cause occurs before the effect; (5) dose-response, meaning that an increasing effect is produced with an increasing dose; (6) plausibility, in that the connection between the cause and the effect is biologically plausible; (7) coherence, meaning that the causal relationship does not conflict with already existing knowledge about the disease and its processes; (8) experimental evidence; and (9) analogy (Rothman, 1986).

Suppose, for instance, that a vaccine has been developed to prevent the transmission of HIV and that the vaccine is now being marketed. Paul Plaintiff has taken the vaccine and is now experiencing a neurological disorder. Suppose that epidemiological studies examining the relationship between the neurological disorder and the HIV vaccine concluded that there might be a causative link between the disorder and the vaccine if the onset of the disorder occurred ten weeks or less after the administration of the vaccine. There are, however, alternative explanations for the occurrence of the neurological disorder in a given population. Additionally, the vaccinated attack rates for later-onset cases are extremely close to the range of unvaccinated baseline rates. If Paul Plaintiff's disorder began within ten weeks after having received the vaccine, and he can prove receipt of the vaccine, it is likely that a court would find in his favor against the manufacturer of the vaccine, notwithstanding the fact that there may exist other explanations for the onset of the disorder in Paul's individual case at that time. If, however, Paul's disorder began more than ten weeks after the administration of the vaccine, he will have a more difficult time proving his case legally, although the vaccine may have actually been the cause of the disorder in his case.

The example of Paul Plaintiff illustrates well the "sensitivity and specificity" of standards of legal causation. If the standard for establishing legal causation is set too high, individuals who have been injured as the result of an exposure will not be compensated. They are, in essence, the false negatives. If the standard is set too low, individuals who have not been injured from the exposure in question will be allowed to recover. These individuals are equivalent to false positives. Figure 11.3 illustrates this dilemma.

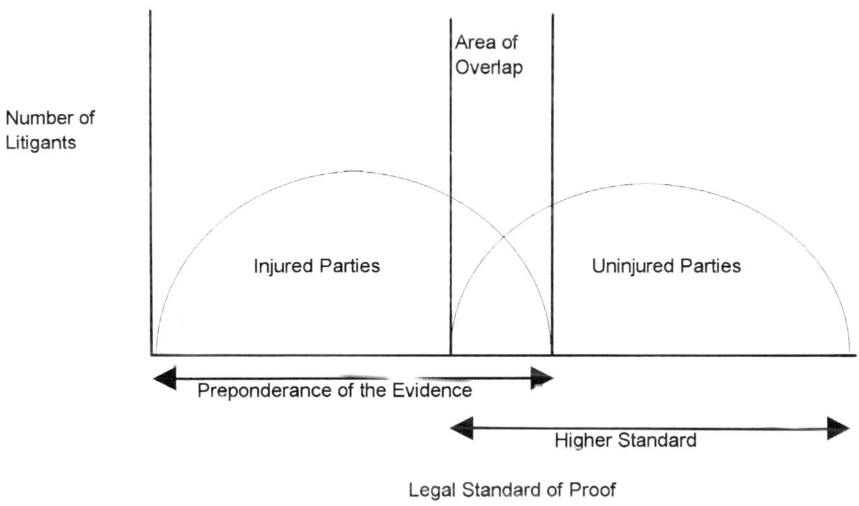

Figure 11.3. "Sensitivity and specificity" of legal standards in relation to causation and recovery.

11.6. CONCLUSION

The legal system often appears very complex and unwelcoming. HIV researchers may ask themselves why they would want to become participants in that system on any level, and why they would wish to subject themselves to the ordeal of cross-examination in the courtroom. The legal system will appear much less threatening, however, if it is viewed as a process, much the same way that the scientific method constitutes a process. It is a process by which the legal system attempts to discover Truth, not Truth for all time, as scientists might wish to do, but Truth in the context of a particular situation, with particular parties, at a specific point in time. The discovery and courtroom procedures can be analogized to the collection and entry of data, and peer review (by judge or jury) of the ultimate conclusions of each side (attorney). By bringing his or her particular expertise to this process, the researcher helps to maintain the integrity of the process and, perhaps, a more accurate result.

CHAPTER TWELVE

The HIV Researcher and Legislative Advocacy

There are multiple opportunities for an HIV researcher to participate in the legislative process as an advocate. The researcher can draft a bill or an amendment to a bill and present the proposal to a legislator; write, call, or visit a legislator to express his or her views on an existing bill or to express an idea for a bill or an amendment; testify at a hearing on an issue or bill, if one is held; involve or organize other interested persons to participate in the process; or hire a lobbyist to represent his or her interests in the legislature (Davies, 1986).

This chapter reviews the legislative process of the federal government and provides a summary of state legislative process. States differ in their processes for the passage and implementation of legislation, and all 50 states cannot be reviewed here. The chapter addresses the ethics of an HIV researcher serving as an advocate in the legislative arena. It concludes with a case example, that of legislation for a needle exchange program. Varying strategies are discussed in the context of the needle exchange example.

12.1. THE LEGISLATIVE PROCESS

Federal Legislation—An Overview

The U.S. Congress consists of the Senate and the House of Representatives. Once a senator or representative agrees to author a bill, he or she will introduce the bill and it will be referred to the appropriate standing committee. The committee may refer the bill to a subcommittee, or hold an open or closed hearing. It is more likely that a hearing will be held if the bill deals with an issue of great importance. The committee must then decide how to proceed on the bill. It has several options, including "pigeonholing" or disregarding the bill, defeating the bill, accepting the bill with or without amendment and reporting it, or rewriting the bill.

With some exceptions for major bills, the bill will be submitted to the floor of the House for general debate, the second reading, and amendment, if necessary. The bill will then proceed to the third reading and either passage or defeat.

The entire process is repeated in the second house. If the versions differ between the houses of Congress, a conference committee may try to work out the differences between the versions. If agreement is reached, the Speaker and the Vice President will sign the bill. The President must then approve the bill, veto or pocket veto the bill, or permit the bill to become law without his signature (Martineau, 1991).

State Legislation—An Overview

Almost all state legislatures are composed of two houses, the senate and the assembly (or house of representatives). Nebraska, unlike other states, has only one house in its legislature. Members of each house belong to committees, much as in the federal system. Each committee is responsible for a given subject area. The committees may be further divided into subcommittees to address particular subject areas or bills, or to take testimony, redraft language, and develop the consensus necessary before a bill is submitted to the full committee and to the floor. Most committees screen a multitude of bills in order to select a few for submission to the floor of the legislative body. Once a bill is selected for submission to the floor, it may be debated, sent back to the committee for modifications, defeated, or signed into law.

The California legislature, for example, consists of the Senate, the smaller of the two houses, and the Assembly. An interested person or group may attempt to persuade a legislator in either house to author or to sponsor a bill. If the legislator agrees to author the bill, the idea or draft bill is sent to the Legislative Counsel, where it is drafted into the actual bill. If the bill is already in bill form when it is sent to the Legislative Counsel, the latter will polish and refine it. The bill will then be returned to the sponsoring legislator. It will undergo its "first reading," after which the bill is sent to the Office of State Printing. No bill may be acted on until it has been in print for at least 30 days.

After the 30-day period, the bill is assigned to the appropriate committee to be heard. Bills passed by committees are eventually explained to the full house by the author, and the bills are then debated. If a bill passes the parent house, it will be sent to the other house, where it will undergo the same process again. If the bill is amended in the second house, it must then go back to the parent house in order to reach agreement on the amendments. If no agreement is reached, the bill moves to a two-house conference committee to resolve the differences. The conference committee holds hearings which are open to the public.

If the bill is passed by both houses, it will go to the governor. The governor must decide whether to sign it into law, to allow it to become law without his or her signature, or to veto it. A veto may be overridden by a two-thirds vote of both houses (Senate Select Committee on Citizen Participation in Government, 1989).

12.2. THE ETHICS OF PARTICIPATING AS AN ADVOCATE

The appropriateness of researchers assuming an advocacy role has often been questioned. Rothman and Poole (1985) have asserted that a researcher's participation in public advocacy is inappropriate. They would entertain the possibility of an epidemiologist participating in the advocacy process only in his or her role as a private citizen (Poole & Rothman, 1990). Last (1991a) holds epidemiologists to the "highest standards of scientific honesty, integrity and impartiality." Although he notes that advocacy, the opposite of impartiality, is often required to address existing health risks, he resolves the apparent conflict by focusing on the need for sound scientific judgment, rather than impartiality (Last, 1991a,b). Weed (1994) justifies advocacy in epidemiology based on the principle of beneficence. Bankowski (1991) explains well the relationship between scientific research and beneficence:

> Epidemiology is a means of quantifying injustice in relation to health care, of monitoring progress towards justice, beneficence, non-maleficence, and respect for persons, as these ethical principles apply to society, and of applying its findings to the control of health problems. That those at the political level charged with safeguarding the public health often neglect or find it inconvenient, or even impractical, to apply epidemiological findings, sometimes because the more vulnerable populations or groups lack the power to assert or safeguard their rights, often because of the complexity of prioritizing resource allocation, does not invalidate epidemiology. Rather, that this happens

> is a reason for emphasizing the relation between ethics and human values and health policy-making, and for an ethics of public health, concerned with social justice as well as individual rights, to complement the ethics of medicine.

Gordis (1991) envisions that the epidemiologist will play role in the policy-making process by presenting data, interpreting the data, and utilizing the data in developing and evaluating policy proposals. He acknowledges that there remains a question as to whether a researcher's credibility will be lessened if he or she takes a strong advocacy position on a particular issue. Gordis notes, however, that

> [a]n additional consideration is that since our [epidemiologists'] data have important societal implications, if we [epidemiologists] want society to continue to support our efforts we will have to demonstrate the value of our research for the health of the public. This can only be done if we broaden our responsibility from the research only role to that of policy-related functions.
>
> Thus, the epidemiologist must also serve as an educator. Her efforts are directed at many target populations including other scientists, legislators, policy makers, lawyers and judges, and the public. Each must be dealt with differently depending on the specific needs of that population and the objectives towards which the educational effort is directed.

Ultimately, each HIV researcher will have to decide for him- or herself the advisability of participating as an advocate. Cogent arguments support the appropriateness of such a role, but there are clearly professional consequences to be considered in assuming that responsibility.

12.3. CASE EXAMPLE: LEGISLATION FOR A NEEDLE EXCHANGE PROGRAM

Preliminary Issues

It is crucial to the success of legislative advocacy efforts that a proposal for a bill or, better yet, a draft of a bill, be presented to a potential sponsor of the legislation in as finished a form as possible. The draft of the bill should be supported by written documentation that explains the need for the bill and provides sufficient documentation to justify a legislator's interest and support of the bill.

Table 12.1 provides a listing of the issues that must be considered prior to contacting a legislator regarding his or her interest and willing-

Table 12.1. Preliminary Issues to Be Addressed Prior to Seeking Legislative Sponsorship for Needle Exchange Legislation

1. Legal issues
   What is current law with respect to each of the following?
   a. Possession of needles and syringes without a prescription
   b. Distribution of needles and syringes
   c. The availability of needles and syringes over the counter
   d. The ability of local government to declare an emergency situation and the implications of such a declaration if one is possible
2. Political issues
   a. Who are the key players on this issue? Where do they stand? Publicly or privately?
   b. Who needs to be on board with this issue to make an advocacy effort successful?
   c. What is the best way to approach various communities (ethnic, religious, civic, etc.) for their support of the issue so that they will urge their legislators to support it?
3. What data support the need for a needle exchange program in the state?
   a. What is the HIV seroprevalence rate?
   b. What is the HIV seroprevalence rate in injecting drug users (IDUs) in the state?
   c. How many IDUs are in treatment?
      - Of the IDUs in treatment, what proportion is receiving HIV-related prevention services?
      - What is the nature and extent of the HIV-prevention services being provided?
   d. How many IDUs are not in treatment?
   e. How many treatment slots are currently available for IDUs and how many are projected to be available over the next 5 to 10 years?
   f. What is the incidence and prevalence of other diseases transmitted through shared needle use?
      - Hepatitis
      - Bacterial endocarditis
   g. What are the current costs for each of the following in the state?
      - Lifetime cost of care per HIV-infected individual

Table 12.1. *Continued*

- The cost of treatment per episode of hepatitis B, hepatitis C, or bacterial endocarditis
- The cost of treatment per treatment episode per IDU and the median/mean/range of number of treatment episodes for IDUs
- The cost of alternative care arrangements for uninfected minor children of HIV-infected IDUs: (1) costs for alternative housing, such as foster care, (2) court costs related to child placement, (3) social service costs
- The cost of care for children infected through vertical transmission from IDU: (1) medical care costs, (2) social service costs, (3) housing costs
- Costs for the cleanup of publicly disposed needles and syringes
- Personnel costs associated with needlestick injuries, such as police injured during a frisk

h. What are the projected costs and benefits of a needle exchange program?

- Actual costs
- Projected costs savings compared to current expenditures resulting from status quo
- The impact on the health care system
- The impact on the social service system
- Potential number of years of life saved and number of lives projected to be saved
- The projected decrease in public disposal of needles and syringes and associated costs savings

ness to sponsor legislation supportive of a needle exchange program. A researcher who supports the implementation of needle exchange programs based on his or her objective assessment of their impact on the transmission of HIV and other bloodborne diseases, will bring invaluable skills and insights to the advocacy process. First, the researcher will be helpful in assisting with the compilation and interpretation of data pertaining to the incidence and prevalence of HIV infection and other infections transmitted via shared needles and syringes in a given community, and the projected impact of a needle exchange program on those rates. Researchers with a background in economics will be able to provide estimates on the cost savings to the medical and social service systems that would result from the implementation of a legalized needle exchange program. Additionally, HIV researchers who have been active in the policy arena previously may be able to identify key players on this issue, and advise the legislator of potential alliances or battles.

It is important to recognize that researchers may have differing views as to the value of a needle exchange program in a particular community. Consequently, some researchers may align themselves with legislators who are opposed to this legislation and provide differing interpretations of existing data. For instance, suppose that a community has a very low rate of injecting drug use, drug treatment is available on demand, and there are extremely low rates of hepatitis B virus and HIV among the injecting drug population of that community. In such a situation, a needle exchange program may not be advisable. Other options may be more viable, including the purchase of needles and syringes through pharmacies.

Drafting the Legislation

Much has been written on strategies for drafting legislation (Davies, 1986). There are a few basic principles that seem to be time-honored techniques.

First, it is helpful to review similar legislation that has been drafted and passed in other jurisdictions. For instance, if an HIV researcher in Montana wished to participate in drafting specific sections of a needle exchange bill, he or she might consult the legislation already in place in Connecticut or New York, where the legislatures have reviewed and implemented legislation permitting such programs.

It is important that the individual or individuals with primary responsibility for drafting a bill have the draft reviewed by other individuals from multiple disciplines for their critical comments. For instance, if a lawyer formulated the initial draft of a needle exchange bill, it will be important that he or she have it reviewed by medical personnel, public health personnel, education personnel, and others to ensure the accuracy of the statements contained in the bill and to get the benefit of varied perspectives from multiple disciplines.

The legislature has an office that will modify the bill to have it conform to the accepted style. The advocates of the bill may be able to access this service with the help of the legislative sponsor of the bill.

It is beyond the scope of this text to address problems of statutory construction: how legislation is to be interpreted when it conflicts with already existing legislation or when it is ambiguous. Basically, problems such as these will be less likely to arise in the future in connection with the needle exchange legislation, once passed, if the bill was drafted clearly and is limited in its scope.

Seeking Sponsorship

A bill is more likely to succeed if it is supported by as broad a coalition of sponsors as possible. For example, legislation favoring the implementation of a needle exchange program is more likely to succeed if it is supported by legislators who represent both rural and urban areas and by legislators from more than one political party. Advocacy efforts will be most effective and efficient if the sponsors of the legislation include legislators who are members of the committees that have jurisdiction over the subject matter of the bill. Efforts at locating sponsors may be enhanced if the individuals seeking sponsorship represent a broad coalition. For instance, if the advocates of the needle exchange legislation include medical personnel, HIV researchers, attorneys, pharmaceutical representatives, HIV-infected individuals, and substance abuse professionals, it will be easier to locate a legislator willing to sponsor the bill than if the sole supporter of the draft bill is an HIV researcher.

Introduction of the Bill and Committee Action

After sponsors of the bill have been located and have signed their names to the bill, it will be introduced. It will most likely be referred to a standing committee. Once the bill has been referred to the committee, the advocates must move into high gear. It is important to request time on the committee agenda to be heard on the issue. In California, for instance, a bill will be heard in committee either in the order in which it appears in the Daily File, or in the order in which the authors of the bills to be considered sign in at the hearing. The committee secretary should be consulted to verify which procedure will be followed (Senate Select Committee on Citizen Participation in Government, 1989).

It is important to remember that even though the needle exchange bill is set for hearing on a particular date, that may not actually come to pass. There may not be a sufficient amount of time to hear all of the bills scheduled. This is particularly true if some of the bills require lengthy debate because of their controversial nature. If the bill is not heard, it will be rescheduled for another time. Because a needle exchange bill is likely to be quite controversial in many localities, it is very likely that it would be scheduled to be heard at a particular time, as a "special order of business" (Senate Select Committee on Citizen Participation in Government, 1989). It is very unlikely that a needle exchange bill would be heard on a "consent calendar," because that designated time is devoted to the review and disposition of bills identified by committee report as noncontroversial.

The most effective lobbying generally occurs while a bill is in committee. It will be important to mobilize supporters of the legislation to write to their representatives, urging their support of the legislation. The HIV researcher may be able to play a key role while the bill is in committee by offering testimony on key points. It will be important to obtain a copy of the committee's analysis of the bill and to prepare the testimony to address the questions raised in that analysis. The committee will give time to both the opponents and proponents of particular legislation. Consequently, the supporters of the needle exchange legislation, including the HIV researcher, should know the arguments that the bill's opponents will make and should be ready to counter them. The researcher should notify the sponsor's office of his or her desire to testify on the bill.

If the committee recommends passage of the bill, it will be sent to the floor of that legislative house with a favorable recommendation. Although the bill will be debated on the floor, participation in the debate is limited to members of the legislature. The public may, however, attend.

If the bill is passed in both houses of the legislature, it will be sent to the governor for signature or veto. It is important that advocates for the bill use this opportunity to communicate their support for the legislation directly to the governor's office, either by phone or by letter. A support letter from a researcher should be short and concise, and can summarize the scientific or public health basis for the implementation of a needle exchange program.

Appropriations

It is important to understand the difference between authorizing expenditures for the implementation of legislation and appropriating monies to do so. The passage of the needle exchange bill, for instance, may explicitly authorize the expenditure of monies for its implementation. However, until money is actually appropriated for the program, it is a program without a real existence.

The process for passing an appropriations bill is the same as that for other legislation. However, even when a bill appropriates monies for a program, the program may not be funded. For instance, suppose the needle exchange legislation passes both houses of the state legislature. The appropriations committee allocates money for that program.However, the governor may decide to veto the needle exchange item as a single item in the appropriations bill.

12.4. CONCLUSION

All too often, legislators must develop a coherent response to a perceived problem without having all of the expertise that would be desired. The issue of needle exchange programs as a response to increased HIV transmission is but one example of such a situation. Legislators may be swayed by the emotions of their constituents, who they have promised to represent. The participation of the HIV researcher in the legislative process ensures that the relevant facts will come before those who are in a position to effectuate change, whether it is by drafting, sponsoring, or supporting legislation. The HIV researcher, by virtue of his or her scientific training, can inject rationality into the process. Legislators may, in fact, be more accountable for their actions where researchers have presented relevant data or have explained the reasons for existing scientific uncertainty.

CHAPTER THIRTEEN

The HIV Researcher in the Regulatory Arena

The HIV researcher can participate in the regulatory process in a number of ways. The researcher can send comments to the appropriate agency once the agency has published the draft of a rule. For example, the Occupational Safety and Health Administration of the United States Department of Labor received many comments in response to its proposed rule governing occupational exposure to bloodborne pathogens (56 Federal Register 64004, 1991). The researcher can also petition the appropriate agency for the issuance, amendment, or appeal of a rule, or participate in negotiated rule-making. Researchers may also be consulted by the agency to assist with the initial conception of the rule, the collection and analysis of relevant data, and the initial review of the draft rule. Figure 13.1 illustrates the possible roles of the HIV researcher as the development of a rule progresses.

This chapter provides an overview of the regulatory process at the federal and state levels, using California as an example of the state process, since the various states have different processes. It also discusses the ethics of a researcher participating in the regulatory process. The final section of the chapter provides an example of a researcher participating in the regulatory process, in the context of HIV.

13.1. THE REGULATORY PROCESS

The Federal Process

The executive branch of the government includes many agencies, each of which has jurisdiction over a particular subject area. Agencies

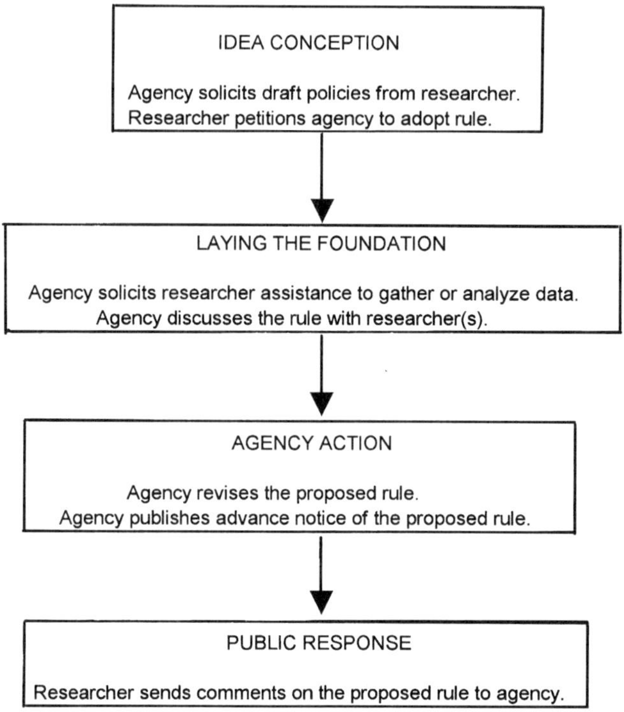

Figure 13.1. Researcher roles during the regulatory process. Not all of the tasks necessary for the promulgation of a rule are illustrated, but only the different stages at which a researcher may participate in the process.

with the designated authority to do so may promulgate regulations in the subject area of jurisdiction.

The Administrative Procedure Act created minimum uniform rule-making procedures which enable the public to participate in the rule-making process. The Act requires that an agency adhere to three basic steps in promulgating rules:

1. The agency must issue notice of the proposed rule-making.
2. The agency must provide an opportunity for the public to comment on the proposed rule.
3. The agency must provide a concise, general statement of the basis and purpose of any rules that are ultimately adopted [5 United States Code section 533(b), 1977].

These three steps are known as the "notice and comment" procedure. The statute requires that the notice of the proposed rule-making include three items:

1. A statement of the time, place, and nature of the public rule-making proceedings
2. A reference to the legal authority which provides the basis for the promulgation of the proposed rule
3. The terms or substance of the proposed rule or a description of the issues to which it relates [5 United States Code section 553(b), 1977].

Exceptions to the notice and comment requirements are

1. Interpretive rules
2. "General statements of policy"
3. "Rules of agency organization, procedure, or practice"
4. When the agency finds "that notice and public procedure thereon are . . . impracticable, unnecessary, or contrary to the public interest"
5. Rule-making on a record
[5 United States Code sections 553(b)(A), (B), 1977].

Although these types of rules are not subject to the notice and comment procedure, their importance should not be minimized. An interpretive rule does not alter substantive rights, but presents the agency's view of what the existing law means. The courts will usually give great deference to an agency's interpretation of the applicable law (Gellhorn & Levin, 1990). Interpretive rules and general statements of policy can be treated as having the force of law if they were promulgated properly (*Chrysler Corporation v. Brown*, 1979).

Any interested person or group may contact the appropriate agency or person to discuss a draft rule (O'Reilly, 1983). A list of the federal regulatory agencies, their functions, responsibilities, personnel, and field offices can be found in *Congressional Quarterly's Federal Regulatory Directory.* It is helpful and most efficient to contact the appropriate agency from the beginning of the process.

Notice and Comment

By the time a proposed rule is in the notice and comment phase, it has been reviewed and revised by numerous people. Consequently, the most useful comments are not those that address whether the rule should be promulgated at all, but rather those that focus on particular problems with the proposed rule. Helpful comments are those that highlight the weaknesses of specific language, acquaint the agency staff with unforeseen practical consequences stemming from the proposed rule, supplies facts and data that may have been overlooked, or seek exceptions for specific circumstances (Edles & Nelson, 1993).

Petition

The Administrative Procedure Act allows an interested person to petition a particular agency for the "issuance, amendment, or repeal of a rule" [5 United States Code section 553(e), 1977]. The petitioning process can be initiated by sending a letter to the appropriate agency. The agency's denial can also take the form of a letter (Koch, 1985). If the petition is successful, it will produce a notice of proposed rule-making. If the agency denies the petition, the agency must issue a brief statement explaining the reasons for the denial. It is unclear whether the agency's denial of the rule-making petition is subject to review by the courts (Edles & Nelson, 1993).

Negotiated Rule-Making

The text of a proposed rule may be open to negotiation. In a typical regulatory negotiation, concerned interest groups and the agency itself send representatives to bargaining sessions that are led by a mediator. The resulting agreement is then forwarded to the agency, which publishes it as a proposed rule and follows through with the rule-making procedure under the Administrative Procedure Act (Gellhorn & Levin, 1990). The process of negotiated rulemaking has been used by the Environmental Protection Agency, the Nuclear Regulatory Commission, and the Department of Agriculture, among others.

California Regulatory Procedures

Notice Procedure

The Office of Administrative Law publishes *The Rulemaking Calendar* each year in March. This publication lists the regulations that agencies are planning to take action on during the upcoming year. Single copies are available from the Office of Administrative Law on request. This calendar is also distributed to those who subscribe to the *California Administrative Notice Register.* Additionally, state agencies are required to maintain a mailing list of those individuals and entities that wish to be notified of proposed regulatory actions.

Agencies will most often draft a revised or new regulation in-house. On some occasions, an agency may issue a "notice of intent" via the *Notice Register* or persons on the agency's mailing list as an informal invitation to participate in the drafting of the new or revised regulation. Once the draft text appears satisfactory, the agency will initiate the more formal notice and public comment procedure.

The published notice of the proposed regulation may not contain the exact text. The text can be requested from the agency promulgating the regulation. The Initial Statement of Reasons, which describes the public problem to be addressed by the regulation and the information supporting the proposed change, is not included in the *Notice Register.* A copy may be requested from the agency. The agency must provide the public with access to any background data on which it is relying to promulgate the regulation.

Generally, an agency must follow the notice and comment procedure each time it wishes to adopt, repeal, or amend a regulation. The public announcement must invite public comment and include the time and place for receiving public comment. However, an agency can pass an "emergency regulation" without going through the notice and comment procedure if it first makes a finding that there exists an immediate threat to the public health and welfare. The Office of Administrative Law must support that finding. In such a situation, the agency has 120 days to adopt the regulation on a permanent basis following the usual public notice and comment procedure. The 120-day deadline can be extended by the Office of Administrative Law for good cause.

Comment Procedure

Comments on the proposed regulation can be in the form of a letter. The letter should focus on the substantive aspects of the proposed change and the extent to which the proposed regulation meets the six statutory standards of necessity, authority, clarity, consistency, reference, and nonduplication. The comment period extends for 45 days.

Sometimes the agency will set a public hearing on the proposed regulation. If no public hearing has been set, the researcher or other member of the public may request one, at least 15 days prior to the end of the public comment period. The public hearing is an excellent opportunity to present arguments in support of or against a proposed regulation. Those who testify should take a written copy of their comments with them, and present them to the agency so that they will have an immediate written record of them.

If the agency makes changes related to the original text following the 45-day comment period, it must afford the public an additional 15 days to comment. The agency must mail a written notice to all individuals who presented written or oral testimony during the original 45-day comment period, as well as anyone who has requested notification of any changes to the originally proposed regulation. The notice advising of the additional 15 days for comment must contain the original text of the regulation, with the changes clearly marked. If the agency decides to make very significant changes, a new notice and 45-day public comment period is required.

Following the notice and comment period, the agency will compile the rule-making record and file it with the Office of Administrative Law. That office will then review the record to ensure that the text of the regulation was made available to the public during the comment period; that the language of the adopted regulation is identical to that presented to the public for comment; that the text of changes related to the original text after the comment period closed was made available to members of the public for an additional 15 days; and that substantive changes were made available to the public for comment for an additional 45 days. The Office of Administrative Law does not have the authority to review regulations relating to rates, prices, or tariffs; public works; or rules directed at a specific person or group of persons.

The Office of Administrative Law must complete its review within 30 days after its receipt of the rule-making record. Approved regulations are filed with the California Secretary of State. Decisions disapproving the regulations are published in the *Notice Register,* and the regulation is returned to the promulgating agency with an explanation as to why it was disapproved. The agency may appeal the disapproval decision by filing a request for review with the Governor's Legal Affairs Secretary, with a copy to the Office of Administrative Law. The Governor will decide the appeal within 15 days after he or she has received the Office of Administrative Law's response to the agency's request.

Petition Process

Like the federal government, California permits a member of the public to petition an agency directly to adopt, amend, or appeal existing regulations. In order to be considered, the petition must be directed to the appropriate agency and must contain a statement describing the action requested, the reason the request is being made, and the basis for the agency's authority to implement the requested action. The agency must acknowledge the petition within 30 days of its receipt and must either deny the petition, with an explanation of its reasoning, or schedule the matter for public hearing. The petitioning individual may, if dissatisfied with the agency's response, request a reconsideration of the request within 60 days from the date of the agency's decision on the original petition.

13.2. THE ETHICS OF REGULATORY ADVOCACY

Arguments both for and against the participation of HIV researchers as advocates in the regulatory policy arena mirror those raised in the judicial and legislative contexts. Gordis (1991) has stressed epidemiologists' educational and interpretive functions, and the need to direct educational efforts to policymakers. The structure of the regulatory process allows the HIV researcher to confine his or her role to the interpretation of science and the evaluation of regulations' impact. As an example, assume that a state or federal agency has promulgated proposed regulations governing procedures to be implemented in a clinical work setting to reduce the occupational risk of HIV transmission. An HIV researcher with substantial knowledge relating to HIV transmission can provide valuable comments regarding the potential effectiveness of the proposed procedures.

13.3. CASE EXAMPLE: REGULATIONS RELATING TO CLINICAL TRIALS

We have examined at length the requirements for the conduct of clinical research with prisoner-participants. Suppose that the Department of Health and Human Services wished to broaden the circumstances in which research could be conducted in prisons. Such a change is fairly substantial and could not qualify as an interpretive rule, a statement of policy, or a rule of agency organization, any of which would be exempt from the notice and comment procedure.

HHS would publish in the Federal Register a notice including a reference to the legal authority providing the basis for the promulgation of the amended regulation; the text of the proposed rule; the place where written comments should be forwarded; and the closing deadline for the receipt of comments if they are to be considered.

Depending on the content of the regulation, the HIV researcher's comments could address the relationship between the broadened areas of research and the benefits and burdens to the inmates that would result from the proposed change. Other researchers might underscore the difficulties of ensuring the personal safety of the research staff conducting research with prisoners and the potential increased complexity of such efforts if the numbers of prisoners participating were to increase as a result of the regulatory expansion. Clearly, a researcher's comments should relate to his or her area of expertise, and should be supported by available data and references. HHS would then publish a response to these comments in the Federal Register, and reasons for incorporating them into the rule or for declining to incorporate them.

13.4. CONCLUSION

The administrative process presents a unique opportunity for HIV researchers to educate policymakers and lawmakers in a meaningful and significant way. Processes are in place by which a researcher can comment on a proposed regulation or suggest the promulgation of a new or better one. This role may be particularly appealing to researchers who would prefer not to assume the role of an "advocate," and who would prefer to maintain the role of an objective onlooker or evaluator.

Conclusion

It seems almost trite to say that there are neither easy issues nor easy solutions in the context of HIV research. HIV has highlighted the multiple problems faced by all societies, including differential access to medical care and biomedical research, discrimination in multiple arenas against segments of society that lack both the political force and the economic base to halt such practices, and the disintegration of family and social networks as a result of debilitating and financially costly illness. Our increasing experience during the HIV pandemic has underscored the complexity of HIV research, as we now grapple to find treatments, cures, preventive therapies, and educational interventions that are both effective and appropriate for persons of diverse races, ethnicities, cultures, languages, religions, ages, genders, and sexual orientation.

There is an old saying that one never steps into the same river twice. As we learn more, the questions may themselves change, necessitating a reexamination of the answers that we thought we once had. The material contained in this book provides a foundation for the development of these new questions and new solutions.

References

Ackerman, T. F. (1989). An ethical framework for the practice of paying research subjects. *IRB, 11,* 1–4.

Ackerman, T. F. (1990). Protectionism and the new research imperative in pediatric AIDS. *IRB, 12,* 1–5.

Adkinson, N. F., Starklauf, B. L., & Blake, D. A. (1983). How can an IRB avoid the use of obsolete consent forms? *IRB, 5,* 10–11.

Altman, D. G., Chalmers, I., & Herxheimer, A. (1994). Is there a case for an international medical scientific press council? *Journal of the American Medical Association, 272,* 166–167.

Altman, L. K. (1993, July 27). Faith in multiple-drug AIDS trial shaken by report of error in lab. *New York Times,* p. C3.

American Medical Association. (1989). Current Opinions of the Judicial Council, Current Opinion 5.05. In McDonald, B. A. Ethical problems for physicians raised by AIDS and HIV infection: Conflicting legal obligations of confidentiality and disclosure. University of California at Davis 22, 557–592.

American Psychological Association. (1982). *Ethical principles in the conduct of research with human participants.* Washington, DC: Author.

Andrews v. Eli Lilly & Company, 97 F.R.D. 494 (N.D. Ill. 1983).

Annas, G. J. (1989). Faith (healing), hope and charity at the FDA: The politics of AIDS drug trials. *Villanova Law Review, 34,* 771–797.

Annas, G. J. (1994). Scientific evidence in the courtroom: The death of the Frye rule. *New England Journal of Medicine, 330,* 1018–1021.

Annas, G. J., & Grodin, M. A. (Eds.). (1992). *The Nazi doctors and the Nuremberg Code: Human rights in human experimentation.* London: Oxford University Press.

Appelbaum, P. S., Lidz, C. W., & Meisel, A. (1987). *Informed consent: Legal theory and clinical practice.* London: Oxford University Press.

Appelbaum, P. S., & Rosenbaum, A. (1989). Tarasoff and the researcher: Does the duty to protect apply in the research setting? *American Psychologist, 44,* 885–894.

Appler, W. D. (1988). The FDA's treatment rule—A glimpse into the future of drug regulation in the U.S.? *Food, Drug, & Cosmetic Law Journal, 43,* 649–658.

Application of American Tobacco Company, 880 F.2d 1520 (2nd Cir. 1989).

Application of R. J. Reynolds Tobacco Company, 136 Misc.2d 282, 328 N.Y.S. 729 (1987).

Arnold, A. J. (1991). Developing, testing, and marketing and AIDS vaccine: Legal concerns for manufacturers. *University of Pennsylvania Law Review, 139,* 1076–1121.

Arras, J. D. (1990). Noncompliance in AIDS research. *Hastings Center Report, 20,* 24–32.

Association of American Medical Colleges. (1990). *Guidelines for dealing with faculty conflicts of commitment and conflicts of interest in research.* Washington, DC: AAMC Ad Hoc Committee on Misconduct and Conflict of Interest in Research.

Avins, A. L., & Lo, B. (1989). To tell or not to tell: The ethical dilemmas of HIV test notification in epidemiologic research. *American Journal of Public Health, 79,* 1544–1548.

Ballard, E. L., Nash, F., Raiford, K., & Harrell, L. E. (1993). Recruitment of black elderly for clinical research studies of dementia: The CERAD experience. *Gerontologist, 33,* 561–565.

Bankowski, Z. (1991). Epidemiology, ethics and 'health for all.' *Law, Medicine & Health Care, 19,* 162–163.

Barinaga, M. (1992). Who controls a researcher's files? *Science, 256,* 1620–1621.

Barry, M., & Molyneux, M. (1992). Ethical dilemmas in malaria drug and vaccine trials: A bioethical perspective. *Journal of Medical Ethics, 18,* 189–192.

Batterman, J. S. (1990). Brother can you spare a drug: Should the experimental drug distribution standards be modified in response to the needs of persons with AIDS? *Hofstra Law Review, 19,* 191–228.

Bayer, R. (1993). The ethics of blinded HIV surveillance testing. *American Journal of Public Health, 83,* 496–497.

Bayer, R., Levine, C., & Murray, T. H. (1984). Guidelines for confidentiality in research on AIDS. *IRB, 6,* 1–7.

Bayer, R., Lumey, L. H., & Wan, L. (1991). The American, British and Dutch responses to unlinked HIV seroprevalence studies: An international comparison. *Law, Medicine & Health Care, 19,* 222–229.

Bayer, R., & Toomey, K. E. (1992). HIV prevention and the two faces of partner notification. *American Journal of Public Health, 82,* 1158–1164.

Beauchamp, T. L., Cook, R. R., Fayerweather, W. E., Raabe, G. K., Thar, W. E., Cowles, S. R., & Spivey, G. H. (1991). Ethical guidelines for epidemiologists. *Journal of Clinical Epidemiology, 44* (Suppl. 1), 151S–169S.

Begay v. United States, 768 F.2d 1059 (9th Cir. 1985).

Bein, P. M. (1991). Surrogate consent and the incompetent experimental subject. *Food, Drug & Cosmetic Law Journal, 46,* 739–771.

Benson, K. R. (1991a). Fraud and misconduct in science: Crimes, misdemeanors, and the nine circles of hell. *Cancer Bulletin, 43,* 319–323.

Benson, K. R. (1991b). Science and the single author: Historical reflections on the problem of authorship. *Cancer Bulletin, 43,* 324–331.

Benson, P. R., Roth, L. H., Appelbaum, P. S., Lidz, C. W., & Winslade, W. J. (1988). Information disclosure, subject understanding, and informed consent in psychiatric research. *Law and Human Behavior, 12,* 455–475.

Bergkamp, L. (1988). Research ethics committees and the regulation of medical experimentation with human beings in the Netherlands. *Medicine & Law, 7,* 65–72.

Berglund, C. A. (1990). Australian standards for privacy and confidentiality of health records in research: Implications of the Commonwealth Privacy Act. *Medical Journal of Australia, 152,* 664–669.

Bigorra, J., & Banos, J. E. (1990). Weight of financial reward in the decision by medical students and experienced healthy volunteers to participate in clinical trials. *European Journal of Clinical Pharmacology, 38,* 443–446.

Binder, M. (1989). Ethical issues in academic science: Lecture to conjoint 521. Washington: University of Washington. Cited in Benson, K. R. (1991). Fraud and misconduct in science: Crimes, misdemeanors, and the nine circles of hell. *Cancer Bulletin, 43,* 319–323.

Birkett, N. (1993). Confidentiality and research. *Canadian Medical Association Journal, 148,* 486–487.

Bjune, G., & Arnesen, O. (1992). Problems related to informed consent from young teenagers participating in efficacy testing of a new vaccine. *IRB, 14,* 6–9.

Boccellari, A., & Zeifert, P. (1994). Management of neurobehavioral impairment in HIV-1 infection. *Psychiatric Clinics of North America, 1,* 183–203.

Boffey, P. M. (1987, December 28). Trial of AIDS drug in U. S. lags as too few participants enroll. *New York Times,* p. A1.

Boruch, R. F. (1984). Should private agencies maintain federal research data? *IRB, 6,* 8–9.

Boruch, R. F., & Cecil, J. S. (1979). *Assuring the confidentiality of social research data.* Philadelphia: University of Pennsylvania Press.

Brahams, D. (1988). Randomised trials and informed consent. *Lancet, 2,* 1033–1034.

Brandt, M. (1985). Racism and research: The case of the Tuskegee syphilis study. In J. W. Leavitt & R. L. Numbers (Eds.), *Sickness and health in America* (pp. 331–343). Madison: University of Wisconsin Press.

Bravender-Coyle, P. (1986). The law relating to confidentiality of data acquired by researchers in the biomedical and social sciences. *University of Tasmania Law Review, 8,* 333–360.

Brennan, T. A. (1990). Ethics of confidentiality: The special case of quality assurance research. *Clinical Research, 38,* 551–557.

Brislin, R. W. (1970). Back-translation for cross-cultural research. *Journal of Cross-Cultural Psychology, 1,* 185–216.

Brock, D. W. (1994). Ethical issues in exposing children to risks in research. In M. A. Grodin & L. H. Glantz (Eds.), *Children as research subjects: Science, ethics, and law* (pp. 81–101). London: Oxford University Press.

Brookmeyer, R., & Gail, M. H. (1994). *AIDS epidemiology: A quantitative approach.* London: Oxford University Press.

Brown, P. (1991, April 27). AIDS vaccines: What chance of a fair trial? *New Science,* pp. 33–37.

Buc, N. L. (1993). Women in clinical trials: Concluding remarks. *Food and Drug Law Journal, 48,* 223–226.

Burchell, H. B. (1992). Vicissitudes in clinical trial research: Subjects, participants, patients. *Controlled Clinical Trials, 13,* 185–189.

Byar, D. P., Schoenfeld, D. A., Green, S. B., Amato, D. A., Davis, R., DeGruttola, V., Finkelstein, D. M., Gatsonis, C., Gelber, R. D., Lagakos, S., Lefkopoulou, M., Tsiatis, A. A., Zelen, M., Peto, J., Freedman, L. S., Gall, M., Simon, R., Ellenberg, S. S., Anderson, J. R., Collins, R., Peto, R., and Peto, T. (1990). Design considerations for AIDS trials. *New England Journal of Medicine, 323,* 1343–1348.

California Association of Hospitals and Health Systems. (1992). *Consent manual* (19th ed.). Dubuque, Iowa: Kendall/Hunt Publishing Company.

California Code of Civil Procedure section 1987.1 (West 1983).

California Department of Health Services. (1993). *California HIV/AIDS epidemiology summary.* Prepared for the AIDS Budget Task Force, April 27, 1993.

California Government Code section 6250 (West 1980).

California Government Code sections 6253(a), 6254 (West 1994).

California Health and Safety Code section 26679 (West 1984).

California Health and Safety Code sections 24170–24179.5 (West 1992).

California Health and Safety Code sections 199.25, 199.30–.40 (West 1990).

California Penal Code section 11165.6 (West 1992 & Suppl. 1994).

Cantwell, A., Jr. (1993). *Queer blood: The secret AIDS genocide plot.* Los Angeles: Aries Rising Press.

Capron, A. M. (1991). Protection of research subjects: Do special rules apply in epidemiology? *Journal of Clinical Epidemiology, 44* (Suppl.), 81S–89S.

Cassileth, B. R., Lusk, E. J., Miller, D. S., & Hurwitz, S. (1982). Attitudes towards clinical trials among patients and the public. *Journal of the American Medical Association, 248,* 968–970.

Cassileth, B. R., Zupkis, R. V., Sutton-Smith, K., & March, V. (1980). Informed consent—Why are its goals imperfectly realized? *New England Journal of Medicine, 302,* 896–900.

Castronovo, F. P., Jr. (1993). An attempt to standardize the radiodiagnostic risk statement in an institutional review board consent form. *Investigative Radiology, 28,* 533–538.

Centers for Disease Control (1990, November). HIV/AIDS surveillance report.

Chalmers, T. C. (1983). The control of bias in clinical trials. In *Clinical trials: Issues and approaches* (pp. 15–127). New York: Dekker.

Chiesi, A., Vella, S., Dally, L. G., Pedersen, C., Lundgren, J. D., & AIDS IN EUROPE Study Group. (1994). *Epidemiology of AIDS dementia complex in Europe.* Presented at the Tenth International Conference on AIDS, Yokohama, Japan, August, 1994.

Christakis, N. A. (1992). Ethics are local: Engaging cross-cultural variation in the ethics for clinical research. *Social Science and Medicine, 35,* 1079–1091.

Christakis, N. A., Lynn, L. A., & Castelo, A. (1991). Clinical AIDS research that evaluates cost effectiveness in the developing world. *IRB, 13,* 6–8.

Christakis, N. A., & Panner, M. J. (1989). Appropriate collaboration between industry and government in the development of an AIDS vaccine. *Law, Medicine & Health Care, 17,* 130–138.

Christakis, N. A., & Panner, M. J. (1991). Existing international ethical guidelines for human subjects research: Some open questions. *Law, Medicine & Health Care, 19,* 214–221.

Chrysler Corporation v. Brown, 441 U.S. 281 (1979).

Cimons, M. (1989a, August 17). Coalition proposes criteria for AIDS drug trials. *Los Angeles Times,* p. 16.

Cimons, M. (1989b, November 9). Lack of volunteers may hurt AIDS drug trials. *Los Angeles Times,* p. A39.

Cimons, M. (1990, August 21). Children's drug trials come of age amid AIDS epidemic. *Los Angeles Times,* p. A5.

Cimons, M., & Steinbrook, R. (1987, November 7). Facing lack of recruits, officials issue call for volunteers to test AIDS vaccine. *Los Angeles Times,* p. 29.

Clark, C. (1993, July 11). Private groups helping test AIDS drugs: U. S. efforts too slow, local activists contend. *San Diego Union-Tribune,* p. B-1.

Classen, W. H. (1986). Institutional review boards: Have they achieved their goal? *Medicine & Law, 5,* 387–393.

Cohen, J. (1994). The HIV vaccine paradox. *Science, 264,* 1072–1074.

Cole, P. (1991). The epidemiologist as an expert witness. *Journal of Clinical Epidemiology, 44* (Suppl. 1), 35S–39S.

Collins and Aikman Corp. v. J. P. Stevens & Co., 51 F.R.D. 219 (D.C.S.C. 1971).

Committee on the Conduct of Science, National Academy of Sciences. (1989). *On being a scientist.* Washington, DC: National Academy Press.

Cooke, R. E. (1994). Vulnerable children. In M. A. Grodin & L. H. Glantz (Eds.). *Children as research subjects: Science, ethics, and law* (pp. 193–214). London: Oxford University Press.

Cooper, E. (1994). *A public policy and legal critique of proposals to mandatory testing of pregnant women and their newborns.* Presented at the 122nd Annual Meeting of the American Public Health Association, Washington, DC.

Cotton, D. J., Powderly, W. G., Feinberg, J., Abrams, D. I., Chaisson, R. E., Wheat, L. J., Finkelstein, D. M., Tallman, V., Zimmer, B., Berzon, R., Fogelman, I., & Phair, J. (1993). Guidelines for the design and conduct of AIDS clinical trials. *Clinical Infectious Diseases, 16,* 817–822.

Council on Scientific Affairs and Council on Ethical and Judicial Affairs. (1990). Conflict of interest in medical center, industry research relationships. *Journal of the American Medical Association, 263,* 2790–2793.

Culliton, B. J. (1990). Dingell: AIDS researcher in conflict. *Science, 248,* 676.

Dal-Re, R. (1992). Elements of informed consent in clinical research with drugs: A survey of Spanish clinical investigators. *Journal of Internal Medicine, 231,* 375–379.

Dalton, R. (1994a, April 4). 2 at UCSD banned from experimentation on patients. *San Diego Union-Tribune,* B-1.

Dalton, R. (1994b, March 1). Med center penalized for flawed procedures. *San Diego Union-Tribune,* p. A1.

Dannenberg, A. L., Vernick, J. S., & Kirk, G. D. (1993). AIDS and confidentiality: Making exemptions to encourage research. *Journal of the American Medical Association, 269,* 47–48.

Daubert v. Merrill Dow Pharmaceuticals, Inc., 113 S.Ct. 2786 (1993).

Davidson, R. A. (1986). Source of funding and outcome of clinical trials. *Journal of General Internal Medicine, 3,* 155–158.

Davies, J. (1986). *Legislative law and process in a nutshell* (2nd ed.). St. Paul, MN: West Publishing Co.

Davis v. Lhim, 124 Mich. App. 291 (1983), *aff'd on rem* 147 Mich. App. 8 (1985), *rev'd* on grounds of government immunity in *Canon v. Thumudo,* 430 Mich. 326 (1988).

Day, J. J., Grant, I., Atkinson, J. H., Brysk, L. T., McCutchan, J. A., Hesselink, J. R., Heaton, R. K., Wernrich, J. D., Spector, S. A., and Richman, D. D. (1992). Incidence of AIDS dementia in a two-year follow-up of AIDS and ARC patients on an initial phase II AZT placebo-controlled study: San Diego cohort. *Journal of Neuropsychiatry and Clinical Neurosciences, 4,* 15–20.

DCCT Research Group. (1989). Implementation of a multicomponent process to obtained informed consent in the Diabetes Control and Complications Trial. *Controlled Clinical Trials, 10,* 83–96.

De Craemer, W. (1983). A cross-cultural perspective on personhood. *Milbank Memorial Quarterly Fund, 61,* 19–34.

de Gans, J., & Portegies, P. (1989). Neurological complications of infection with HIV type I. *Clinical Neurology and Neurosurgery, 91,* 197–217.

Deitchman v. E. R Squibb & Sons, Inc., 740 F.2d 556 (7th Cir. 1984).

Delgado, R., & Leskovac, H. (1986). Informed consent in human experimentation: Bridging the gap between ethical thought and current practice. *UCLA Law Review, 34,* 67–130.

Department of Defense. (1985, October 25). Memorandum for secretaries of the military departments, etc.: Policy on identification, surveillance and disposition of military personnel infected with human t-lymphotropic virus type III (HTLV-III).

Department of Defense. (1991, March 19). Directive 6485.1, Human immunodeficiency virus-1 (HIV-1).

Department of Defense. (1993, December 22). Directive 1332.14, Enlisted administrative separations.

Department of Justice v. Tax Analysts, 109 S.Ct. 2841 (1989).

Dickens, B. M. (1991). Issues in preparing ethical guidelines for epidemiological studies. *Law, Medicine & Health Care, 19,* 175–183.

Drahos, P. (1989). Ethics committees and medical research: The Australian experience. *Medicine & Law, 8,* 1–9.

Dresser, R. (1993). Sanctions for research misconduct: A legal perspective. *Academic Medicine, 68* (Sept. Suppl.), S39–S43.

Dresser, R. S., & Robertson, J. A. (1989). Quality of life and non-treatment decisions for incompetent patients: A critique of the orthodox approach. *Law, Medicine & Health Care, 17,* 234–244.

Dubler, N. N., & Sidel, V. W. (1989). On research on HIV infection and AIDS in correctional institutions. *Milbank Quarterly, 67,* 171–207.

Dunbar, M. M. (1991). Shaking up the status quo: How AIDS activists have challenged drug development and approval procedures. *Food, Drug, & Cosmetic Law Journal, 46,* 673–706.

Earle v. Kuklo, 26 N.J. Super. 471 (App. Div. 1953).

Edgar, H., & Sandomire, H. (1990). Medical privacy issues in the age of AIDS: Legislative options. *American Journal of Law & Medicine, 16,* 155–222.

Edles, G. J., & Nelson, J. (1993). *Federal regulatory process: Agency practices and procedures* (2nd ed.). Englewood Cliffs, NJ: Prentice Hall Law & Business.

Efron, B., & Feldman, D. (1991). Compliance as an explanatory variable in clinical trials. *Journal of the American Statistical Association, 86,* 9–17.

Eigo, J. J. (1990). Expedited drug approval procedures: Perspective from an AIDS activist. *Food, Drug, & Cosmetic Law Journal, 45,* 377–384.

Ellenberg, S. S., Cooper, E., Eigo, J., Finkelstein, D., Hoth, D. F., Nusinoff-Lehrman, S., & Sacks, H. (1992). Studying treatments for AIDS: A panel discussion at the 1990 annual meeting of the Society for Clinical Trials, *Statistics in Medicine, 13,* 272–292.

Ellenberg, S. S., & Foulkes, M. A. (1994). Clinical trials: The utility of large, simple trials in the evaluation of AIDS treatment strategies. *Statistics in Medicine, 13,* 405–415.

Ellenberg, S. S., Myers, M. W., Blackwelder, W. C., & Hoth, D. F. (1993). The use of external monitoring committees in clinical trials of the National Institute of Allergy and Infectious Diseases. *Statistics in Medicine, 12,* 461–467.

El-Sadr, W., & Capps, L. (1992). The challenge of minority recruitment in clinical trials for AIDS. *Journal of the American Medical Association, 267,* 954–957.

Epstein, L. C., & Lasagna, L. (1969). Obtained informed consent. *Archives of Internal Medicine, 123,* 682–688.

Faden, R., Kass, N., & McGraw, D. (in press). Women as vessels and vectors: Lessons from the HIV epidemic. Cited in DeBruin, D. A. (1994). Justice and the inclusion of women in clinical studies: A conceptual framework. In A. C. Mastroianni, R. Faden, & D. Federman (Eds.), *Women and health research: Ethical and legal issues of including women in clinical studies,* (Vol. 2, pp. 127–150). Washington, DC: National Academy Press.

Falk, T. C. (1988). AIDS public health law. *Journal of Legal Medicine, 9,* 529–546.

Farnsworth v. Proctor and Gamble Company, 785 F.2d 1545 (11th Cir. 1985).

FDC Reports. (1994). *The Blue Sheet, 37* (31).

Federal Centre for AIDS Working Group on Anonymous Unlinked HIV Seroprevalence Research. (1992). Revised guidelines on ethical and legal considerations in anonymous unlinked HIV seroprevalence research. *Canadian Medical Association Journal, 10,* 1743–1744.

Federal Rules of Civil Procedure 26(b), 45(b) (West 1983).

Federal Rules of Evidence 401, 501, 702, 705 (West 1992).

Feinleib, M. (1991). The epidemiologist's responsibilities to study participants. *Journal of Clinical Epidemiology, 44* (Suppl. 1), 73S–79S.

Finkel, M. J. (1991). Should informed consent include information on how research is funded? *IRB, 13,* 1–3.

Finlinson, H. A., Robles, R. R., Colon, H. M., & Page, J. B. (1993). Recruiting and retaining out-of-treatment injecting drug users in the Puerto Rico AIDS prevention project. *Human Organization, 52,* 169–175.

Fisher, M., Friedman, S. B., & Strauss, B. (1994). The effects of blinding on acceptance of research papers by peer review. *Journal of the American Medical Association, 272,* 143–146.

Flannery, E., & Greenberg, S. N. (1994). Liability exposure for exclusion and inclusion of women as subjects in clinical studies. In A. C. Mastroianni, R. Faden, & D. Federman (Eds.), *Women and health research: Ethical and legal issues of including women in clinical studies* (Vol. 2, pp. 91–102). Washington, DC: National Academy Press.

Fleming, T. R., & DeMets, D. L. (1993). Monitoring of clinical trials: Issues and recommendations. *Controlled Clinical Trials, 14,* 183–197.

Fletcher, J. C. (1993). Women's and fetal rights and interests: Ethical aspects. *Food & Drug Law Journal, 48,* 213–221.

Florida Statutes Annotated section 455.2146 (1991).

Florida Statutes Annotated section 827.04 (2) (1994).

Food and Drug Administration. (1977). *General considerations for the clinical evaluation of drugs* (FDA Publication 77-3040). Washington, DC: United States Government Printing Office.

Forsham v. Harris, 445 U.S. 169 (1980).

Fowler, F. J., Massagli, M. P., Weissman, J., Seage, G. R., III, Cleary, P. D., & Epstein, A. (1992). Some methodological lessons for surveys of persons with AIDS. *Medical Care, 30,* 1059–1066.

Francis, D., & Chin, J. (1987). The prevention of acquired immunodeficiency syndrome in the United States. *Journal of the American Medical Association, 257,* 1357–1366.

Freedman, B. (1992). Suspended judgment: AIDS and the ethics of clinical trials: Learning the right lessons. *Controlled Clinical Trials, 13,* 1–5.

Freedman, B., Fuks, A., & Weijer, C. (1993). In loco parentis: Minimal risk as an ethical threshold for research upon children. *Hastings Center Report, 23*(2), 13–19.

Freedom of Information Act, 5 United States Code Annotated section 552 (West 1977 & Supp. 1993).

Fried, C. (1974). *Medical experimentation: Personal integrity and social policy* (pp. 31–34). Amsterdam: North–Holland.

Fruman, L. S. (1991). AIDS and the physician's duty to warn (part 2). *Medicine & Law, 10,* 515–526.

Fulford, K. W. M., & Howse, K. (1993). Ethics of research with psychiatric patients: Principles, problems and the primary responsibilities of researchers. *Journal of Medical Ethics, 19,* 85–91.

Garfinkel, S. L. (1988). AIDS and the Soundex code. *IRB, 10*(5), 8–9.

Gelber, R. D., Lenderking, W. R., Cotton, D. J., Cole, B. F., Fischl, M. A., Goldhirsch, A., & Testa, M. A. (1992). Quality-of-life evaluation in a clinical trial of zidovudine therapy in patients with mildly symptomatic HIV infection. *Annals of Internal Medicine, 116,* 961–966.

Gellhorn, E., & Levin, R. M. (1990). *Administrative law and process in a nutshell* (3rd ed.). St. Paul, MN: West Publishing Co.

Glantz, L. H. (1992). In G. J. Annas & M. A. Grodin (Eds.), *The Nazi doctors and the Nuremberg Code* (pp. 183–200). London: Oxford University Press.

Gordis, L. (1991). Ethical and professional issues in the changing practice of epidemiology. *Journal of Clinical Epidemiology, 44*(Suppl. 1), 9S–13S.

Gostin, L. (1991). Ethical principles for the conduct of human subject research: Population-based research and ethics. *Law, Medicine & Health Care, 19,* 191–201.

Grady, C. (1991). Ethical issues in clinical trials. *Seminars in Oncology Nursing, 7,* 288–296.

Gray, J. N. (1989). Pediatric AIDS research: Legal, ethical, and policy influences. In J. M. Siebert and R. A. Olson (Eds.). *Children, adolescents, and AIDS* (pp. 179–227). Lincoln, Nebraska: University of Nebraska Press.

Gray, J. N., & Melton, G. B. (1985). The law and ethics of psychosocial research on AIDS. *Nebraska Law Review, 64,* 637–688.

Green, S. B., Ellenberg, S. S., Finkelstein, D., Forsythe, A. B., Freedman, L. S., Freeman, K., Lefkopoulou, M., Schoenfeld, D., & Smith, R. P. (1990). Issues in the design of drug trials for AIDS. *Controlled Clinical Trials, 11,* 81–87.

Grodin, M. A. (1992). Historical origins of the Nuremberg Code. In G. J. Annas & M. A. Grodin (Eds.), *The Nazi doctors and the Nuremberg Code: Human rights in human experimentation* (pp. 121–144). London: Oxford University Press.

Grodin, M. A., & Alpert, J. J. (1988). Children as participants in medical research. *Pediatric Clinics of North America, 35,* 1389–1401.

Grodin, M. A., Kaminow, P. V., & Sassower, R. (1986). Ethical issues in AIDS research. *Quality Review Bulletin, 12,* 347–352.

Guinan, M. E. (1993). Black communities' belief in AIDS as "genocide:" A barrier to overcome for HIV prevention. *Annals of Epidemiology, 3,* 193–195.

Halbreich, U., & Carson, S. W. (1989). Drug studies in women of childbearing age: Ethical and methodological considerations. *Journal of Clinical Psychopharmacology, 9,* 328–333.

Hammerschmidt, D. E., & Keane, M. A. (1992). Institutional review board (IRB) review lacks impact on the readability of consent forms for research. *American Journal of the Medical Sciences, 304,* 348–351.

Hammett, T. M., & Dubler, N. N. (1990). Clinical and epidemiologic research on HIV infection and AIDS among correctional inmates: Regulations, ethics, and procedures. *Evaluation Review, 14,* 482–501.

Healy, B., NIH Director. (1993, April 7). Quoted in S. Squires, Army to test AIDS drug despite objections. *Washington Post,* p. A1.

Hedrick, T. E. (1988). Justifications for the sharing of social science data. *Law and Human Behavior, 12,* 163–171.

Hendrix, C. W., & Boswell, R. N. (1992). Letter to Col. Donald Burke, Director, Division of Retrovirology, Re: Gp160 phase I immunotherapy data presentation, dated October 21, 1992.

Herek, G. M., Kimmel, D. C., Amaro, H., & Melton, G. B. (1988). Avoiding heterosexist bias in psychological research. *American Psychologist, 46,* 957–963.

Herxheimer, A. (1988). The rights of the patient in clinical research. *Lancet, 2,* 1128–1130.

High, D. M. (1992). Research with Alzheimer's disease subjects: Informed consent and proxy decision making. *Journal of the American Geriatrics Society, 40,* 950–957.

Hilts, P. J. (1992, December 31). U.S. accuses AIDS scientist: Investigators say Gallo made a false key report. *San Diego Union-Tribune,* p. A1.

Hoch v. C.I.A., 593 F. Supp. 675 (D.C.D.C. 1984).

Hogue, C. R. (1991). Ethical issues in sharing epidemiological data. *Journal of Clinical Epidemiology, 44*(Suppl. 1), 103S–107S.

Holder, A. R. (1983). Can teenagers participate in research without parental consent? In T. Silber (Ed.), *Ethical issues in the treatment of children and adolescents* (pp. 133–139). Thorofare, NJ: Slack.

Holder, A. R. (1989). Researchers and subpoenas: The troubling precedent of the Selikoff case. *IRB, 11*(6), 8–11.

Holder, A. R. (1993). Research records and subpoenas: A continuing issue. *IRB, 15*(1), 6–7.

Hurley, P., & Pinder, G. (1992). Ethics, social forces, and politics in AIDS-related research: Experience in planning and implementing a household seroprevalence survey. *Milbank Quarterly, 70,* 605–628.

Hutchinson, C. T. (1993). 'Daubert' confirms judge's gatekeeper role. *Product Safety & Liability Reporter, 21,* 12–15.

Ickovics, J. R., Ethier, K., Meisler, A. W., & Rodin, J. (1994). *Recruitment, adherence and retention in AIDS clinical trials: A prospective study.* Presented at the Annual Meeting of the Society of Behavioral Medicine, Boston, April, 1994.

Inmates of New York State with HIV v. Cuomo et al., No. 90-Civ-252 (N.D.N.Y. 1990).

In re Grand Jury Subpoena Dated Jan. 4, 1984, 750 F.2d 223 (2nd Cir. 1984).

Isaacman, S. H. (1993). HIV surveillance: Taking advantage of the disadvantaged. *American Journal of Public Health, 83,* 597–598.

Jablonski v. United States, 712 F.2d 391 (9th Cir. 1983).

Johnson, D. (1989, November 15). Condemning many to an early grave, *Los Angeles Times,* p. B7.

Johnstone, J. M. (1988). Treatment IND safety assessment: Potential legal and regulatory problems. *Food Drug & Cosmetic Law Journal, 43,* 533–540.

Jones, B., & Kenward, M. G. (1989). *Design and analysis of cross-over trials.* London: Chapman & Hall.

Jones, J. H. (1992). The Tuskegee legacy: AIDS and the black community. *Hastings Center Report, 22*(6), 38–40.

Kass, N. E., Faden, R. R., Fox, R., & Dudley, J. (1992). Homosexual and bisexual men's perceptions of discrimination in health services. *American Journal of Public Health, 82,* 1277–1279.

Keeton, R. E. (1973). *Trial tactics and methods* (2nd ed., pp. 390–412). Boston: Little, Brown.

Keeton, W., Dobbs, D., Keeton, R., & Owen, D. (1984). *Prosser and Keeton on the Law of torts* (5th ed., pp. 320–321). St. Paul, MN: West Publishing Co.

Kegeles, S. M., Catania, J. A., Coates, T. J., Pollack, L. M., & Lo, B. (1990). Many people who seek anonymous HIV-antibody testing would avoid it under other circumstances. *AIDS, 4,* 584–588.

Kelly, J. A., St. Lawrence, J. S., Smith, S., Hood, H. V., & Cook, D. J. (1987). Stigmatization of AIDS patients by physicians. *American Journal of Public Health, 77,* 789–791.

Kissinger v. Reporters Committee for Freedom of the Press, 445 U.S. 136 (1980).

Knapp, S., & Van de Creek, L. (1990). Application of the duty to protect to HIV-positive patients. *Professional Psychology: Research and Practice, 21,* 161–166.

Koch, C. H., Jr. (1985). *Administrative law and practice.* St. Paul, MN: West Publishing Co.

Kodish, E., Lantos, J. D., & Siegler, M. (Supp. 1990). Ethical considerations in randomized controlled clinical trials. *Cancer, 65,* 2400–2404.

Kolata, G. (1988a, March 15). Doctors and patients take AIDS drug trial into their own hands. *New York Times,* C3.

Kolata, G. (1988b, December 18). Recruiting problems in New York slowing U. S. trials of AIDS drug. *New York Times,* 1-1.

Kolata, G. (1989, March 6). Group will import unapproved drugs for treating AIDS. *New York Times,* A1.

Kolata, G. (1990a, November 8). AIDS drug trials may be revamped. *New York Times,* p. A24.

Kolata, G. (1990b, March 26). Radical change urged in testing of AIDS drugs. *New York Times,* p. A1.

Koska, M. T. (1992, January 5). Outcomes research: Hospitals face confidentiality concerns. *Hospitals,* pp. 32–34.

Kuzma, S. M. (1992). Criminal liability for misconduct in scientific research. *University of Michigan Journal of Law Reform, 25,* 357–421.

Laband, D. N., & Piette, M. J. (1994). A citation analysis of the impact of blinded peer review. *Journal of the American Medical Association, 272,* 147–149.

Lamb, D. H., Clark, C., Drumheller, P., Frizzell, K., & Surrey, L. (1989). Applying *Tarasoff* to AIDS-related psychotherapy issues. *Professional Psychology: Research and Practice, 20,* 37–43.

Lara, M. D. C., and de la Fuente, J. R. (1990). On informed consent. *Bulletin of Pan-American Health Organization, 24,* 419–424.

Last, J. M. (1991a). Epidemiology and ethics. *Law, Medicine & Health Care, 19,* 166–173.

Last, J. M. (1991b). Obligations and responsibilities of epidemiologists to research subjects. *Journal of Clinical Epidemiology, 44*(Suppl. 1), 95S–101S.

Lavelle-Jones, C., Byrne, D. J., Rice, P., & Cuschieri, A. (1993). Factors affecting quality of informed consent. *British Medical Journal, 306,* 885–890.

Leiken, S. L. (1989). Immunodeficiency virus infection, adolescents, and the institutional review board. *Journal of Adolescent Health Care, 10,* 500–505.

Leikin, S. (1993). Minors' assent, consent, or dissent to medical research. *IRB, 15,* 1–7.

Levine, C. (1988). Has AIDS changed the ethics of human subjects research? *Law, Medicine & Health Care, 16,* 167–173.

Levine, C. (1989, November 15). AIDS crisis sparks a quiet revolution. *Los Angeles Times,* p. B7.

Levine, C. (1990). Women and HIV/AIDS research: The barriers to equity. *Evaluation Review, 14,* 447–463.

Levine, C. (1991a). Children in HIV/AIDS clinical trials: Still vulnerable after all these-years. *Law, Medicine & Health Care, 19,* 231–237.

Levine, C. (1991b). Women and HIV/AIDS research: The barriers to equity. *IRB, 13*(1–2), 18–23.

Levine, C., Dubler, N. N., & Levine, R. J. (1991). Building a new consensus: Ethical principles and policies for clinical research on HIV/AIDS. *IRB, 13,* 1–17.

Levine, R. J. (1988). Protection of human subjects of biomedical research in the United States: A contrast with recent experience in the United Kingdom. *Annals of the New York Academy of Sciences, 530,* 133–143.

Levine, R. J. (1991). Informed consent: Some challenges to the universality of the western model. *Law, Medicine & Health Care, 19,* 207–213.

Levine, R. J. (1992). Clinical trials and physicians as double agents. *Yale Journal of Biology & Medicine, 65,* 65–74.

Levy, R., & Bredesen, D. E. (1988). Central nervous system dysfunction in acquired immunodeficiency syndrome. *Journal of Acquired Immune Deficiency Syndromes, 1,* 41–64.

Lichter, P. R. (1989). Biomedical research, COI and the public trust. *Ophthalmology, 96,* 575–578.

Lo, B. (1990). Assessing decision-making capacity. *Law, Medicine, & Health Care, 18,* 193–201.

LoVerde, M. E., Prochazka, A. V., & Byyny, R. L. (1989). Research consent forms: Continued unreadability and increasing length. *Journal of General Internal Medicine, 4,* 410–412.

Lurie, P. (1995). *Ethical aspects of HIV vaccine trials.* Presented at the Second International Conference on Engineered Vaccines for Cancer and AIDS, San Francisco, March 3, 1995.

Lurie, P., Bishaw, M., Chesney, M. A., Cooke, M., Fernandes, M. E. L., Hearst, N., Katongole-Mbidde, E., Koetsawang, S., Lindan, C. P., Mandel, J., Mhloyi, M., & Coates, T. J. (1994). Ethical, behavioral, and social aspects of HIV vaccine trials in developing countries. *Journal of the American Medical Association, 271,* 295–301.

Lynch, M. T. (1988). The nurse's role in the biotherapy of cancer: Clinical trials and informed consent. *Oncology Nursing Forum, 15*(Suppl.), 23–27.

Lynoe, N., Sandlund, M., Dahlqvist, G., & Jacobsson, L. (1991). Informed consent: Study of quality of information given to participants in a clinical trial. *British Medical Journal, 303,* 610–613.

McArthur, J. C. (1987). Neurologic manifestations of AIDS. *Medicine, 66,* 407–437.

McCarthy, C. R., & Porter, J. P. (1991). Confidentiality: The protection of personal data in epidemiological and clinical research trials. *Law, Medicine & Health Care, 19,* 238–241.

McCormick, W. C. (1990). Impact of a change in confidentiality law on enrollment of persons with AIDS in a clinical research study. *Clinical Research, 38,* 545–550.

McIntosh v. Milano, 168 N.J. Super. 466 (1979).

McKenna, R. M. (1988). The impact of product liability law on the development of a vaccine against the AIDS virus. *University of Chicago Law Review, 55,* 943–964.

Macklin, R. (1989). The paradoxical case of payment as benefit to research subjects. *IRB, 11,* 1–3.

Macklin, R., & Friedland, G. (1986). AIDS research: The ethics of clinical trials. *Law, Medicine, & Health Care, 14,* 273–280.

Maddocks, I. (1992). Ethics in aboriginal research: A model for minorities or for all? *Medical Journal of Australia, 157,* 553–555.

Mariner, W. K. (1990). The ethical conduct of clinical trials of HIV vaccines. *Evaluation Review, 14,* 538–564.

Marquis, D., & Stephens, R. (1989). The doctor's unproven beliefs and the subject's informed choice: Another commentary. *IRB, 11,* 8–9.

Martineau, R. J. (1991). *Drafting legislation and rules in plain English.* St. Paul, MN: West Publishing Co.

Marwick, C. (1983). 'Confidentiality' issues may cloud epidemiologic studies of AIDS. *Journal of the American Medical Association, 250,* 1945–1946.

Meade, C. D., & Howser, D. M. (1992). Consent forms: How to determine and improve their readability. *Oncology Nursing Forum, 19,* 1523–1528.

Melton, G. B. (1988). When scientists are adversaries, do participants lose? *Law and Human Behavior, 12,* 191–198.

Melton, G. B. (1989). Ethical and legal issues in research and intervention. *Journal of Adolescent Health Care, 10*(Suppl.), 36S–44S.

Melton, G. B., & Gray, J. N. (1988). Ethical dilemmas in AIDS research: Individual privacy and public health. *American Psychologist, 43,* 60–64.

Melton, G. B., Levine, R. J., Koocher, G. P., Rosenthal R., & Thompson, W. C. (1988). Community consultation in socially sensitive research: Lessons from clinical trials of treatments for AIDS. *American Psychologist, 43,* 573–581.

Mendelson, J. H. (1991). Protection of participants and experimental design in clinical abuse liability testing. *British Medical Journal, 86,* 1543–1548.

Merkatz, R. B. (1993). Women in clinical trials: An introduction. *Food & Drug Law Journal, 48,* 161–166.

Merkatz, R. B., Temple, R., Subel, S., Feiden, K., & Kessler, D. A. (1993). Women in clinical trials of new drugs: A change in Food and Drug Administration policy. *New England Journal of Medicine, 329,* 292–296.

Merton, V. (1993). The exclusion of pregnant, pregnable, and once-pregnable people (a.k.a. women) from biomedical research. *American Journal of Law & Medicine, 19,* 369–451.

Meyers, C. (1991, January 30). AIDS scientists say clash in Colorado shows need for U. S. protection of confidentiality in research. *Chronicle of Higher Education,* p. A19.

Miller, B. (1991). The ethics of random clinical trials. In T. A. Mappes & J. S. Zembaty (Eds.), *Biomedical ethics* (3rd ed., pp. 231–239). New York: McGraw–Hill.

Mirkin, B. L. (1975). Drug therapy and the developing human: Who cares? *Clinical Research, 23,* 110–111.

Mitchell, S. C., & Steingrub, J. (1988). The changing clinical trials scene: The role of the IRB. *IRB, 10,* 1–5.

Moini, S., & Hammett, T. M. (1990). *1989 update: AIDS in correctional facilities.* Washington, DC: United States Department of Justice, National Institute of Justice.

Moreno, J. D. (1994). Ethical issues relating to the inclusion of women of childbearing age in clinical trials. In A. C. Mastroianni, R. Faden, & D. Federman (Eds.), *Women and health research: Ethical and legal issues of including women in clinical studies* (Vol. 2, pp. 29–34). Washington, DC: National Academy Press.

Morrissey, J. M., Hofmann, A. D., & Thorpe, J. C. (1986). *Consent and confidentiality in health care of children and adolescents: A legal guide.* New York: The Free Press.

Moros, D. A., & Rhodes, R. (1991). Panel discussion: The ethics of surrogate decision making. *Mount Sinai Journal of Medicine, 58,* 398–402.

Morrow, G., Gootnick, J., & Schmale, A. (1978). A simple technique for increasing cancer patients' knowledge of informed consent to treatment. *Cancer, 42,* 793–799.

Murphy, D. (1993). Women in clinical trials: HIV-infected women. *Food and Drug Law Journal, 48,* 175–179.

Murphy, T. F. (1991). Women and drug users: The changing faces of HIV clinical drug trials. *Quality Review Bulletin, 17*(1), 26–32.

Muss, H. B., White, D. R., Michielutte, R., Richards, F. II, Cooper, M. R., Williams, S., Stuart, J. J., and Spurr, C. L. (1979). Written informed consent in patients with breast cancer. *Cancer, 43,* 1549–1556.

Newhard, J. A. (1988). Immunity from AIDS awaits immunity for vaccine manufacturers: How products liability law may affect the development of an AIDS vaccine. *Toledo Law Review, 19,* 885–922.

New Jersey Statutes Annotated 9:6–1 (1993).

Newton, L. H. (1990). Ethical imperialism and informed consent. *IRB, 12*(3), 10–11.

Nigg, N. G., & Radulescu, G. (1994). Scientific misconduct in environmental science and toxicology. *Journal of the American Medical Association, 272,* 168–170.

Nolan, K. (1990). AIDS and pediatric research. *Evaluation Review, 14,* 464–481.

Norris Mfg. Co. v. R. E. Darling Co., 29 F.R.D. 1 (D.C. Md. 1961).

Office for Protection from Research Risks. (1988). PRR Report, Policy on informing those tested about HIV serostatus, June 10, 1988.

Onek, J. (1994). *Scientific misconduct—Representing institutions and academics in scientific misconduct investigations.* Presented to the National Health Lawyers Association, April 8, 1994.

O'Reilly, J. T. (1983). *Administrative rulemaking: Structuring, opposing, and defending federal agency regulations.* Colorado Springs, CO: Shepard's/McGraw–Hill.

Osmond, D. (1992). Ethical and legal issues of vaccine clinical trials. *FOCUS: A guide to AIDS research and counseling, 8,* 1–4.

Owens, J. F. (1987). Informed consent in the clinical research setting: Experimentation on human subjects. *Medical Trial Techniques,* 33, 335–350.

Palca, J. (1990). African AIDS: Whose research rules? *Science, 250,* 199–201.

Palca, J. (1992). The case of the Florida dentist. *Science, 255,* 392–394.

Pascal, C. B. (1994). *Scientific misconduct investigations: The federal perspective.* Washington, DC: National Health Lawyers Association.

Peppin, P. (1991). Drugs/vaccine risks: Patient decision-making and harm reduction in the pharmaceutical company duty to warn action. *Canadian Bar Review, 70,* 473–516.

Perley, S., Fluss, S. S., Bankowski, Z., & Simon, F. (1992). The Nuremberg Code: An international overview. In G. J. Annas & M. A. Grodin (Eds.), *The Nazi doctors and the Nuremberg Code* (pp. 149–173). London: Oxford University Press.

Peterson, B. T., Clancy, S. J., Champion, K., & McLarty, J. W. (1992). Improving readability of consent forms: What the computers may not tell you. *IRB, 14*(6), 6–8.

Pocock, S. J. (1992). When to stop a clinical trial. *British Medical Journal, 305,* 235–240.

Pogash, C. (1993). Kill or cure? *California Lawyer,* June, 48–51, 100–102.

Poole, C., & Rothman, K. J. (1990). Epidemiologic science and public health policy (letter). *Journal of Clinical Epidemiology, 43,* 1270.

Popper, K. R. (1965). *The logic of scientific discovery.* New York: Harper & Row.

Portegies, P., Enting, R. H., de Gans, J., Algra, P. R., Derix, M. M. A., Lange, J. M. A., and Goudsmit, J. (1993). Presentation and course of AIDS dementia complex: 10 years of follow-up in Amsterdam, the Netherlands. *AIDS, 7,* 669–675.

Porter, J. P., Glass, M. J., & Koff, W. C. (1989). Ethical considerations in AIDS vaccines. *IRB, 11,* 1–4.

Porter, R. J. (1992). Conflict of interest in research: Personal gain—The seeds of conflict. In R. J. Porter & T. E. Malone (Eds.), *Biomedical research, collaboration, and conflict of interest* (pp. 135–149). Baltimore: John Hopkins University Press.

Portney, L. G., & Watkins, M. P. (1993). *Foundations of clinical research: Applications to practice.* Norwalk, CT: Appleton & Lange.

Potler, C., Sharp, V. L., & Remick, S. (1994). Prisoners' access to HIV experimental trials: Legal, ethical, and practical considerations. *Journal of Acquired Immune Deficiency Syndromes, 7,* 1086–1094.

Privacy Act, 5 United States Code Annotated section 552a (West 1977 & Supp. 1993).

Public Citizens Health Research Group. (1994). Army AIDS vaccine studies: Scientific research or market research? *Health Letter,* December, 11–12.

Public Health Service, United States Department of Health and Human Services (1987). *A public health challenge: State issues, policies and programs,* Vol. 1, pp. 4-1 to 4-31.

Public Health Service, United States Department of Health and Human Services. (1990). Grants Policy Statement.

Purtilo, R., Sonnabend, J., & Purtilo, D. T. (1983). Confidentiality, informed consent and untoward social consequences in research on a "new killer disease' (AIDS). *Clinical Research, 31,* 462–472.

Raskin, D. E. (1988). Psychiatric and psychological aspects of AIDS. *Delaware Lawyer, 7,* 38–40.

Reiser, S. J., & Knudson, P. (1993). Protecting research subjects after consent: The case for the "research intermediary." *IRB, 15*(2), 10–11.

Relman, A. S. (1989). Economic incentives in clinical investigation. *New England Journal of Medicine, 320,* 933–934.

Rivas, M. S. (1991). The California AIDS initiative and the Food and Drug Administration: Working at odds with each other? *Food, Drug & Cosmetic Law Journal, 46,* 107–127.

Rivera, R., Reed, J. S., & Menius, D. (1992). Evaluating the readability of informed consent forms used in contraceptive clinical trials. *International Journal of Gynecology and Obstetrics, 38,* 227–230.

Robertson, J. (1994). Ethical issues related to the inclusion of pregnant women in clinical trials (I). In A. C. Mastroianni, R. Faden, & D. Federman (Eds.), *Women and health research: Ethical and legal issues of including women in clinical studies* (Vol. 2, pp. 18–22). Washington, DC: National Academy Press.

Roht, L. H., Selwyn, B. J., Holguin, A. H., & Christensen, B. L. (1982). *Principles of epidemiology: A self-teaching guide.* New York: Academic Press.

Roizen, B. (1988). Why I oppose drug company payment of physician/investigators on a per patient/subject basis. *IRB, 10*(1), 9–10.

Rose, C. D. (1993, July 2). NIH proposes research-ethics rules. *San Diego Union-Tribune,* p. C1.

Rosenthal, R., & Blanck, P. D. (1993). Science and ethics in conducting, analyzing, and reporting social science research: Implications for social scientists, judges, and lawyers. *Indiana Law Journal, 68,* 1209–1228.

Rosenthal, R., and Rosnow, R. L. (1984). Applying Hamlet's question to the ethical conduct of research: A conceptual addendum. *American Psychologist, 39,* 561–563.

Rosnow, R. L., Rotheram-Borus, Ceci, S. J., Blanck, P. D., & Koocher, G. P. (1993). The institutional review board as a mirror of scientific and ethical standards. *American Psychologist, 48,* 821–826.

Rothman, K. J. (1976). Causes. *American Journal of Epidemiology, 104,* 588–592.

Rothman, K. J. (1986). *Modern epidemiology.* Boston: Little, Brown.

Rothman, K. J., & Poole, C. (1985). Science and policy making. *American Journal of Public Health, 75,* 340–341.

Sacket, D. L. (1983). On some prerequisites for a successful clinical trial. In S. H. Shapiro & T. A. Louis (Eds.), *Clinical trials: Issues and approaches* (pp. 72–74). New York: Dekker.

Sandman, P. M. (1991). Emerging communication responsibilities of epidemiologists. *Journal of Clinical Epidemiology, 44* (Suppl. 1), 41S–50S.

Schoepf, B. G. (1991). Ethical, methodological and political issues of AIDS research in Central Africa. *Social Science & Medicine, 33,* 749–763.

Schroeder, K. (1983). A recommendation to the FDA concerning drug research on prisoners. *Southern California Law Review, 56,* 969–1000.

Schulte, P. (1991). Ethical issues in the communication of results. *Journal of Clinical Epidemiology, 44* (Suppl. 1), 57S–61S.

Schwartz, R. L. (1985). Informed consent to participation in medical research employing elderly human subjects. *Journal of Contemporary Health Law, 1,* 115–131.

Seligmann, J., Gosnell, M., Copola, V., & Hager, M. (1983, April 18). The AIDS epidemic: The search for a cure. *Newsweek,* pp. 74–79.

Senate Select Committee on Citizen Participation in Government. (1989). *The legislative process: You really do matter: A citizen's guide.* Sacramento, CA: Senate Select Committee.

Settle, N. D. (1994). *Remedies for scientific misconduct.* Washington, DC: National Health Lawyers Association.

Shapiro, M. F., and Charrow, R. D. (1985). Scientific misconduct in investigational drug trials. *New England Journal of Medicine, 312,* 731–736.

Shapiro, M. F., & Charrow, R. P. (1989). The role of data audits in detecting scientific misconduct: Results of the FDA program. *Journal of the American Medical Association, 261,* 2505–2511.

Shilts, R. (1987). *And the band played on.* New York: St. Martin's Press.

Shimm, D. S., & Spece, R. G., Jr. (1991a). Conflict of interest and informed consent in industry-sponsored clinical trials. *Journal of Legal Medicine, 12,* 477–513.

Shimm, D. S., & Spece, R. G., Jr. (1991b). Industry reimbursement for entering patients into clinical trials: Legal and ethical issues. *Annals of Internal Medicine, 115,* 148–151.

Shipp, A. C. (1992). How to control conflict of interest. In R. J. Porter & T. E. Malone (Eds.), *Biomedical research, collaboration, and conflict of interest* (pp. 163–184). Baltimore: Johns Hopkins University Press.

Shorr, A. F. (1992). AIDS and the FDA: An ethical case for limiting patient access to new medical therapies. *IRB, 14,* 1–4.

Shtasel, D. L., Gur, R. E., Mozley, P. D., Richards, J., Taleff, M. M., Heimberg, C., Gallacher, F., & Gur, R. C. (1991). Volunteers for biomedical research: Recruitment and screening of normal controls. *Archives of General Psychiatry, 48,* 1023–1025.

Sieber, J. (1992). *Planning ethically responsible research: A guide for students and internal review boards.* Beverly Hills: Sage Publications.

Sieber, J. E. (1988). Data sharing: Defining problems and seeking solutions. *Law and Human Behavior, 12,* 199–206.

Sieber, J. E., & Sorensen, J. L. (1992). Conducting social and behavioral AIDS research in drug treatment clinics. *IRB, 114,* 1–5.

Siegal, H. A., Carlson, R. G., Falck, R., Reece, R. D., & Perlin, T. (1993). Conducting HIV outreach and research among incarcerated drug abusers: A case study of ethical concerns and dilemmas. *Journal of Substance Abuse Treatment, 10,* 71–75.

Silva, M. C., & Sorrell, J. M. (1988). Enhancing comprehension of information for informed consent: A review of empirical research. *IRB, 10,* 1–5.

Silverman, W. A. (1989). The myth of informed consent: in daily practice and in clinical trials. *Journal of Medical Ethics, 15,* 6–11.

Simberkoff, F. S., Hartigan, P. M., Hamilton, J. D., Deykin, D., Gail, M., Bartlett, J. G., Feorino, P., Redfield, R., Roberts, R., Collins, D., DeMets, D., Pritchett, W., Spritz, N., Wenzel, R. P., & VA Cooperative Study Group on AIDS Treatment. (1993). Ethical dilemmas in continuing a zidovudine trial after early termination of similar trials. *Controlled Clinical Trials, 14,* 6–18.

Simel, D. L., & Feussner, J. R. (1992). Suspended judgment: Clinical trials of informed consent. *Controlled Clinical Trials, 13,* 321–324.

Simmons, J. C., Acting Director, Office of Compliance, Center for Biologics Evaluation and Research, FDA. (1995). Letter to Dennis J. Carlo, Executive Vice President, Immune Response Corporation, dated January 9, 1995.

Simon, R. (1993). High court throws out rigid rules excluding scientific evidence, says focus must be on methods, principles. *Product Safety & Liability Reporter, 21,* 5–11.

Sinrod, E. J. (1994). Expediting access to government information relative to immigration proceedings. *Interpreter Releases, 71,* 669–679.

Smeltzer, S. C. (1992). Women and AIDS: Sociopolitical issues. *Nursing Outlook, 40,* 152–157.

Southgate, M. (1987). Conflict of interest and the peer review process. *Journal of the American Medical Association, 258,* 1375.

Specter, M. (1989, June 5). AIDS patients insist on treatment role: Researchers report difficulty conducting traditional drug trials. *Washington Post,* p. A12.

Spiers, H. R. (1991). Community consultation and AIDS clinical trials, Part III. *IRB, 13*(5), 3–7.

Squires, B. P. (1993). Confidentiality and research. *Canadian Medical Association Journal, 148,* 487.

Stanley, B., & Stanley, M. (1988). Data sharing: The primary researcher's perspective. *Law and Human Behavior, 12,* 173–179.

Steinbrook, R. (1989, September 25). AIDS trials shortchange minorities and drug users. *Los Angeles Times,* p. I-1.

Stoy, D. B. (1994). Recruitment and retention of women in clinical studies: Theoretical perspectives and methodological considerations. In A. C. Mastroianni, R. Faden, & D. Federman (Eds.), *Women and health research: Ethical and legal issues of including women in clinical studies* (Vol. 2, pp. 45–51). Washington, DC: National Academy Press.

Strom, B. L. (1989). *Pharmacoepidemiology.* Edinburgh: Churchill Livingstone.

Susman, E. J., Dorn, L. D., & Fletcher, J. C. (1992). Participation in biomedical research: The consent process as viewed by children, adolescents, young adults, and physicians. *Journal of Pediatrics, 121,* 547–552.

Susser, M. (1991). What is a cause and how do we know one? A grammar for pragmatic epidemiology. *American Journal of Epidemiology, 133,* 635–648.

Svensson, C. K. (1989). Representation of American blacks in clinical trials of new drugs. *Journal of the American Medical Association, 261,* 263–265.

Tankanow, R. M., Sweet, B. V., & Weisikoff, J. A. (1992). Patients' perceived understanding of informed consent in investigational drug studies. *American Journal of Hospital Pharmacy, 49,* 633–635.

Tarantola, D., Mann, J., Mantel, C., & Cameron C. (1994). Projecting the course of the HIV/AIDS pandemic and the cost of adult AIDS care in the world. In E. H. Kaplan & M. L. Brandeau (Eds.), *Modeling the AIDS epidemic: Planning, policy, and prediction* (pp. 3–23). New York: Raven Press.

Tarasoff v. Regents of the University of California, 17 Cal. 3d 425 (1976).

Taub, H. A. (1986). Comprehension of informed consent for research: Issues and directions for future study. *IRB, 8,* 7–10.

Thomas, S. B., & Quinn, S. C. (1991). The Tuskegee syphilis study, 1932 to 1972: Implications for HIV education and AIDS risk education programs in the black community. *American Journal of Public Health, 81,* 1498–1504.

Thompson v. County of Alameda, 27 Cal. 3d 741 (1980).

Thong, Y. H., & Harth, S. C. (1991). The social filter effect of informed consent in clinical research. *Pediatrics, 87,* 568–569.

Tobias, J. S. (1988). Informed consent and controlled trials. *Lancet, 2,* 1194.

Torres, C. G., Turner, M. E., Harkess, J. R., & Istre, G. R. (1991). Security measures for AIDS and HIV. *American Journal of Public Health, 81,* 210–211.

Totten, G., Lamb, D. H., & Reeder, G. D. (1990). *Tarasoff* and confidentiality in AIDS-related psychotherapy. *Professional Psychology: Research and Practice, 21,* 155–160.

Traver, L. B., & Cooksey, D. R. (1988). Defense argument. In J. A. Girardi, R. M. Keese, L. B. Traver, & D. R. Cooksey, Psychotherapist responsibility in notifying individuals at risk for exposure to HIV. *Journal of Sex Research, 25,* 1–27.

United States Department of Commerce, Bureau of the Census. (1993). *Statistical abstract of the United States* (113th ed.). Washington, DC: Government Printing Office.

United States Department of Health and Human Services, Public Health Service. (1991, June). *Technical instructions for medical examination of aliens in the United States.* Atlanta: Centers for Disease Control.

United States Public Health Service. (1991). Consultation on international collaborative human immunodeficiency virus (HIV) research. *Law, Medicine, & Health Care, 19,* 259–263.

Valdisseri, R. O., Tama, G. M., & Ho, M. (1988). The role of community advisory committees in clinical trials of anti-HIV agents. *IRB, 10*(4), 5–7.

Van de Kamp, J., California State Attorney General, at a press conference, Washington, DC, September 30, 1987, cited in California initiates program to allow experimental drugs. *AIDS Policy & Law, 2* (October 7, 1987).

Vogue Instrument Corp. v. Lem Instruments Corp., 41 F.R.D. 346 (D.C.N.Y. 1967).

Vollmer, W. M., Hertert, S., & Allison, M. J. (1992). Recruiting children and their families for clinical trials: A case study. *Controlled Clinical Trials, 13,* 315–320.

Washington Research Project v. Department of Health, Education, and Welfare, 504 F.2d 238 (D.C. Cir. 1974).

Weed, D. L. (1994). Science, ethics guidelines, and advocacy in epidemiology. *Annals of Epidemiology, 4,* 166–171.

Weiss v. Solomon, R.J.Q. 731 (1989).

Weiss, R. B., Vogelzang, N. J., Peterson, B. A., Panasci, L. C., Carpenter, J. T., Gavigan, M., Sartell, K., Frei, E. III, and McIntyre, O. R. (1993). A successful system of scientific data audits for clinical trials: A report from the Cancer and Leukemia Group B. *Journal of the American Medical Association, 270,* 459–464.

Weithorn, L. A., & McCabe, M. A. (1988). Emerging ethical and legal issues in pediatric psychology. In D. Routh (Ed.), *Handbook of pediatric psychology* (pp. 567–606). New York: Guilford Press.

Weithorn, L. A., & Scherer, D. G. (1994). Children's involvement in research participation decisions: Psychological considerations. In M. A. Grodin & L. H. Glantz (Eds.), *Children as research subjects: Science, ethics, and law* (pp. 133–179). London: Oxford University Press.

Weitz, R. (1987). The interview as legacy: A social scientist confronts AIDS. *Hastings Center Report, 17*(3), 21–23.

Wells, F. (1987). Promotion by the drug companies: The industry replies. *Journal of the Royal College of Physicians of London, 37,* 271.

Whitely, W. P., Rennie, D., & Hafner, A. W. (1994). The scientific community's response to evidence of fraudulent publication: The Robert Slutsky case. *Journal of the American Medical Association, 272,* 170–173.

Wilborn, E. (1990). Developments under the Freedom of Information Act—1989. *Duke Law Journal, 1990,* 1113–1155.

Winston, M. E. (1991). AIDS, confidentiality, and the right to know. In T. A. Mappes & J. S. Zembay, (Eds.), *Biomedical ethics* (3rd ed, pp. 173–180). New York: McGraw–Hill.

Wion, A. H. (1979). The definition of "agency records" under the Freedom of Information Act. *Stanford Law Review, 31,* 1093–1115.

Woody, K. J. (1981). Legal and ethical concepts involved in informed consent to human research. *California Western Law Review, 18,* 50–79.

World Health Organization, Council for International Organizations of Medical Sciences (CIOMS). (1982). *Proposed international guidelines for biomedical research involving human subjects.* Geneva: CIOMS.

World Health Organization, Global Programme on AIDS. (1993). *A checklist of ethical, practical and legal criteria.* Geneva: World Health Organization.

World Medical Association. (1991a). Declaration of Helsinki. *Law, Medicine & Health Care, 19,* 264–265.

World Medical Association. (1991b). The Nuremberg Code. *Law, Medicine & Health Care, 19,* 266.

Young, D. R., Hooker, D. T., & Freeberg, F. E. (1990). Informed consent documents: Increasing comprehension by reducing reading level. *IRB, 12,* 1–5.

Young, F. S., Norris, J. A., Levitt, J. A., & Nightingale, S. T. (1988). The FDA's new procedures for use of investigational drugs in treatment. *Journal of the American Medical Association, 260,* 2267–2270.

Zak, M. (1991). Compensating victims of biomedical injuries: Comparative analysis of the United States and New Zealand. *Wisconsin International Law Journal, 9,* 191–225.

Zelen, M. (1990). Randomized consent designs for clinical trials: An update. *Statistics in Medicine, 9,* 645–656.

21 Code of Federal Regulations Parts 312, 314.500–.510, 812 (1994).

21 Code of Federal Regulations Parts 50 & 56 (1994).

32 Code of Federal Regulations Part 58.6 (1991).

42 Code of Federal Regulations sections 50.101, 50.103, 50.105 (1993).

45 Code of Federal Regulations Part 46 (1993).

56 Federal Register 25000 (1991).

56 Federal Register 64004 (1991).

5 United States Code Annotated sections 552, 552(a) (West Supp. 1994).

5 United States Code Annotated sections 553(b), (e) (West 1977).

8 United States Code Annotated section 1182 (1990).

21 United States Code Annotated section 872 (West 1981).

21 United States Code Annotated sections 355(I), 360j(g)(2) (West Supp.1994).

42 United States Code Annotated section 241(d) (West 1990).

42 United States Code Annotated sections 241, 289b, 290dd–23789g (West Supp. 1994).

Index